The Lion's Share

This is the most in-depth analysis of inequality and social polarization ever attempted for a preindustrial society. Using data from the archives of the Venetian *Terraferma*, and compared with information available for elsewhere in Europe, Guido Alfani and Matteo Di Tullio demonstrate that the rise of the fiscal-military state served to increase economic inequality in the early modern period. Preindustrial fiscal systems tended to be regressive in nature, and increased post-tax inequality compared to pre-tax – in contrast to what we would assume is the case in contemporary societies. This led to greater and greater disparities in wealth, which were made worse still as taxes were collected almost entirely to fund war and defence rather than social welfare. Though focused on Old Regime Europe, Alfani and Di Tullio's findings speak to contemporary debates about the roots of inequality and social stratification.

Guido Alfani is Professor of Economic History at Bocconi University. His recent works include *Calamities and the Economy in Renaissance Italy: The Grand Tour of the Horsemen of the Apocalypse* and, with Cormac Ó Gráda, *Famine in European History*.

Matteo Di Tullio is a research fellow in early modern history at Pavia University and a member of the Dondena Centre at Bocconi University. He is the author of *The Wealth of Communities: War, Resources and Cooperation in Renaissance Lombardy*.

Cambridge Studies in Economic History

Editorial Board

Cambridge Studies in Economic History comprises stimulating and accessible economic history which actively builds bridges to other disciplines. Books in the series will illuminate why the issues they address are important and interesting, place their findings in a comparative context, and relate their research to wider debates and controversies. The series will combine innovative and exciting new research by younger researchers with new approaches to major issues by senior scholars. It will publish distinguished work regardless of chronological period or geographical location.

A complete list of titles in the series can be found at:
www.cambridge.org/economichistory

The Lion's Share

Inequality and the Rise of the Fiscal State in Preindustrial Europe

Guido Alfani

Università Commerciale Luigi Bocconi, Milan, Italy

Matteo Di Tullio

Università degli Studi di Pavia, Italy

CAMBRIDGE
UNIVERSITY PRESS

CAMBRIDGE
UNIVERSITY PRESS

Shaftesbury Road, Cambridge CB2 8EA, United Kingdom

One Liberty Plaza, 20th Floor, New York, NY 10006, USA

477 Williamstown Road, Port Melbourne, VIC 3207, Australia

314–321, 3rd Floor, Plot 3, Splendor Forum, Jasola District Centre, New Delhi – 110025, India

103 Penang Road, #05–06/07, Visioncrest Commercial, Singapore 238467

Cambridge University Press is part of Cambridge University Press & Assessment, a department of the University of Cambridge.

We share the University's mission to contribute to society through the pursuit of education, learning and research at the highest international levels of excellence.

www.cambridge.org
Information on this title: www.cambridge.org/9781108476218

DOI: 10.1017/9781108568043

First published 2019

A catalogue record for this publication is available from the British Library

Library of Congress Cataloging-in-Publication data
Names: Alfani, Guido, 1976– author. | Di Tullio, Matteo, author.
Title: The lion's share : inequality and the rise of the fiscal state in preindustrial Europe / Guido Alfani, Universita Commerciale Luigi Bocconi, Milan, Matteo Di Tullio, Universita degli Studi di Pavia, Italy.
Description: Cambridge, United Kingdom; New York, NY: Cambridge University Press, 2019. | Series: Cambridge studies in economic history | Includes bibliographical references and index.
Identifiers: LCCN 2018038842 | ISBN 9781108476218 (hardback)
Subjects: LCSH: Venice (Italy) – Economic conditions – To 1797. | Fiscal policy – Italy – Venice – History. | Income distribution – Italy – Venice – History. | Equality – Italy – Venice – History.
Classification: LCC HC308.V4 A44 2019 | DDC 330.945/311–dc23
LC record available at https://lccn.loc.gov/2018038842

ISBN   978-1-108-47621-8   Hardback

Contents

Figures

Tables

Acknowledgements

In writing this book, we have accumulated vast debts of gratitude towards many colleagues who have kindly provided advice and support. We would first like to express our sincere thanks to Samuel K. Cohn, Alessio Fornasin, Maria Fusaro, Matthieu Scherman and Andrea Zannini for their comments on early versions of the manuscript. Further valuable advice came from the anonymous referees selected by Cambridge University Press. Andrea Caracausi, Claudio Lorenzini, Marcella Lorenzini and Germano Maifreda were generous with their advice about historical sources and useful literature; Carlo Devillanova and Paola Profeta provided counsel about public finance and taxation theory; and Richard Paping kindly provided information about urbanization rates in the Dutch Republic.

We are also grateful to the colleagues who have taken part at seminar presentations of our research and provided useful feedback, at Bocconi University, Geneva University, the London School of Economics, the Stone Center of the City University of New York and Yale University. Early versions of this research were also presented at the XVIIIth World Economic History Conference held in Boston in 2018 and at the Twelfth European Social Science History Conference held in Belfast in the same year. We are particularly grateful for the long conversations we had with Peter Lindert and Branko Milanovic, from whose expertise on inequality we profited greatly, and with Francesca Trivellato, who shared her deep knowledge of Venetian history.

The research leading to these results has received funding from the European Research Council under the European Union's Seventh Framework Programme (FP7/2007–2013)/ERC Grant agreement No. 283802, EINITE (Economic Inequality across Italy and Europe, 1300–1800). Given the large amount of new archival research that was required to complete our project, it is a sure fact that without European generosity this book would never have been written, or would have been much more limited in scope.

To come to life, a book also needs the right research environment. We are grateful to Bocconi University, and particularly to the Dondena Centre that hosted the EINITE project, for providing such an environment. Our gratitude of course extends to the many colleagues and friends at Bocconi who provided continuous support, encouragement and advice. Part of the book was written during a period spent abroad at the Institute for the Advanced Studies in the Humanities of the University of Edinburgh, in summer 2017, to which we are also grateful.

Special thanks go to the Bocconi Library, particularly to the staff of the interlibrary loan service, whose competence has always been a crucial asset for our research. We are also grateful to the staff of the many archives that we consulted for their help in chasing the historical sources we needed.

Finally, our largest and most obvious debt is towards our families, who have patiently supported us throughout the long years needed to complete this book.

Introduction

For centuries, the Lion of Saint Mark, the symbol of Venice, was encountered in all corners of the Mediterranean and beyond, fluttering on the flags of one of the largest merchant fleets of the Old World as well as marking the boundaries of a powerful maritime empire. Born out of a scatter of islands in a well-protected lagoon during the early Middle Ages, Venice came to be the main protagonist in one of the most stunning histories of Western civilization. As such, it has been the object of an enormous number of studies, some of which remain classic examples of scholarship, inspiring generations of historians of all kinds.

But the city of Venice was not alone in this history, and indeed it is not the main character in this book, and it is not our aim to provide a general account of her fascinating history – nor yet an account focusing primarily on Venice's maritime endeavours, which are still the better known to international historians. Instead, we focus on some specific aspects of Venetian history, some of which have been hitherto neglected – distribution and inequality – or have been studied from perspectives different from ours – poverty – or have never been connected to the kind of issues that we intend to explore – the fiscal state. And we develop our analyses mostly on the relatively vast domains of Venice in the Italian mainland, the *Terraferma*, although always in close connection with developments in the central institutions of the state, particularly regarding taxation. The Lion of Venice extracted tributes in the *Terraferma*, but lions of another kind also prowl this book: the economic elites which during the Middle Ages and the early modern period, until the very end of the Republic in 1797, never ceased to increase their share of the overall wealth, also profiting from what were – if seen from our modern perspective, but maybe *not* from that of the contemporaries – the iniquities of the fiscal system.

By placing distribution at the centre of the analysis, we aim to integrate and to enrich our understanding not only of Venetian history, but of European history more generally. Indeed, what we propose here is the

1

most thorough attempt ever made to measure inequality and the prevalence of both poverty and wealth in a preindustrial society, as well as to explore the inner workings of distributional change, from ca. 1400 and throughout the entire early modern period. As such, this book helps to fill in a gap in our knowledge of topics which are crucial to many current debates, not only in social and economic history but also more generally in the social sciences. Indeed, we set for ourselves the ambitious task of identifying the main factors explaining long-term inequality change in preindustrial times – and possibly even later.

The Changing Fortunes of a Composite State: An Overview

If seen from the year 1600, in the exact middle of the time period we cover, the Venetian state had three main components: the capital city of Venice itself with the *Dogado* (i.e. the lagoon area plus a strip of coastal lands nearby); the *Stato da Terra* (which we will usually refer to as the *Terraferma*), that included the territories ruled by Venice in Italy, from the city of Bergamo in the West to the boundary at the Isonzo River in the East, and finally the *Stato da Mar*. The latter included mostly Istria and Dalmatia, the Ionian Islands, Crete and many smaller Aegean islands. Cyprus had been conquered by the Ottomans in 1571, but more generally, the extent and the composition of the *Stato da Mar* changed significantly during the time period considered here. For example, Crete was lost to the Ottomans in 1669, while Morea (the Peloponnese peninsula in Greece) was conquered in 1685, albeit only temporarily as the Ottomans recovered it in 1715 (Lane 1973a; Cozzi 1995; Scarabello 1995; Arbel 2013; Fusaro 2015).

The vicissitudes of the *Stato da Mar* are relevant to our study only in the measure in which they affected fiscal developments (for example, by leading to changes in the fiscal burden) and the composition of public expenditure, which in turn helped to shape wealth distribution in the *Terraferma* and promoted inequality growth, as is demonstrated in Chapter 4. From this perspective, the War of Candia (1645–69) is particularly important, not only because it led to a very significant and lasting increase in the public debt, but also because it can be considered a turning point in the economic fortunes of the Republic of Venice, as discussed in the text that follows. More relevant to our study are changes in the composition of the *Stato da Terra*, which however, in the time period that we work on, are very limited. The expansion of Venice towards the rich and fertile Po plain began in 1338, with the annexation of Treviso. But the quickest and most successful phase of expansion occurred during

1404–06, when the large cities of Padua, Verona and Vicenza were acquired. Important acquisitions were made in the following twenty years, both to the north (Belluno and Friuli) and to the west (southern Trentino and eastern Lombardy). Expansion westwards was completed in 1449, with the incorporation of Crema (Lane 1973a; Knapton 2012; 2013). At the onset of the Italian Wars (1494–1559), Venice aspired to acquire further territories and indeed, some other areas in Lombardy fell temporarily under its rule (Cremona and the Geradadda), but all this came to an end with the catastrophic defeat at the battle of Agnadello (1509) by the League of Cambrai, an alliance temporarily uniting against Venice the Kingdom of France, the Empire and some of the main Italian states. In the aftermath of Agnadello, Venice lost almost all the *Terraferma*, but in the following years, through astute diplomacy and a substantial military effort, it managed to recover all but the most recent acquisitions (Mallett and Hale 1984; Knapton 2012; Alfani 2013a). Thereafter, and until the end of the Republic, the boundaries of the *Terraferma* remained basically unchanged.

The Venetian state was a 'composite' state not only because of the aforementioned distinction between *Dogado, Stato da Terra* and *Stato da Mar*, but also because the *Terraferma* (similarly to the *Stato da Mar*) was far from constituting a homogeneous whole. Instead, the very procedure through which it was pieced together, which built upon agreements with the local communities and territories and involved at least some elements of 'voluntary choice' (Knapton 2013, 86),[1] led to a complex territorial and administrative structure. To some degree at least, this complex structure managed to resist attempts at rationalization and uniformity promoted by the central state throughout the early modern period. This is clearly visible, for example, in differences between local fiscal systems and in the type of relationship entertained by various kinds of territories with the central fiscal authorities, as discussed in detail in Chapter 1. This is also why, as Marino Berengo (1999, 3–4) had suggested, it might be better to use the definition of *Dominante* ('dominant city') for Venice, instead of that of 'capital city', as the latter tends to imply a higher degree of administrative and political centralization than that found in the Venetian state. Surely, in many instances this allowed for a useful flexibility, especially regarding the management of the *Stato da Mar* (Fusaro

[1] Voluntary, of course, up to a point and to different degrees according to each territory. So, for example, the first territory acquired, Treviso, as well as Padua which was conquered after a bitter war against the earlier rulers (the Carrara family), enjoyed less autonomy and experienced a somewhat disadvantaged situation compared to, say, the big cities of eastern Lombardy (Bergamo and Brescia), at the boundary with the State of Milan (about this, see Knapton 2013, 88).

2015) – but in the *Terraferma*, it also betrayed, in Michael Knapton's (2013, 86) words, the 'adaptation of a city-state mentality to the regional state', which might also have imposed certain limits to long-term development.

Indeed, even the way in which we refer to the political entity subject to the dominion of Venice is somewhat controversial. Recently, Maria Fusaro has advocated the use of the word 'empire' to qualify Venice's way of governing the subject territories – as indeed they were subjects of the *Dominante*: 'the hierarchy of government was very clear, as all these disparate territories were ultimately ruled by the same governing body, the *Senato* (...). And the ultimate authority of Venice was unquestioned in three fundamental political spheres: foreign and defence policy; state finance, on which defence is utterly dependent; and the administration of justice' (Fusaro 2015, 5). However, this definition seems to be more proper to the *Stato da Mar* than to the *Stato da Terra*. On the mainland, Venice's way of exerting dominion does not seem to be all that different from what was found in other Italian regional states which had grown from a powerful city-state – think, for example, of the Florentine State and of its administrative and fiscal division between the *contado* and the much more independent and varied *distretto*, a division maintained until the end of the eighteenth century (Cohn 1999; Tanzini 2012; Alfani and Ammannati 2017).[2] So we could simply refer to this political entity as 'the Venetian State', similarly to what studies of other composite Italian political entities, like the 'Sabaudian State' or again, the 'Florentine State' have done recently. However, it seems necessary to recognize that there is also an element of uniqueness in this specific state – after all, as rightly underlined again by Fusaro, this was 'the longest-lived and most stable republic and was also the only one of all the Italian regional states to hold possessions outside of Italy for centuries' (Fusaro 2015, 22). Hence we will resort to a classic definition, which was also that used by contemporaries to define this state: Republic of Venice. But it will be clear throughout the discussion that this is a book primarily about the *Terraferma*, and also that the 'republican' character of the state, if it has any meaning at all, certainly does not exert any visible influence on the way in which concentration of wealth and resources developed in time and in comparison with other Italian or European areas.

Another aspect worth clarifying is that in the period covered by this study the Republic of Venice went through phases of expansion and of decline. We have already mentioned the dynamic period when the

---

[2] More generally about the prevalence of 'composite states' across Europe, see Elliott (1992).

Terraferma was acquired. Although territorial expansion in Italy had ended after Agnadello in 1509, in the following two centuries Venice was anything but blessed by enduring peace – but it was mostly on the defensive, in attempts to protect its *Stato da Mar* from the aggressive expansion of the Ottoman Empire. From the beginning of the sixteenth to the early eighteenth centuries, the Republic fought no fewer than five large-scale wars with the Ottomans who, after the conquest of Constantinople in 1453, were pressing westwards, from the Balkans to Egypt and across the eastern Mediterranean. The first of such wars occurred in 1537–40, and cost Venice some important bases in Greece, particularly Nauplion. The second, in 1570–73, led to the loss of Cyprus, notwithstanding the great naval victory of Lepanto in 1571. More than seventy years passed before the long and harsh War of Candia (1645–69), when Venice ultimately lost the island (nowadays Crete) but increased its domains in Dalmatia and Albania. Shortly afterwards, Venice went on the offensive, conquering Morea and strengthening further her control over Dalmatia (1684–99). But Morea was lost in a final war against the Ottomans (1714–18). After this second 'Morean War', the Republic of Venice set out to pursue neutrality and was never again involved in major international conflicts, until the coming of Napoleon and the final dissolution of this proud and ancient state in 1797 (Lane 1973a; Cozzi 1995; Scarabello 1995; Arbel 2013).

Of all the conflicts against the Ottomans, the War of Candia has particular importance, as it seems to mark a turning point not so much in the military fortunes of the Republic (given the success of the First Morean War), as in economic potential and social and institutional dynamism. From the point of view of the central administration of the state, the war favoured a large increase in the per capita fiscal pressure but an even more marked, and ultimately more important, increase in the public debt – which proved to be very difficult to repay quickly, also due to the huge expenditures sustained for the two subsequent Morean Wars. In other words, as clearly shown by Luciano Pezzolo (2006a, 2007), the War of Candia was ruinous for public finances and imposed enduring limits to the destination of the growing public expenditure – as in the post-war decades, interest payments on the public debt accounted for 35–40% of the central budget of the Republic, subtracting resources from alternative uses. This was not without distributive consequences of its own, given the high concentration of the shares of the public debt, mostly owned by the economic elites of Venice and of the *Terraferma*, as discussed in Chapter 4.

The War of Candia also helped to establish the process of relative decline of the Republic. This requires further and more general discussion as indeed, the timing and the causes of the decline not only of Venice, but of all or almost all the main Italian states is the subject of debate. According to the classic reconstruction of Fernand Braudel (1984), Venice had been the (almost) undisputed centre of the European and Mediterranean 'world-economy' since at least the Black Death of 1348 and up to the opening of the main Atlantic trade routes from the late fifteenth to the early sixteenth century. The situation, however, would have been aggravated by the arrest of the expansion on the Italian mainland after Agnadello, as well as by the growing hostility of the Ottoman Empire in the Mediterranean and the Levant. Consequently, after a temporary displacement westwards, from which Genoa profited thanks to its means and financial skills and its privileged relationship with the Spanish crown, during the seventeenth century the centre of the European economy became solidly placed in the North, in the Low Countries and especially the city of Amsterdam. This is the process which recent literature refers to as the 'Little Divergence' (Van Zanden 2009; Alfani and Ryckbosch 2016), to distinguish it from the 'Great Divergence' of Western Europe from East Asia (and all the rest) (Pomeranz 2002; Acemoglu et al. 2005). However, although there is no doubt that in the seventeenth century Venice did not enjoy the same position of economic centrality as it had two or three centuries earlier, the situation is much more nuanced than this simple story suggests.

Many historians – mostly Italian – have elaborated the notion of 'relative decline' to describe the fortunes of Italy during the seventeenth century (Sella 1997; D'Amico 2004; Lanaro 2006).[3] According to Paolo Malanima (2006), the century when Italy as a whole faced its deepest crisis was not the seventeenth, as held by earlier scholarship, but the eighteenth. This, however, leads to another question: when exactly did the relative decline of the main Italian economies begin? Indeed, it has been argued that by the late sixteenth to early seventeenth century, these economies were still very strong and competitive (Alfani 2013a). It has also been argued that the devastating plague of 1630, which killed about 35% of the population of the affected areas and possibly as much as 40% in the *Terraferma* (see discussion in Chapter 3, as well as Fornasin and Zannini 1999; Zannini 2010, 152), was hugely instrumental in precipitating the situation. It affected central-northern Italy (a similarly severe plague affected the rest of Italy in 1656–57) and some other Southern European areas far more heavily than any mortality crisis experienced by Northern Europe during the seventeenth century. And it

---

[3] For the Republic of Venice, some of these views had already been expressed by Luzzatto (1967) and Rapp (1976).

did so at the worst possible moment, when competition in trade and manufacture from the most economically dynamic areas of Northern Europe had become particularly acute (Alfani 2013b). A recent quantitative study provided further proof of this, focusing on urban economies (Alfani and Percoco 2018).

In the case of the Republic of Venice, an indisputable merit of the scholarship of the last few decades has been to demonstrate how the conquest of the *Terraferma* became a great opportunity for development, for the *Dominante* itself and also for the subject cities and territories, and not only to replace declining international trade across the Mediterranean, but also in a much more positive and innovatory way (see, for example, Zannini 2010, 167–71; Demo 2013). These opportunities started to become apparent from the sixteenth century, when investment in waterworks and in land drainage allowed for the expansion of rice in the western part of the *Terraferma*, and more generally helped to trigger a long phase of agrarian innovation (think, for example, not only of the expansion of the mulberry tree and the subsequent cultivation of silkworms but also, from the seventeenth century, the spread of maize) which led to increases in land productivity and revenues (Ciriacono 1994; Knapton 1995, 429–47; Zannini 1999, 2010). But the new opportunities went much beyond land investment. As argued by Paola Lanaro (2006, 20–21), 'recent historical research has tried to highlight the ability of merchants and merchant entrepreneurs from Venice and from the mainland to react to the restructuring of the [European] economy ... these studies have brought to light Venetian businessmen's innovative ability to look for new products, new technologies, new professionally organized systems, and new markets'. This is clear from looking at textile manufactures, a sector revolutionized by the introduction of silk during the sixteenth century (Molà 2000) but where also the somewhat more traditional woollen productions remained strong (Demo 2013, 300–01) – at least until the 1630 plague.

The catastrophic plague brought about the complete disappearance of the production of woollen cloth in Verona and caused lasting damage to that of Treviso and Bassano. In Venice, the average yearly production of woollen cloth in 1645–49 was still 45% lower than in 1625–29 (Panciera 1996, 15, 22, 42–43). Even silk suffered as in Venice this sector, which had been booming in the pre-plague years, had to face its first crisis ever (Panciera 2006, 191). True, part of the production of woollen cloth had moved from the city to the country, especially towards the hilly areas close to the Alps (Demo 2013, 302), a process which the plague had only accelerated, while in the case of silk the sector resumed growing from the second half of the seventeenth century, especially in the western

Terraferma (Bergamo and Brescia: see Mocarelli 2006, 323–24).[4] And it is also true that growth in other sectors compensated at least partly for the decline in textile production and export. This is the case, for example, of Venice's glass beads (Trivellato 2006). Nevertheless, '[After the plague] the deconstructing of urban industry was an obstacle to recovery' (Lanaro 2006, 49) and the plague-induced damage suffered by the urban economies was not without enduring consequences for the whole system, as argued by Alfani and Percoco (2018). Indeed, beyond manufacture, also the agrarian sector seems to have been stagnating overall in the post-plague decades (Knapton 1995, 429).

As already discussed, the 1630 plague also wrecked other Italian economies. Unique to the Republic of Venice, however, is the fact that it was shortly followed by the War of Candia. This war, which it seemed in certain phases that Venice could actually win, is a clear testament to the Republic's enduring wealth and ability both to concentrate sizeable resources and to project military power across the sea – but because in the end Venice lost and had to give up Crete, it was ultimately an enormous waste of money, which badly damaged state finances in a period when the economy was still suffering from the plague. Additionally, the loss of many commercial bases as well as the hostility of the Ottomans, which continued well beyond the end of the war, affected negatively Venetian trade in the eastern Mediterranean area (Sella 1968; Fusaro 2012). This is why in the case of the Republic of Venice, the War of Candia can be assumed together with the plague to be the turning point in a process which, from then on, would lead the economic fortunes of the *Terraferma* as a whole (and allowing for some locally diverging tendencies) towards relative decline.[5] This path is reflected in urbanization rates (a popular rough indicator of economic development). Beginning from a very high level of 21–23% of the population living in cities with at least 5,000 inhabitants in the sixteenth and early seventeenth centuries, urbanization rates dropped to 15% in the aftermath of the 1630 plague, then slowly recovered to little over 18% by 1700, stagnating thereafter (Zannini 2010; Alfani and Percoco 2018). In relative terms, the *Terraferma* moved from being one of the most urbanized areas of Europe, to a condition of relative disadvantage compared not only to the most advanced northern European countries, but also to some other northern Italian areas (see Chapter 4 for a more detailed discussion, and particularly Table 4.1).

---

[4] About the long-term consequences of the relocation towards the foothills of Veneto of the textile industries, see Zalin (1987) and Fontana and Gayot (2004).

[5] About the economic difficulties of Venice and the *Terraferma* during the eighteenth century, see Zannini (2010), 161–67.

Inequality in Preindustrial Europe: An Expanding Research Field

Until recently, economic inequality has been a topic seriously under-researched by social and economic historians and economists alike. Although many classical economists, from Ricardo to Marx, put distribution at the centre of their analyses, modern economists have tended to view inequality as 'an inevitable outcome of the market as a coordinating mechanism, and a necessary outcome for the market to function as an incentive mechanism' (Wade 2014, 118). Famously, Nobel Prize economist Robert Lucas (2004) went as far as to claim that 'Of the tendencies that are harmful to sound economics, the most seductive, and in my opinion the most poisonous, is to focus on questions of distribution.' However, the Great Recession, beginning in 2008, and subsequent events, helped to heighten the perception of inequality, and in many countries throughout the world it became a prime topic in political debates. Inequality has also become a matter of debate among economists, largely as a consequence of Thomas Piketty's efforts to '[place] study of distribution and of the long-run back at the center of economic thinking' (Piketty 2015, 68).

Knowledge of long-run dynamics has long been a feature of research on inequality, due to Simon Kuznets' (1955) seminal article, in which he argued that income inequality followed an inverted-U path through the industrialization process (the so-called 'Kuznets curve'), with a rising phase at the beginning of industrialization. This path would be the consequence of economic development, and particularly of the transfer of workforce from a traditional (agrarian) sector to an advanced (industrial) one. This approach generated a sizeable amount of research on historical inequality, which, however, covered mostly the nineteenth and twentieth centuries: the period during which the Kuznets curve was expected to manifest itself. These studies usually found some evidence of rising inequality during the nineteenth century followed by decline in the early decades of the twentieth century (see Williamson 1985 for Britain; Piketty, Postel-Vinay and Rosenthal 2006, 2014 for France; Rossi, Toniolo and Vecchi 2001 for Italy; Prados de la Escosura 2008 for Spain; Williamson and Lindert 1980 for the United States). Earlier periods were not covered by these studies and indeed, in his 1955 article Kuznets seemed to imply that before ca. 1800 or 1750 at the earliest, income inequality was relatively low and stable over time.

This implication, however, was wrong. A seminal article by Jan Luiten Van Zanden published in 1995 (forty years after Kuznets'!) was for a long time the only attempt to reconstruct inequality change for a large area (the province of Holland in the Netherlands) throughout the early modern period.[6] Van Zanden found that inequality had started to increase from the sixteenth century – much earlier than the industrial revolution. However, it seemed possible to explain Holland's case with arguments that were 'kuznetsian' in nature, notably as the outcome of long-term economic growth (Van Zanden 1995; Soltow and Van Zanden 1998) – after all, during the early modern period the Dutch Republic went through its Golden Age. Van Zanden postulated the existence of a 'super-Kuznets curve' spanning many centuries, with a long phase of inequality growth followed by inequality decline only during the twentieth century (Van Zanden 1995, 662). In the following years, very few studies of tendencies in preindustrial inequality appeared, the main exception being the attempt of Phil Hoffman et al. (2002) to estimate 'real' inequality from data on prices and consumption. Indeed, from 1995, fifteen years would pass before a new study of preindustrial economic inequality measured from wealth or income distributions reconstructed from archival data was published by an international journal. In 2010, inspired by Van Zanden's work, one of the authors of this book demonstrated that in the district of Ivrea in the Sabaudian State (north-western Italy), wealth inequality had been growing throughout the early modern period – but this area mostly faced economic stagnation, not growth, during the sixteenth and the seventeenth centuries (Alfani 2010a). This led us to question the relationship between inequality and economic growth in the long run, as well as to start looking in different directions to find possible drivers of change in preindustrial inequality. This constituted the main research question of the project *EINITE – Economic Inequality across Italy and Europe 1300–1800*,[7] which thanks to the generous funding of the European Research Council was able to launch a vast campaign of archival research during 2012–16. This book is also an outcome of EINITE.

It seems fair to state that the project EINITE, whose activities began in a period when inequality was, as seen earlier, still far from becoming a fashionable topic in the social sciences, has played an important role in promoting the study of this aspect of human societies among historians specializing in the preindustrial period. Indeed, since 2010 the studies providing new quantitative information, laboriously collected from the archives, about preindustrial inequality have multiplied and many of them involved a member of the EINITE team or one of the project's close associates. These works covered many areas of Europe, from the

[6] Before 1995, only local studies for single years of very short periods were available – see, for example, the classic works by David Herlihy: Herlihy (1978) and Herlihy and Klapisch-Zuber (1985).
[7] www.dondena.unibocconi.it/EINITE

Low Countries (Hanus 2013; Ryckbosch 2016; Alfani and Ryckbosch 2016; Alfani 2017) to Spain (Santiago-Caballero 2011; Fernández and Santiago-Caballero 2013; García-Montero 2015; Nicolini and Ramos Palencia 2016a, 2016b; Alfani 2017), Portugal (Reis 2017), Sweden (Bengtsson et al. 2018) and Poland (Malinowski and Van Zanden 2017). Italy, however, has attracted the greatest amount of research, from the Sabaudian State in the northwest (Alfani 2010a, 2010b, 2015, 2017) to the Florentine State in the centre (Alfani and Ryckbosch 2016; Alfani and Ammannati 2017) and the Kingdom of Naples (Apulia) in the south (Alfani and Sardone 2015; Alfani 2017). Some non-European areas were also researched, from Anatolia under the Ottoman Empire (Coşgel and Boğaç 2012; Canbakal 2013) to the pre-revolutionary Unites States (Lindert and Williamson 2016) and Japan in the late Tokugawa period (Saito 2015). Finally, wealth and income inequality feature quite largely in Bas Van Bavel's (2016) recent study of the consequences of the development of market economies in human history, which covers areas from Iraq to parts of Western Europe.

This recent wave of research on preindustrial inequality does not show any sign of stopping. On the contrary, it seems to be gaining momentum. This is because the new research is not only filling in a gap in our knowledge, but it is changing very significantly the way in which we look at long-term trends in economic inequality. A particularly important point, is that overall the aforementioned studies do not confirm the Kuznetsian paradigm.[8] Indeed, in almost all areas subject to large-scale reconstructions, inequality was found to have been on the rise since at least the beginning of the early modern period, so that on the eve of industrialization it was already relatively high. If we move from preindustrial times to the modern world, it is now obvious that Kuznets' 'promise' of automatic inequality decline as countries progressed going through the industrialization process has also been disproved by the trends of the recent decade (Atkinson, Piketty and Saez 2011; Alvaredo et al. 2013; Piketty 2014, 2015). The day might have come to conclude, as Peter Lindert (2000) suggested a while ago, that the Kuznets curve is now obsolete.[9]

This, however, raises many questions about the causes of inequality change, which can no longer be simply indicated in economic growth (or

---

[8] Kuznets' hypothesis referred to income inequality; however, it stands to reason that it can also be applied to wealth (Lindert 1991, 215–19, as well as further discussion in Chapter 3, Section 3.1). Indeed, a growing number of empirical studies suggest that the concentration of wealth also followed an inverted-U path during the Industrial Revolution, growing during the nineteenth century and later declining, especially in the period between the two world wars (Williamson and Lindert 1980; Piketty, Postel-Vinay and Rosenthal 2006, 2014; Piketty 2014; Roine and Waldenström 2015).

[9] Similar views have also been expressed by Alfani (2009a, 2015).

decline). In this sense, studies of preindustrial inequality contribute very significantly to current debates on recent trends: see, for example, the new take on the general Kuznetsian argument proposed by Branko Milanovic (2016a), who argued for the existence of 'Kuznetsian waves' in the very long run, or Walter Scheidel's (2017) broad and fascinating overview of catastrophes as the main (or even, as Scheidel seems to argue, the only) cause of inequality decline in human history. Both these recent encompassing studies were stimulated by the new information that had just been made available by the aforementioned studies. This seems to demonstrate that, in their common enquiry about inequality in the long run, economic historians and other social scientists still badly need new studies and more information, as each piece that we add to the puzzle seems to necessitate looking for two or three new ones to complete the picture. From this point of view the Republic of Venice, with its peculiarities and the excellent quality and abundance of its surviving archival documentation, offers particularly rich opportunities for discovering new facts and for making – we hope – an important contribution to the debate about the determinants of inequality levels and, even more importantly, the fundamental causes of long-term inequality change.

As a conclusion to this synthetic overview of recent studies of preindustrial inequality – a more in-depth discussion, especially of the literature on the possible causal factors of inequality growth in history, is proposed in Chapter 4 – it seems useful to remember two key empirical findings relevant to the part of European history covered by this book:

1. From ca. 1450 or 1500 until 1800, economic inequality (of both wealth and income) seems to have tended to increase almost monotonically across Europe. This was the case for wealth inequality in the Sabaudian State, the Florentine State and the Kingdom of Naples in Italy, as well as for some parts of central Spain and (somewhat less clearly) for Catalonia. It was also the case for income inequality in the Dutch Republic and the southern Low Countries, as well as Spain. Indeed, of all the areas covered by recent research, only in Portugal was income inequality found to be overall declining during the early modern period – although Jaime Reis (2017) does distinguish two phases: inequality decline during 1575–1700, followed by some inequality increase in the eighteenth century.

2. Before 1450, a phase of sustained inequality decline was triggered by the Black Death epidemic of 1347–51. In the five centuries from 1300 to 1800, this was the only event capable of reducing inequality in Europe. The evidence we have covers mostly Italy – the Sabaudian State, the Florentine state, as well as seemingly some other areas from the Marches to Emilia-Romagna, at least if the provisional measures

produced by the EINITE project are confirmed – but some hints at inequality decline in the post–Black Death period are also available for parts of southern France and the southern Low Countries.

As will be seen in Chapter 3, the case of the Republic of Venice fits perfectly within this general scheme, which is indeed reassuring. However, our study is far from being purely confirmative of earlier findings. Instead, the wealth of information available for this European state, as well as the analytical approach that we have followed, allows us to provide a much more detailed and nuanced description at the local level of these continental tendencies. It also gives us the opportunity to experiment a new approach towards the identification of the causes of the tendency for economic inequality to grow during the early modern period – and beyond, as the research on the nineteenth and twentieth centuries reveals that inequality, especially of wealth, continued to grow up until 1913: the eve of a new continental catastrophe, World War I.

Before proceeding to the specific case of inequality in the Republic of Venice, a final point needs to be clarified. Historians of mentalities and of culture have rightly suggested that the perception of wealth (for example, as positive or negative) and even the position of the rich in human societies changed over time (Todeschini 2002, 2004; Le Goff 2010). Additionally, and possibly more importantly for this book, to members of any given society the actual meaning of a condition of inequality is grounded in the deeper cultural context specific to that society. Preindustrial Europeans were well aware that their economies and societies were highly unequal, but this did not lead to social unrest – indeed, as recently argued by Samuel K. Cohn (2006), most medieval and early modern popular revolts do not seem to have been caused by economic reasons, but by 'political' claims. Consequently, we have to understand how the high economic inequality typical of Western Europe (as well as of other world areas) could occur in a social and cultural context that made it acceptable. A crucial point to consider is that Old Regime societies were intrinsically hierarchic – but they were also perceived as just, according to their own criterion of justice which was not one of 'fairness' (which implies equality of some sort: for example, Rawls 1971) but of *aequitas* ('equity'). *Aequitas* does not decree that everyone must receive the same treatment as all others, but that which is due to him or her according to his or her condition or *status* (Levi 2003; Alfani 2009b; Alfani and Frigeni 2016). This is the principle of 'distributive justice' that we have to consider, if we are to understand the actual significance of a condition of inequality in late medieval and early modern European societies.

In such societies, then, it was not the simple imbalance in the distribution of wealth and resources, but the violation of 'justice' in the reciprocal relationship between each component of the society, that would have been perceived as the violation of an implicit social contract and consequently, caused a social breakdown. Coherently with this, fiscal systems that we would immediately qualify as unfair were instead accepted, insofar as they made the rich pay more than the poor (although proportionally *less* than the poor, as detailed in Chapter 4). We should also consider that it would be wrong to try and present Old Regime societies as individualistic societies – they were not. On the contrary, individual members of such societies perceived themselves as part of a group (communities based on a village, a parish or a quarter; family and kinship group; neighbourhoods; institutions such as confraternities or guilds; etc.) (Bossy 1973; Dyer 1995; Lynch 2003). It is only in this super-individual context, further complicated by the presence of specific relief institutions with functions of redistribution towards the poorest strata of society (see Chapter 2), that a profoundly unequal distribution of wealth and income, beyond being 'just' in some abstract sense, could also prove to be compatible with a generalized (albeit not universal) access to the resources necessary to achieve living conditions deemed acceptable (Di Tullio 2018). Indeed, during the long time period that we cover, a process of transformation 'from the community to the individual' began and progressed in time, a process which would help to bring forward the modern society (Bossy 1970, 1973; Lynch 2003). This crucial transformation is not directly analysed in this book, but it contributed to the background against which the distributive changes that we describe have occurred. Indeed, to some level which would be worthy of future research, the process of social polarization that we found to have characterized the entirety of the early modern period probably contributed not only to the waning of the networks of solidarity typical of Old Regime societies, but also determined a change in the perception of inequality itself – some evidence of which begins to be noticeable in Western Europe from the eighteenth century (Alfani and Frigeni 2016).

An Unequal Republic?

Until now, the Republic of Venice has never been the object of a systematic study of inequality and distribution. Like other Italian areas, it has seen studies of changes in property structures both at the local and the regional level, studies conducted especially during the 1960s (Beltrami 1961; Tagliaferri 1966) but of which there are also some recent examples: see the important research conducted by Germano Maifreda (2002) on the Veronese territory and by Jean-François Chauvard (2005, 2009) on Venice. However, these studies did not assess directly the issue of household inequality, favouring instead aspects such as the spread of Church or 'Venetian' property across the *Terraferma* (see further discussion in Chapter 3). An important large-scale project, funded by the Benetton Foundation and coordinated by Gaetano Cozzi and Danilo Gasparini during the 1990s and early 2000s, focused on the countryside of the province of Treviso during the fifteenth and sixteenth centuries, going as far as to collect information about the property of each household in the province – exactly the kind of information that we need. But the related publications focused on landscape history, agrarian contracts and property structures, not on inequality and wealth distribution[10]. These topics were instead present in Matthieu Scherman's (2009, 2013) study of the city of Treviso during 1434–1507 and indeed, we were able to incorporate his careful reconstructions into our analysis. Scherman's works (especially his 2009 article), together with the study of the city of Padua during 1549–1642 by Alfani and Caracausi (2009), seem to be the only earlier attempts at measuring inequality in parts of the *Terraferma*.

At least a specific segment of the overall distribution, the poor, had been the object of a considerable amount of research, of which the better known examples are surely Brian Pullan's (1971, 1992) seminal studies, although many other scholars provided useful contributions (for example, Lanaro 1982a; Scherman 2009; D'Andrea 2013). At the other extreme, the rich and the paths of upward social mobility leading to great wealth have been the object, among others, of a classic study by James S. Grubb (1996) of merchant families of Verona and Vicenza during the Renaissance. A more detailed analysis of the literature on the poor and the rich in the *Terraferma* is provided in Chapter 3. However, also in this case, the approach followed by earlier studies was deeply different from ours. Indeed, our aim is to provide the first attempt to estimate the prevalence of poverty and wealth, as well as overall inequality, in the Republic of Venice – more precisely, in the *Terraferma* – in the long run of history, and to do so by a careful process of reconstruction of the complete local and supralocal distributions, beginning from new archival data and using adequate analytical methods.

Our main historical sources are the famous Italian *estimi*, or property tax records, which have been employed also by other recent works on preindustrial inequality (see, for example, Alfani 2010a, 2015; Alfani and Ammannati 2017). The *estimi* of the *Terraferma* have been the object of intense research, especially about their characteristics and their meaning

---

[10] Detailed information about the thirteen books resulting from this project can be found here: www.fbsr.it/publication-category/campagne-trevigiane-in-eta-moderna/. For a recent synthesis of this research, see Knapton (2010).

within the overall social, economic and institutional framework of a preindustrial society (Borelli 1980, 1986a; Zangheri 1980; Borelli et al. 1982; Maifreda 2009). These sources, which we discuss in greater detail in Chapter 1, allowed us to reconstruct the wealth distributions at the household level. Beginning with such distributions, and by applying simple statistical instruments like the Gini index of inequality (whose properties are recalled in Chapter 3), we explore in detail both the changes in overall inequality and the dynamics experienced by each segment of society. Although our study is statistically rigorous, it is also meant to be accessible to scholars and students from all corners of the social sciences and the humanities, as preindustrial inequality is really a field in which the only fruitful way of proceeding seems to be by bridging the gaps between the disciplines. Hence we pay particular attention to explaining the meaning of our measures, and some of the most technical sections are concentrated in the Appendix. Overall we propose what currently is not only the first assessment of long-term distributional changes in any part of the Republic of Venice, but also the most detailed and in-depth analysis of this kind ever attempted for *any* preindustrial European or world area.

Reconstructing inequality and social polarization across the *Terraferma* would in itself be a worthy task – but for us, it is only a necessary step towards the exploration of the determinants of the tendency for inequality and polarization to grow continuously that we have found in this area, a tendency which is not dissimilar from that reported for other parts of Italy and Europe during the early modern period. Differently from other recent studies, which identified in economic growth/decline the main source of inequality change or which paid particular attention to exogenous shocks (which are indeed crucial to explaining certain specific dynamics, like the considerable and long-lasting drop in inequality found in the fourteenth century, caused undoubtedly by the Black Death: see Alfani and Ammannati 2017; Alfani and Murphy 2017; Scheidel 2017), we focus on institutions, and particularly on the fiscal system. The so-called 'rise of the fiscal state', a process which characterized the early modern period and which has attracted considerable recent attention (Bonney 1999; Yun-Casalilla and O'Brien 2012), had crucial distributive consequences that have never been the object of specific research. We build upon previous studies of the Venetian fiscal system to provide the first-ever attempt to measure the degree of 'regressiveness' of preindustrial taxation. Indeed, the Republic of Venice is the Italian pre-unification state whose fiscal system in the late Middle Ages and the early modern period is better known, mostly due to the pioneering research pursued by Michael

Knapton (1981a, 1981b, 1982) and Luciano Pezzolo (1990, 2006a, 2012). By bringing together our analyses of distributions and of the characteristics of the fiscal system, we are able to provide novel insights into the causes of long-term inequality growth which are valid not only for the Republic of Venice, but for all those states that, in Europe and beyond, during the early modern period experienced the rise of the fiscal state and a substantial increase in per capita taxation.

The book is structured in four chapters, plus a statistical appendix where we detail the way in which we obtained our reconstruction of the overall wealth distribution across the *Terraferma*. Whenever possible, we begin our analyses from the local level (that of each single community), then expanding it to the *Terraferma* as a whole, making use of the afore-mentioned reconstruction to provide a comparison with other Italian and European areas.

In Chapter 1, we provide a general overview of the development of the fiscal system of the Republic of Venice, in connection with the process known as the 'rise of the fiscal-military state'. We discuss the central fiscal system beside the local ones, which had many common points but also some differences. This reflects in the kind of information that we have available for each area and period, as seen in the concluding section of the chapter.

In Chapter 2 we focus on the extremes of society: the poor and the rich. We begin by providing a general account of the social stratification found across the Republic (or at least, its Italian component), later focusing on the characteristics and the numbers of both the poor and the rich. We show that throughout the period, the tendency was for both categories to grow as a share of the overall population. This was especially the case for the rich, while the poor became less prevalent as a consequence of the 1630 plague – although possibly as a result of the extermination of the lowest strata of the society rather than through redistribution and better access to resources.

In Chapter 3 we provide a general description of the long-term trends in inequality and in social polarization across the *Terraferma*, which proved to be entirely similar to those found in other Italian states, particularly the Sabaudian State and the Florentine State. We explore in detail the dynamics affecting different components of the society, and we show that the increase in time of the numbers of the poor and the rich is only one aspect of a more general process of social polarization, with the progressive emptying of the middle ranks of society. We also provide a detailed and in-depth account of a range of relevant issues, such as the distributive consequences of the 1630 plague.

Finally in Chapter 4, we look for the long-term determinants of the growth in both inequality and social polarization found in Chapters 2 and 3. We begin by extending the comparison to other European areas, and particularly the Low Countries: the other extreme of the Little Divergence. On both sides of the Little Divergence the tendency for inequality to grow is found to be similar, which has implications for the current debates about the causes of inequality growth in preindustrial times. We formulate the new hypothesis that during the early modern period, the main cause of inequality growth across Europe was the rise of the fiscal-military state. Hence we build upon the reconstruction in Chapter 1 to provide the first-ever assessment of the redistributive consequences of a preindustrial fiscal system. Subsequently we discuss the redistributive (and inequality-promoting) character of military spending and expenditure for servicing the debt. We also provide estimates of social spending, which is found to be a marginal component of the budget of the central state. We conclude by discussing the implications of our findings for current research on long-term inequality growth.

Indeed, when referring to 'long-term' inequality growth, we might include the last couple of centuries – as the forces which were able to promote or to contain inequality in the past are still active today: think of the fiscal systems and of public expenditure. Of course, the social, economic, institutional and cultural context of a preindustrial European state is very different from that of contemporary societies – but this is not to negate that, for example, seeing the consequences on economic inequality and social polarization of increases in fiscal pressure in a context of highly regressive taxation does not lead to questions (and maybe even some answers) about more recent dynamics, as well as about current proposals for tax reform. As ever in historical research, our questions are driven by our personal experience, and there is no doubt whatsoever that many scholars, as well as the civil society, are now wondering about the nature and the consequences of inequality growth, and about whether and how we should intervene. Our historical enquiry does provide, we believe, some useful and original insights into this debate – but as we also have the ambition to tell a good story, we will save them for the conclusion so as not to deprive the reader of what we hope will be the pleasure of accompanying us, through the book, in an intellectual lion hunt.

1 The Venetian Fiscal System
Centre and Periphery

This chapter aims to give an overview of the developments of the Venetian fiscal system between the late Middle Ages and the early modern period. Such developments, although an integral part of the process of the gradual emergence all over Europe of the modern fiscal state, are nevertheless remarkably localized in their specifics. Particular attention will be paid to local taxation, which on account of its heterogeneous characteristics is often overlooked when attempting a synthesis, but is crucial to understanding the sources available for the study of the distribution of property and wealth. Indeed, the local property tax records (*estimi*) are the main historical sources used in the chapters that follow.

1.1 The General Development of the Republic's Fiscal System: Venice and the Birth of the Domain on the *Terraferma* (Late Fourteenth to Fifteenth Centuries)

Late medieval fiscal systems were based on assumptions which were quite different from those common today. A first point to consider is that they reflected the composite nature of most states – and within such composite states, a high degree of conflictive negotiation between centre and periphery occurred. Indeed, as Bartolomé Yun-Casalilla (2012, 15) recently put it, there could be 'no centralization without negotiation', and taxation was always a crucial feature of such negotiation. As will be seen, the Republic of Venice was no exception. Another important frequent feature of these early fiscal systems, which seems to be particularly apparent in the case of the Republic, was the propensity of the ruling elites to transfer the onus of taxation to the peripheries. Cities tended to saddle with the fiscal burden those who lived in the *contado* (i.e. the rural areas subject to the authority of a given city); the capital city tried to increase taxation in the provinces; the powerful merchant classes were inclined to favour direct taxation on real estate; the patricians taxed the poor and so on (Borelli 1980; Zangheri 1980; Lanaro 1982b; Herlihy and Klapisch-Zuber 1985; Bonney 1999; Cohn 1999; Yun-Casalilla and O'Brien

2012). In Italy, this was the legacy of the age of the communes, which became the heritage of the regional states of the Renaissance and was questioned only in the early modern period, with the organization of a more complex centralized administration of finance (De Maddalena and Kellnbenz 1984; Chittolini, Molho and Schiera 1994; Dubet and Legay 2011; Dincecco 2011). The increase in taxation played a key role in the birth of modern public finance and consequently in the state-building process.[1]

This was by no means a linear process, and it developed in different ways in the various states in Italy. In the case of the Republic of Venice – but the same could be said, for example, for the State of Milan – it generated a polycentric administration which left the system of medieval rights almost unchanged (Berengo 1999).[2] Moreover, in the case of the Republic, the dialectics leading to the rise of the regional state encouraged the development of new administrative exceptions, allowing specific 'new' frontier areas or peripheral territories the right to negotiate their own administration directly with the *Dominante* (the city of Venice). They were the so-called separate lands: non-urban communities or territories which, either because of their own exceptional strategic, demographic or socio-economic characteristics or because Venice wished to limit the power of one of the subject cities, obtained a 'separation' from the *contado* to which they belonged and were often in charge of administrating their own legal and fiscal systems (Chittolini 1983).

These fiscal privileges were not only reaffirmed by the Republic but also continually extended in line with the process of the consolidation of consent, a very common feature in the Italian states of the early modern period (Ventura 1964; Di Tullio and Fois 2014, 69–75). This was carried out according to a distributive model which overlapped the administrative geography, where the closer to the Venetian lagoon, the more the resemblance to the fiscal system of Venice, while the further from the *Dominante,* especially in the mountains (e.g. the valleys of Bergamo and

---

[1] Historiography has paid considerable attention to the study of public finance in Italian states. It would be impossible to mention, even briefly, all these studies; however, see the historiographical syntheses in Di Vittorio (1993), Felloni (1999), De Luca, Pezzolo and Sabatini (2003) and Pezzolo (2006a). For an international comparison, see Bonney (1999), Piola Caselli (2008), Dincecco (2011), Yun-Casalilla and O'Brien (2012) and Béguin (2015).

[2] On the dynamics between central governments and local jurisdictions during the formation of regional states see the seminal works by Giorgio Chittolini (1979a; 1979b, 7–50). For Venice, in particular, see Varanini (1979, 1980), which partly follows Ventura (1964). Some historiographic summaries, especially of the relationship between Venice and the *Terraferma,* are found in Grubb (1986), Knapton (1998) and Varanini (2011). More generally, for Italy, see the recent summary in Gamberini and Lazzarini (2012), and for the Republic of Venice, see Knapton (2012).

Brescia or the Friuli), the more the right to autonomy was respected. This game of privileges and alliances was in stark contrast to the apparent uniformity and equity of the Venetian system of direct taxation, as it penalized the territories closer to the capital and politically more loyal, such as the rich countryside round Padua, and made the tax distribution unfair (Knapton 1982, 19).

While acknowledging the aforementioned polycentrism and the persistence of local characteristics, we must not overlook the efforts of the *Dominante* to establish a single fiscal system throughout the *Terraferma*, which were facilitated by the very similar characteristics already shared by the various cities prior to the ascendancy of Venice. During the Middle Ages a concentration of fiscal powers increasingly passed into the hands of the cities[3] (later replaced by the seigneurial chamber), which based their revenue mostly on indirect taxation (consumer goods and customs duties) and on levies on salt.[4] With the annexation of the *Terraferma*, Venice tried to absorb and harmonize these local systems, concentrating taxation on duties and allowing the direct taxes (the so-called *gravezze*), although becoming increasingly important, to continue to be predominantly extraordinary and weigh more heavily on the rural areas (Knapton 1982, 20).[5] Thus a marked administrative decentralization was maintained, both at a provincial and at a local level, delegating to the local communities the right to distribute and collect tributes. Also here, as in most of Italy and Europe, throughout the early modern period, the political centre, whether a feudal domain or a republic, continued to delegate this administrative function to the local communities (Mannori 1990, 1997).[6]

Already in the fourteenth century, Venice had had the opportunity of trying out the organization of its future fiscal administration in some areas, thanks in particular to the direct control of Treviso and to the indirect influence exerted on the seignories through tariff agreements or the levying of monopolies. These preliminary experiments were followed

[3] Especially after the Black Death, as shown by Cohn (1999) for the case of the Florentine State.
[4] For the importance of this tax, as well as for the part it played in the political domination of the territory, see Mainoni (2001).
[5] For a comparison with the State of Milan in the fifteenth and sixteenth centuries, see Di Tullio (2011), Di Tullio and Fois (2014) and Di Tullio, Maffi and Rizzo (2015).
[6] This also happened with the management of the military, as the burden of armies, both in peacetime and in wars, was often almost completely the responsibility of rural communities, on which fell the tax burden for the upkeep of the soldiers and their billets. On this subject see Knapton (1981a, 1986) and Ongaro (2017). For a comparison with the State of Milan see Covini (1987, 1998), Rizzo (1987, 2001, 2008), Maffi (1999, 2007), Colombo (2008), Buono (2009), Di Tullio (2014a) and Buono, Di Tullio and Rizzo (2016).

by the fiscal organization of the newly conquered territories, which occupied the Republic during the first decades of the fifteenth century until the Peace of Lodi (1454). In this phase of ongoing warfare, agreements were reached between Venice and the municipal institutions of the various provinces on their new and diverse responsibilities, almost always preceded by the renewal of the *estimi*. These were used to calculate the fiscal capacity, both of the various parts of a territory (general *estimi* and provincial *estimi*) and of individual taxpayers (community *estimi*); see later (Knapton 1981b, 386–87). This is what happened in Bergamo and Verona, but we have evidence of similar renewals in the same years also for other cities on the *Terraferma*: Padua (Favaretto 1998), Treviso (Cavazzana Romanelli and Orlando 2006) and Vicenza.[7] To ingratiate the new subjects, the *estimi* were renewed on the basis of the local old customs, but very soon it became clear that this was merely a way of sweetening the pill. In fact, the wartime requirements demanded a new direct tax, apportioned locally on the basis of the *estimi*. It was the so-called *colta ducale* or *dadia delle lanze*, introduced in 1417, which permitted the equipping of a permanent army and led to the Republic's first real increase in ordinary expenses. Until the beginning of the sixteenth century, the *dadia delle lanze* was the most important direct tax, usually levied as an exceptional tax. It originated from a military contingent of cavalry given by Padua to Venice for the war against King Sigismund of Hungary, but gradually every *contado* and city on the *Terraferma* (except for Brescia and perhaps for some years also Bergamo) had to pay this tribute (Pezzolo 1998, 56; Maifreda 2002, 66).

The fiscal system that emerged remained virtually unchanged in the second half of the fifteenth century, with some exceptional requirements resulting from short-lived wars. The onus on the *Terraferma* increased, this time exponentially, during the long Italian Wars (1494–1559). With the advance of the French and the crushing defeat of Agnadello (1509), Venice had to cope with the temporary loss of its Italian provinces and their slow and difficult recovery, and was unable to prevent the situation from degenerating into more or less blatant episodes of fiscal revolt. The beginning of the sixteenth century, in fact, proved to be a turning point in the relationship between Venice and the *Terraferma*. Not so much for the fiscal system, which was still modelled on that of the fifteenth century, or because of the increase in the tax burden, which partly reflected the inflation and population growth of the sixteenth century,[8] but above all, on account of Venice's growing dependence on its mainland dominions.

---

[7] ASVi, *Estimi*, f. 1.
[8] On the demographic dynamics of the period, see Alfani (2013a, 2016a).

From them Venice obtained its principal revenues and consequently the administration of its territory had to be reformed. In this period the provincial fiscal chambers were established, meeting places between the patricians of the Republic and the local elite, mainly for the purpose of administering the new and ever-increasing direct taxation (Knapton 1982, 17–19 and 23–27).[9]

Despite the renewed interest in the *Terraferma*, Venice's aim to shape the previous fiscal systems to its own financial requirements failed to establish a uniform administrative organization, let alone the same system of tax distribution at a local level. On the contrary, it was the object of ongoing bargaining between Venice and subject cities and territories. As was common in Italy, the political centre aimed just to secure the levy on the subject territories of a certain quota agreed on each year. How the sum was distributed within a province or even among taxpayers was not something in which the fiscal chamber would or could intervene. Only when an unfair distribution of the taxes risked damaging the state, because the amounts agreed on were either not levied or were collected with difficulty and at the risk of impoverishing a sector of the taxpayers, did Venice intervene. This happened especially when, with the increasingly heavy burden of taxes and the emptying of the coffers of the local communities, it became necessary to prevent a growing number of bankruptcies. This involved strict control by the state over the management of local finances and enforcing, if not exactly uniformity, at least a certain standardization in the system of the distribution of taxes, above all by means of the *estimi*. For all these reasons, it is necessary to distinguish between the central (state) fiscal system and that of the peripheries, which though increasingly inclined to align with the directives of Venice, still maintained some kind of autonomy – greater or smaller, depending on their collocation and geopolitical role, and on the bargaining power of the local elites.

Another aspect to clarify is that the Venetian fiscal system was based on the concept of the solidarity of the whole body. The centre fixed the yearly amount of taxation, while locally it was the individual bodies, jointly responsible to the fiscal chamber, that determined the actual allocation

[9] Analogous processes took place also in Lombardy and in Piedmont. In Milan, for example, the well-known (and controversial) *estimo* of Charles V was completed and later the complex systems of *equalanza* were organized. On the *estimo* of Charles V and the evolution of the fiscal system in Lombardy in the sixteenth century see Di Tullio (2011) and Di Tullio and Fois (2014). On the *equalanza* see Vigo (1979), Rizzo (2008) and Colombo (2008). In Piedmont, the Savoys started a similar process with the introduction of a tax known as *tasso* in 1562. In Piedmont, however, in comparison with other areas, the communities were allowed greater freedom in finding resources to pay the quota of the dues – a situation which helped to determine a substantial uniformity in local *estimi* between the Middle Ages and the end of the early modern period (Alfani 2013c, 2014).

of the taxes among their members. In other words, it was the individual bodies which ultimately established who paid taxes and how they would be paid. So although the fiscal system of the *ancien regime* might seem rather muddled and complicated, it actually worked perfectly in favour of the hierarchies and the structures of privilege that permeated society. A different taxation was guaranteed (1) between the various bodies of the state, (2) between the cities and the rural areas and (3) among the various communities and the privileged classes within them (the *clero* and the Venetians, for example. Note that the *clero* included religious institutions, such as the monasteries, and only occasionally individual members of the clergy) or the separate lands. The fiscal chamber was not primarily interested in the local systems of tax distribution, but in receiving from every fiscal body the sums established (Pezzolo 2006a, 31–37; Di Tullio 2011). Indeed, a considerable portion of the taxes never passed through the central fiscal chamber, either because collection and distribution were contracted out to individuals or because they were administered locally. This applied both to the management of the military and to the corvées (the maintenance of roads, canals and irrigation ditches, etc.), which although serving a public interest were the responsibility of the rural people and did not touch the budgets either of the Venetian fiscal chamber or of the main cities (Knapton 1982, 22), although it was often the citizens or Venetians owning property in the countryside who benefitted from the system. We should also remember that many local communities, both in Italy and elsewhere in Europe, were apt to pay the taxes levied by the state first of all with sums from the municipal coffers, obtained from collecting rents or rights, or even from the sale of communal assets, and only secondly resorted to raising tributes among their own members (Cattini 1984; Di Tullio 2014a).

We find, therefore, in the fiscal system of the Republic both an original polycentricity and an astute policy pursued by Venice that tended to further its own interests, precisely by recognizing these local rights, which only at first sight seem to be unfavourable to the capital. Let's take as an example the duties, that is, the set of taxes that affected the transit and consumption of goods. From the fifteenth century to the end of the Republic, these indirect taxes made up most of the core revenue of the Venetian fiscal chamber: between 60% and 75% of the revenues of the different budgets of the Republic in the period 1480–1780, but about 80% to 85% if we consider only the revenues from Venice and the *Terraferma* (Pezzolo 2006a, 47–49). As already discussed, after the conquest of the territories on the *Terraferma* Venice adopted a conservative approach, maintaining the pre-existent system, for two main reasons. First, the *Dominante* wished to keep its good relations with local elites, who saw that their privileges were confirmed. Second, Venice had no intention of upsetting a system which was mainly in its favour and based on previously stipulated agreements. This conservative approach proved to be advantageous for Venetian commerce, which already in earlier decades had implemented and entrenched its privileges and now, with the ostensible recognition of local protectionist rights, was in fact guaranteeing its own success, restricting possible competition from free trade within the newly acquired areas. By encouraging the provincial markets of the main cities, whose range of operations was limited to their own *contadi* and was dedicated mainly to obtaining supplies of food, the expansion of new medium- and long-range trade of manufactured goods potentially in competition with Venice was restricted (Knapton 1982, 28–29).

From a different angle, this affected the process of economic 'regionalization' in the Republic. Indeed, in Italy the process of the formation of an economic region (but the same applies to the formation of states) always brought into play conflicting interests, which reflected on the way in which the different Italian states developed. So, for example, the State of Milan was the result of the conflict between various local bodies and the mediation imposed by the dominant feudal family – the Visconti. In Tuscany and in the Republic of Venice it was the urban oligarchies of the respective capital cities which played a central role in the process, although with different results in the two areas. In Tuscany the early establishment of an integrated regional economy went hand in hand with the ascendency of Florence over the other cities in the region. On the Venetian *Terraferma* the results were more varied.[10] In Veneto, economic regionalization had already begun before the Venetian conquest, creating, even though in a context of political fragmentation, a well-defined but polycentric economic area. But in general, a consequence of Venice's attempt to limit the types of production in the subject cities, also with the policy of duties mentioned earlier, was that the sphere of political control did not coincide with the development of an economically integrated region (defined as one made up of interdependent areas organized according to a division of labour on a geographical scale). For example, the Republic's domains in Lombardy were not part of the Veneto economic region, though maintaining important economic ties with the State of Milan.[11] In the end, the *Terraferma* was organized in a series of

---

[10] Malanima (1983), with whom Mirri (1986) agreed. Later there was ample debate on the subject, in an attempt to reconsider and tone down this schematic interpretation. See Corritore (1993), Romani (1994), Lanaro (1999), Epstein (2000) and Beonio-Brocchieri (2000).

[11] On the permanence of what were often ancient autonomous economic spaces in the area of the Republic, see Knapton (1992), Varanini (1992) and Lanaro (1999).

'economic basins' which interacted with each other, maintaining, however, some distinguishing structural features and their own institutional rights (Lanaro 1999, 23–30; 2003a, 2003b; Mocarelli 2006; Caracausi 2008, 211–12).

1.2   The Rise of the Venetian Fiscal State (Sixteenth to Eighteenth Centuries)

During the early modern period, states across Europe managed to increase their financial means, mostly by introducing institutional innovations which led to more effective fiscal systems and to an ability to sustain larger public debts. This phenomenon, to which historiography has paid considerable attention, is known as 'the rise of the fiscal state' (Bonney 1999; Glete 2002; Yun-Casalilla and O'Brien 2012) and is the result of the gradual organization of costly bureaucratic states, of the need to provide support for international commerce (Yun-Casalilla 2012) and, above all, of the underlying 'military revolution' (Roberts 1956; Parker 1988; Downing 1992; Rogers 1995). The new method of warfare and the consequent increase in expenses for equipment and military billets, as well as for the logistics of defence in general, enormously increased the expenditure of early modern states and obliged the treasuries to reorganize public finance and the forms of taxation. In Italy as elsewhere, the increased control of the centre over the fiscal system[12] was aimed primarily at freeing the central treasuries from their dependence on the 'private' property of the ruling families.[13]

Because of the form of state which is peculiar to an oligarchic Republic, this process was slightly different in Venice, not only because here there was not a specific ruling family using the revenues of its patrimony to manage the state but also because originally the Republic had founded its success on trade rather than on extensive territorial possessions. This was why, when it extended its dominion to the *Terraferma*, Venice followed economic and fiscal policies that had previously characterized its overseas possessions. First, the fulcrum of Venetian policy was the defence of the capital's commerce (by gaining control over competing centres, also with the right to impose customs favourable to Venetian goods). Second, the

---

[12] For the Republic of Venice see Mallett and Hale's classic 1984 work. To contextualize the debate on the military revolution in Italy, see Pezzolo (2006b), Rizzo (2007) and Alfani (2013a). More generally on the evolution of public finance in Europe see Dincecco (2011).

[13] This is what happened, for example, in the State of Milan (Di Tullio and Fois 2014). The situation in the duchies of the Po Valley was different, as here the mixing of the prince's property and public finance continued to determine the size of the revenues (De Maddalena 1961; Romani 1978; Podestà 1995, 2007).

subject territories had to contribute to financing the expenses for admin-istration and defence through the Venetian salt monopoly and with tributes that mainly taxed consumer goods. This does not mean, how-ever, that the Republic did not base its revenue also on patrimonial revenues, modest though these were. Traditionally Venice did not usually administer large patrimonies, preferring to cope with the urgent need for ready money by selling the spoils of its conquests. So, when it had extended its dominion on the *Terraferma*, Venice acquired most of the possessions and rights belonging to the ancient noble families (Carrara and della Scala) of Padua, Verona and Vicenza, but soon sold them off, and it did the same with the huge assets of the commune of Treviso. This policy of vending on a large scale continued throughout the early modern period, with estates either confiscated or obtained through wars and the purchase of territory (Knapton 1982, 22–23 and 35–36).

The principal source of revenue for the Republic was therefore taxes, which, with due caution, can be defined as either 'direct' or 'indirect'. In an attempt to classify the different tributes, it might be helpful to take into consideration the structure of the general budgets of the Republic of Venice which differentiated between the *gravezze* (taxes based on assets, i.e. on the *estimi*, the poll taxes or other direct taxation) and the 'duties' (which included taxes on trade, consumption and production). It is, however, only a summary classification, in view of the crucial role played by the local communities in deciding where the burden of taxes actually fell and the changes to the taxable income made by the state's fiscal chamber. Think of the salt tax or the duty on milling, which, although formally taxes on consumption, were often levied simply on a per capita basis, changing from an 'indirect' to a 'direct' criterion of taxation (Pezzolo 2006a, 45). Given these clarifications, it can be said that the Venetian revenue from taxes originated mainly from duties rather than direct taxes, both centrally and locally. Between the sixteenth and eight-eenth centuries, hardly never less than 60% of the national revenue was obtained from duties, with peaks of more than 75% in 1670. This struc-ture is similar to that of the Republic of Genoa in the fourteenth century, of Florence in the early fifteenth century and elsewhere in Europe, that of England (Pezzolo 2006a, 47–49). The Kingdom of Naples (Piola Caselli 1997, 170) and the State of Milan were closer to the structure of the French budget, with greater importance given to direct taxes.[14]

---

[14] In the State of Milan, at the beginning of the sixteenth century, duties were the principal revenue, but only marginally more than direct taxes. During the century, the latter became preponderant (Di Tullio and Fois 2014).

The expansion of Venice on the *Terraferma* was accompanied by the increasing fiscal control of the territory. In a kind of vicious circle Venetian expansion resulted in an increase in expenditure due to the administration of the state, which could be guaranteed only by the control of and the increase in the tax levy in the territory, to prevent the central finances from imploding and to ensure that the mercantile supremacy of Venice was not undermined and was instead extended to the new territories. The preponderant importance of duties in the Venetian budget in the late medieval and Renaissance periods meant that most of the burden involved in the construction of a territorial state was sustained by ordinary means, above all by the revenue from customs – the economic life-blood of the Republic – and second, by forced loans and by the increase in direct taxation. Duties were levied mostly on agricultural products and their transport on the *Terraferma*. Also in Venice itself, the emphasis on avoiding damage to the trade of high-value goods meant that as much as possible of the fiscal burden took the form of duties on goods of mass consumption, such as the agricultural products, which increasingly came from the *Terraferma* (Knapton 1982, 44).

State revenue from taxation in the *ancien regime* tended to cover principally the upkeep of the centre, while almost all the responsibility of the administration of the periphery was delegated to the local institutions, even when it was required by the state, such as in the case of the pay and the expenses of rectors (*rettori*, i.e. the representatives of Venice in the subject communities, whose functions depended on the specific post) and other officials (Borelli 1982). The provinces also suffered because of the 'extraordinary' components of taxation, i.e. the temporary introduction of new tributes, partially managed with recourse to the public debt (which benefitted from the availability of large amounts of capital from commerce) (Knapton 1982, 44). Often, these exceptional burdens took the form of loans which should have been returned once the emergency was over, but instead became part of the assets of the fiscal chamber. This process became so common that in the early part of the sixteenth century a decision was made to regularize it, turning these forced loans into direct ordinary tax, the *sussidio* (subsidy) (Pezzolo 1998, 56–57).

The Republic of Venice was not an exceptional case in being obliged to bring in a new direct tax to cope with the state's growing need for cash.[15] As we have seen, it was a feature of Europe, which in those years affected also other Italian states, for example Milan, where in 1537 the '*mensuale*'

---

[15] See Pezzolo's recent summary (2012) on the connection between the fiscal state and the military revolution. Recent historiography has begun to question the other side of the coin: the redistributive repercussions of the military revolution among civilians (Parrot 2012; Alfani 2013a).

was introduced, or the Sabaudian State, where from 1562 the '*tasso*' was collected. In both cases, the new tributes soon became the main form of ordinary direct taxation in these states (Vigo 1979; Pezzolo and Stumpo 2008; Di Tullio 2011; Alfani 2013c). The process of allocating the burden of these new taxes was similar, as in theory it was based on the actual ability of each province or community to pay. However, in practice some differences are to be found in the way provincial quotas were allotted. In the case of the Republic of Venice they were allocated according to a traditional system, that is, levied by the central chamber on the basis of previous knowledge of the territories and subject to bargaining between the various fiscal bodies (Del Torre 1986). In the case of the State of Milan, it instead led to a completely new attempt to recalculate the wealth of each province using the laborious process of the *estimo* of Charles V, even though it does not automatically follow that in Lombardy taxes were distributed more fairly than elsewhere (Coppola 1973; Zappa 1986; Di Tullio 2011).

Thus, after the first distribution of the *sussidio* in 1529, following petitions and protests by diverse provinces, a new distribution was reached in 1535, which was re-adjusted and finally established in 1542 (Table 1.1). The resulting provincial taxes were the consequence not only of bargaining between Venice and the local elites, but also of the direct mediation of the Venetian patricians. The most significant reduction of the tax quota was actually in those provinces where the estates of the Venetians were important, such as in Padua, Treviso and in the Polesine (Pezzolo 1998, 58–59). Venice, however, took other factors into consideration when establishing the redistribution of taxes. For example, the quota was stable in the province of Bergamo, where there were virtually no Venetian landowners, but which was on the all-important frontier with the State of Milan. In the case of Friuli, which was one of the key suppliers of wood to the Venetian lagoon, the possibility of producing large quantities of wood depended on a particular equilibrium between woods and meadows, which had to be protected from an excessive tax burden (Lorenzini 2011; Zannini 2012).

The *sussidio* and the increase in revenues in the second half of the sixteenth century were only a foretaste of their sudden increase in the seventeenth century. In the first decades of that century, Venice was once again involved in various wars (in particular that of Gradisca in 1615–17 against the Hapsburgs and various wars against the Spanish between 1619 and 1629 during the Thirty Years' War), and its revenues increased from about two and a half million ducats around 1600 to three and a half at the beginning of the 1620s. The situation was exacerbated by the plague in 1629–30, which made the tax collection by the central fiscal offices more difficult and caused a further per capita increase of the fiscal pressure (Pezzolo 1994, 322–23). The economic situation added to the mortality

Table 1.1 *Provincial division of the ordinary 'subsidy' (ducats)*

Province	1529	1535	1542	1542/1529 (% change)
Brescia	22,000	24,000	25,000	+13.6
Vicenza	15,000	15,500	16,800	+12.0
Padua	13,000	12,300	10,300	–20.8
Treviso	13,000	12,600	10,300	–20.8
Verona	12,500	14,000	14,700	+17.6
Bergamo	8,000	7,300	8,000	—
Friuli	7,000	6,000	5,500	–21.4
Polesine	3,000	2,200	2,200	–26.7
Crema	2,600	2,200	2,600	—
Belluno	1,500	1,500	1,700	+13.3
Cologna	1,000	1,000	1,000	—
Feltre	1,000	1,000	1,300	+30
Bassano	400	400	600	+50.0
Tot.	100,000	100,000	100,000	

Sources: Our elaboration from Del Torre (1986), 82 and Pezzolo (1998, 57).

crisis, with the progressive reduction in overseas trade, mainly due to increasing competition by the French, English and Dutch. It has been suggested that in this international situation the plague of 1629–30 (perhaps the worst since the Black Death, resulting in the death of about 35% of the entire population of northern Italy) caused great harm to the principal economies of northern Italy, including Venice (Alfani 2010c, 2013b; Alfani and Percoco 2018). From a fiscal point of view, the crisis in overseas trade meant the re-dimensioning of what had always been the main factor of Venetian public finance, obliging the Republic to find alternative sources, in particular increasing levies on consumer goods in the capital and on the *Terraferma*. The state revenues returned to levels prior to the plague in the 1660s only, reaching around 3,740,000 ducats in 1665 and increasing to four million in 1670 (Pezzolo 1994, 322–23).

It was in these years that Venice, in a final attempt to keep its possessions in the Aegean Sea, was heavily involved in the War of Candia (1645–69), when it had to face the Ottoman Empire, then at the height of its power. The war brought about a rise in extraordinary taxation, which was mainly collected by means of direct taxation and forced loans. In the period 1645–58 the *Terraferma* had to supply exceptional subsidies, *'campatici'* and *'tanse'*,[16] for a theoretical sum of 3,730,000

[16] The *'campatico'* was a tax on landed property calculated with a fixed sum based on the different qualities of land. The *'tansa'*, instead, was paid on the basis of the occupation and estimated wealth of the various taxpayers (Pezzolo 2000, 224).

ducats (Pezzolo 2000, 223–24). The urgent need for a dependable collection of taxes prompted the Venetian fiscal chamber to transfer the onus of taxation onto direct taxes, which were mostly on land and on 'heads' (the *testatico*, a sort of fixed per capita tax), rather than onto other items of wealth, as they were objectively more difficult to calculate. If, therefore, until the seventeenth century, in a situation in which the Republic of Venice was still at the centre of a thriving international trade, the preponderant importance of duties in the public budget had meant partially transferring the costs of the state to foreign merchants and their clients, between the sixteenth and seventeenth centuries increasing military commitments in Italy and in the eastern Mediterranean coincided with the economic down-sizing of the port of Venice, as the growing demand for taxes on the *Terraferma* indicates. In particular, the Republic resorted to increasing duties on domestic consumption, especially on the food consumed within the city walls (duties on wine, salt and cereals) but, as already pointed out, landowners were also hit, especially by the introduction of the *campatico* and the intensifying of tithes (Pezzolo 2006a, 57–60). The growth of the fiscal burden weighed on the ever weaker local finances, badly hit by the war and definitely weakened by the ongoing requests of extraordinary contributions. This situation was common to most of the Italian and European local communities in that period. The local communities were effectively the basic units of the fiscal system and for many early modern states it would have been complicated to secure stable revenues without their mediation.[17] Indeed, often this was the case even after the fiscal reforms and the introduction of the modern cadastre[18] in the eighteenth and nineteenth centuries (Capra 1980; Zangheri 1980, 71–130; Alimento 2008; Pezzolo 2012, 271–73).

As we have seen, from the second half of the sixteenth century until the 1620s, Italian and European states managed to greatly increase their revenues in absolute terms (Figure 1.1). However, at least in northern Italy, a phase of contraction and readjustment followed. Not by chance, it began from the plague in 1629–30 and at least in the Republic of Venice, it ended around the 1660s. A generalized increase in taxes characterized the eighteenth century. If a comparison is made with Europe, different dynamics are found in the Republic of Venice and in France, as the latter

---

[17] For the Republic of Venice, for example, see Pederzani (1992). For a comparison with the Papal States see Tabacchi (2007). For the Kingdom of Naples, see Bulgarelli (2012). For a comparison with Europe, see De Vries (1976).

[18] In the modern cadastres, introduced by many Italian states during the eighteenth century, the evaluation of the assets was based on the assessment of each 'parcel' (portion of territory), geometrically measured by public surveyors and drawn on a cadastral map (Zaninelli 1963).

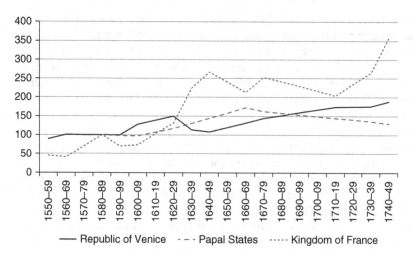

Figure 1.1 The trend of the state revenues of some Italian and European states (indexes based on values in kg of silver. 100 = 1580–89). *Sources:* Our elaboration based on Pezzolo (2006a, 43).

greatly increased its overall revenues in the seventeenth century while the Republic managed this only in per capita terms (see later). Divergence continued during the eighteenth century and would be even clearer if a comparison were made between Venice on one side, and England and Holland on the other side (Pezzolo and Stumpo 2008). This being said, the Republic still performed better compared to most other Italian states, such as the State of Milan (Di Tullio and Fois 2014) and the Papal States – but surely not compared to the rising power of northern Italy, the Sabaudian State, where fiscal revenues steadily grew in both per capita and absolute terms throughout the early modern period (Alfani and Ryckbosch 2016, 151).

The tendency for increasing taxation in the Republic of Venice is more clearly visible if we consider it in per capita terms. Additionally, as the estimates of the state revenues we have are expressed in kilograms of silver, we need to take into account the depreciation of silver that characterizes most of the early modern period. One simple way of doing this is to apply to silver the 'consumer price index' developed by Malanima for central-northern Italy.[19] If we do that and if we take into account the available population estimates, we get – for the Italian territories of the Republic only – a picture of moderate increase in per capita taxation from

[19] Malanima, *Consumer Price Index (1250–2010)* (revision 2015). Available at www.paolo malanima.it.

the 1550s to 1609 (+6.5%). The per capita burden grew much more markedly in the aftermath of the 1630 plague and during the War of Candia of 1645–69 (+43.2% between 1609 and 1710). Indeed, if we compare the estimated level of per capita taxation in the 1550s to that of 1710, we detect an overall increase of 52.5%.[20] However, a possible problem with these figures is that Malanima's consumer price index is based on prices from the Florentine State and the State of Milan, not from the Republic of Venice (Malanima 2011, 173). Consequently, we prefer another estimate, provided by Pezzolo (2006a, 66), which expresses per capita taxation as the daily wages of labourers in the construction industry needed to cover the tax due to the central state. These measures suggest an increase in per capita taxation of 16.1% from 1550–70 to 1620–29, and of 48.8% from 1620–29 to 1760–80 (overall +69.3% from the mid-sixteenth to the mid-eighteenth century). This way of measuring per capita taxation accounts for inflation, and also has the virtue of allowing for international comparisons (see Chapter 4, Figure 4.4 and related discussion). This being said, the two series of estimates of per capita taxation discussed earlier show a largely coherent trend.

To assess correctly the extent of the increase in taxation in the Republic of Venice during the seventeenth and the eighteenth centuries we should include in the analysis local taxation (as the communities could either, at least theoretically, reduce local taxes or get into debt). Some additional information about this will be provided in the following sections. A final point to consider is the overall efficiency of the fiscal system. Regarding the difference between the tax stipulated by the fiscal chamber and that actually collected, it has been pointed out that the transaction costs of the Venetian fiscal system were not as heavy as elsewhere – so this difference was practically insignificant. The flexibility of the Venetian fiscal system has been viewed favourably, because unlike other states in Europe, but in tune with other Italian states, it envisaged the role of local elites in supporting the increase in taxes during the early modern period, even though to the detriment of some local autonomy – a feature found also in the relationship between the government and the trade guilds, both in the cities of the *Terraferma* and in Venice itself (Caracausi 2008, 213). The War of Candia was a turning point, as a sharp increase in military expenditure led to an increase in per capita taxation but also, and more

---

[20] This estimate relates to the Italian territories only, as we do not have good estimates of the population of the entire state. This means that we could calculate the per capita fiscal burden only for those years for which we have the possibility of excluding revenues from the *Stato da Mar* (in particular, we used the data from Pezzolo 2006a, 47). The population estimates we use are an elaboration from the same sources used in the Appendix, Table A.3.

importantly, in the public debt (see Chapter 4). This was possible thanks to the substantial trust the citizens had in the Republic. The coincidence of those people lending money with members of the political elite in Venice made it feasible to invest in the Republic, which had never declared a state of bankruptcy, and also, thanks to the relative social peace in the state and the regular flow of income from duties, had always regularly paid interest (Lane 1973b; Mueller 1997; Pezzolo 2006a). This confidence, which guaranteed the investments in the state's public debt, made it possible to administer more tranquilly the ordinary and above all the exceptional taxes, which might have had serious repercussions on the territory. However, this could be read in a different light, in other words, that Venice, from the seventeenth century onwards, chose to bridge the budget deficit by increasing borrowing, rather than resorting to taxation as in previous years (Gullino 1982, 77). It is unclear how much this was due to voluntary renunciation, or to an inability to organize a stricter system of control over the *Terraferma*.

1.3   Between Continuity and Change: The Local Fiscal Systems

In the transition from the centre (Venice) to the periphery (the *Terraferma* and Venice's overseas possessions) the responsibility for tax collection passed from the Venetian fiscal chamber to those of the various major cities in the province and the political control of the procedure from the centre of the state (the Council of Ten and the Senate, up to the end of the sixteenth century, then afterwards de facto only the latter) to the city rectors. The intermediate and municipal institutions played an important role, both regarding the solidarity of the bodies towards the fiscal chamber and because it often fell to the municipal councils to nominate the tax collectors, and, more generally, the tricky administration of the local budget, with the consequences already mentioned (Maifreda 2002, 61–62).

The mandate of the local institutions was not so clear when it came to the collection of duties, either domestically or abroad. Once an agreement was reached on the amount of the taxation, the fiscal chamber could adopt various methods for its collection. The Republic could administer it directly with its own officials, as usually happened with monopolies. Alternatively it could enter into agreements with the territorial bodies, which accepted to pay a specific sum to Venice and then operated the collection independently if they wanted to do so, or instead opted to cover it with revenues from their own budget.[21] The method commonly used, however, was to contract the tax collection at public auction to the best bidder, who paid a sum to the chamber and took over the responsibility of the collection himself.[22] Unlike France, where tax farming was the per-quisite of a small number of courtiers and more like Holland, the procure-ment of duties in Venice almost always mirrored the local administrative boundaries and social milieu. Among the most important taxes on the *Terraferma*, only the salt taxes and the duty on tobacco were contracted in the capital, while the others were sanctioned by the fiscal chambers of the *Terraferma* and contracts were awarded locally (Pezzolo 2006a, 26–27).[23]

The contract system was very common because it suited both Venice and the local fiscal chambers. The farmer of the duties guaranteed the payment by instalments of the revenue, and took on the risks inherent in its collection. Thus he not only ensured the revenue but also shifted attention away from the true promoter of the tax levy (the state and/or the fiscal chamber), making the tax collector carry the blame for the rapacity of taxation. In this case, 'Venice in the eyes of its subjects was the distant source of justice and wisdom of the government' (Pezzolo 1998, 54). Furthermore, even subtracting the farmer's fee, a higher revenue was obtained from a contract than if it had gone directly into the chamber collecting the sum, which made it possible to plan ahead the revenues and any related expenditure. In comparison to the advantages for the Treasury, problems could arise for the population, which had to bear the costs of collecting taxes and the stress of having agents roaming round the country in search of goods to tax which would be the most profitable for the tax farmer. Thus delegating the tax collection to private individuals could further the injustice of taxation or unfair competition, as tax collectors could succumb to the pressure exerted by local potentates (whom they often knew because they lived in the area) or could even be in cahoots with smugglers.

With the collection of direct taxes the responsibility of the local bodies increased considerably. As we have already seen, the central authorities of

[21] The agreements were mainly adopted with regard to the separated lands, which under-took to pay to the chamber the previously negotiated annual sum, in place of the actual payment of the specific duty. This privilege enabled taxpayers to avoid the presence of tax collectors on their own land and, often, to obtain a discount on the actual amount they should have paid (Pezzolo 1998, 54–55).

[22] This system was in force in many Italian and European states. In France, each year a general tax farmer was nominated who had a contract for most of the taxes (Hamon 1994; Di Tullio and Fois 2014). Employing contractors to collect taxes was also in force at lower levels of the state fiscal system, that is, at the level of the individual fiscal body. See Di Tullio (2014a).

[23] For a detailed reconstruction of the contract system, besides the norms, see Caracausi (2008, 213–35).

the state decided the total amount of the tax and established how it was to be allocated within the provinces,[24] in agreement with the territorial bodies, which in turn distributed it among the local communities. It was the latter which actually organized the collection. The *estimo* was the means used to distribute a large part of the tax to be collected among the different bodies of the state and among the taxpayers.

In the Republic of Venice, as in other parts of central and northern Italy, there were various levels of *estimo*. Once Venice had divided the taxes between the various provinces of the state, each of these allotted them among their constituent parts (cities, *contado*, valleys, *clero*, separated lands, etc.), usually based on a general *estimo*, which established the quotas of the entire body, but not of individual households. Once the amount from provincial bodies was established, each one could fix a further territorial *estimo* to distribute, for example, the taxes between the communities that made up the same *contado*, or between those that constituted the intermediate fiscal jurisdictions called '*quadre*' (Zamperetti 1987; Pederzani 1992; Rossini 1994; Favaretto 1998). Finally, the taxes were apportioned among the individual taxpayers, or rather the single households that made up a community, and a municipal *estimo* was compiled for this purpose. However, within this compartmental system, which made the whole body jointly liable to the fiscal chamber (Faccini 1988; Colombo 2008), each body had the right to allocate the taxes imposed by the centre as it thought best, so long as the due amounts were handed over to the fiscal chamber on time. This was why at a local level the general principles and the fiscal objectives imposed by the centre could be completely reversed, and a tax conceived to be direct could be collected, in full or in part, increasing duties or taxes on salt consumption, and could therefore be allocated per head, per household or per *estimo* (Pezzolo and Stumpo 2008; Di Tullio 2011, 2014a). As a matter of fact, also at a local level everything possible was done to shift the onus of taxation onto classes which were remote from the local political elite or to transfer to other bodies the amount due. This was especially common among city dwellers, who not only enjoyed certain privileges compared to country people, on whom the tax burden mainly fell, but also transferred most of the taxes they should have paid onto duties, which hit also those residing in rural areas (Collins 1988; Pezzolo 1990). In addition there was the well-known practice of transferring rural wealth to the urban *estimi*,

---

[24] According to the traditional division between city, *clero* and territory (Maifreda 2009, 83), except for Bergamo, where the allocation was between the city and the various parts of the territory (the plain and the valleys). The case of Treviso was slightly different, because there the fiscal body of foreigners was added (Grubb 1982; Scherman 2009, 2013).

thanks to the widespread encroachment of urban property into the countryside on the one hand, and on the other, the acquisition of citizenship by members of the local rural elites, who could therefore transfer their assets to the city lists and thus pay less tax. So, while the already privileged citizens saw their tax base increase and based the allocation of taxes also on duties, the country people had to cope with taxation which became increasingly onerous as the state required more and more money, and was allocated on an ever-decreasing tax base (due to the increase of urban property) and without being able to shift tributes onto duties.

The transfer of real estate to the cities by rural communities should have triggered a renewal of the general *estimi*, but this did not happen very often and, incredible as it seems, was never the focus of country people's demands, even though it was the basic reason for the perpetuation and extension of the fiscal privileges of the city dwellers (Zamperetti 1987). In this respect, in the Republic of Venice, as elsewhere in Italian states, those who sided with the country people on the issue of citizen's privileges were the elites of Venice and the fiscal chambers, but only from the sixteenth century onwards, when most of the real estate was already in the hands of the citizens. It was only in the 1530s that, for example, taxes had to be paid on lands owned and managed directly (*condotte a boaria*) by city dwellers (Maifreda 2002, 120–21). These measures by the state in favour of the country people were based more on the need to increase revenues and to guarantee the collection of taxes than on any desire for fiscal equity. If the rural communities were overtaxed, they would not be able to collect the required sums and the first to suffer would be the state treasury. This was why the onus had to be spread and borne also by the citizens and by those bodies which were traditionally exempt. For this reason during the sixteenth century various reforms were introduced, which forbade the transfer of estates from rural to urban *estimi* or to those recording property belonging to the *clero* (at least that acquired after a certain date). At the same time various systems to rebalance the tax burden were encouraged and, for example, the introduction of the ordinary subsidy (*sussidio*) was an opportunity to re-examine the fiscal burden on the various provinces of the *Terraferma* and promote the reform of the general *estimi* (Del Torre 1986; Pezzolo 1998).

As well as the ordinary and extraordinary taxes defined in terms of money (although often paid in kind), the country people were also often subject to various corvées: by no means an insignificant liability. They were required to contribute by supplying food, carts and lodgings for the Venetian rectors, for troops stationed in the *contado* and for various public representatives. They also had to supply labour for the upkeep of all the local 'public' facilities (roads, bridges, etc.), meaning that the state costs borne by the rural communities were extremely high and often the cost for military logistics and generally for corvées was more than that paid annually for levies. In the two years 1589–90 in various communities in the Bergamo area, the tributes to the fiscal chambers amounted to less than one third of the expenses, compared to the 40% spent on the *carreggi* (mandatory transport services of goods such as wood, grain or fodder), the militia and the upkeep of roads. In roughly the same period, in the community of Santa Sofia in the Verona area, about 10% of the expenses covered the *dadia delle lanze*, while twice that amount went towards the costs of billeting, the maintenance of forts, roads and *carreggi* (Pezzolo 2006a, 69).

So generally speaking, over the seventeenth century, as seen for the revenues of the Venetian fiscal chamber, there was also an increase in taxes locally. This can be inferred from the progressively greater demands made by the communities in general, or on the basis of the levy per *lire* of the *estimo*, which was meant to cover the overall amount required by the state and by the intermediate and local authorities. In the areas of Padua and Treviso, the taxes for every *lira* increased 2/2.5 times between 1550 and 1650. In various communities in the area of Verona expenses grew by the same amount between 1570 and 1626. Finally, in Nanto in the area of Vicenza, a peak in expenses around 1647 was followed by a stable period until the 1670s (Pezzolo 2006a, 71–3).[25] There were several reasons for this; among them was certainly the already mentioned increases in state taxes, following the increase in military expenses, likewise the progressive loss in assets and various municipal revenues. However, the whole process was deeply affected by the nature of the relationship between the various territories and Venice, which differed from one province to another, and by some specific aspects in the relationship between the main cities and the *contado*, which now will be briefly discussed. Particular attention will be paid to the areas which will be the object of the analysis in the following chapters (the provinces of Bergamo, Padua, Verona and Vicenza).

Bergamo

In 1427 Bergamo, formerly part of the State of Milan, was conquered by the Republic of Venice. From the outset Venice exercised extreme care in

---

[25] Similar examples of the increase in expenditure and taxation of local communities are found in other parts of Italy, for example in the state of Milan already in the sixteenth century (Di Tullio 2014), but above all in the following century (Colombo 2005). For a more general discussion on the subject, especially during the Italian Wars, see Alfani (2013a).

imposing on Bergamo its fiscal and administrative policy, for various reasons related to the province's two specific characteristics: it bordered on the State of Milan and was the scene of repeated clashes, and it had poor agricultural yields. Compared to other provinces on the *Terraferma*, Bergamo was particularly privileged. Various communities of the *contado* were recognized as separate lands in the mountains or as semi-autonomous jurisdictions on the plain, which won the right to administer taxation independently from the city of Bergamo (Pederzani 1992; Pezzolo 1998, 50). Special treatment was reserved for the city itself, granting customs agreements for local manufactured goods in transit from the Venetian lagoon with the aim of both strengthening the ties between Venice and the merchants of Bergamo, and limiting, as far as possible, smuggling over the borders with Milan and Switzerland, which, however, remained a constant scourge (Pezzolo 1998, 51).

The fiscal structure did not greatly differ from that in other areas of the *Terraferma* and was based principally on tolls and duties, perhaps also due to the extensive urban property on the plain of Bergamo, which would have made taxation based on direct levies ineffective (Pezzolo 1998, 52; Gioia 2004). The Venetian government structured the fiscal system along the lines of the pre-existent one, which originated in feudal times, and, compared to the rest of the *Terraferma*, put more importance on the so-called *imbottato*, a tax theoretically on the production of cereals and wine. In the second half of the sixteenth century, Venice's need for revenue led to the introduction of other duties that were particularly heavy on the production of textiles, which, together with wine, constituted Bergamo's main exports (Pezzolo 1998, 53). However, the Italian Wars and the financial requirements of the sixteenth century made it necessary to review the citizens' privileges by reforming the *estimo generale* of the whole province, dating back to 1476. This was by no means simple, obstructed as it was by the merchants, in particular, who grew rich during the difficult phases of the war. The new *estimo*, however, was eventually issued in 1547, establishing until the decline of the Republic the allocation of taxes between the various fiscal bodies in the Bergamo province and considerably increasing the fiscal burden in the city, mainly to the benefit of the valleys (Silini 1996). At the same time the gradual loss of estates from rural *estimi* was curtailed and the citizens had to contribute jointly and severally with the communities of the *contado* where their property was located (Pederzani 1992, 149; Pezzolo 1998, 60–61). As well as guaranteeing more revenues, Venice's assault on the prerogatives of the citizens was necessary to broaden the rural consensus, not so much among the farmers and farm labourers as among a sort of rural 'bourgeoisie' who had grown rich by trafficking in the shadow of big absentee patrician landowners. This happened principally in the politically more dynamic areas on the plain, Romano and Martinengo, or in the centres in the valleys, which, as elsewhere, campaigned in favour of the creation of territorial fiscal bodies, aiming to unite and institutionalize the claims of the rural communities against the privileges of the citizens.[26]

Venice's support of the rural communities hinged, however, on the need to avoid an excessively disproportionate fiscal burden, such as had already caused the erosion of municipal and collective properties, which had been used as collateral to guarantee loans in funding the billeting of armies and war taxes, but never paid back. For this reason, as in other states of northern Italy, Venice also intensified its efforts to control local finances, preventing the wealthy, in particular, from appropriating what remained of common property (Pederzani 1992, 408–23). Between the end of the sixteenth century and the eighteenth, Venice's capacity to impact on the local administration of finances and taxation, in Bergamo as elsewhere, was increased by the redrawing of the lines of conflict, which no longer focused on the wrangling between the various fiscal bodies, typical of the second half of the sixteenth century, but on the distribution of taxes within the provinces and the single communities and, more generally, on the way public money was spent (Pezzolo 2000, 227–30). This was the result of a closure by the leaders of the territorial bodies, which, as in the case of the lock-outs in the city councils (Lanaro 1992; Cattini and Romani 2005), had produced an elite that tended to shift the tax burden onto the lower orders, reproducing the very system against which these institutions had been established (Zamperetti 1987, 319). A possible solution to these problems was found in the extension of access to the community councils to include the households listed on the *estimo* that would have been hit by the fiscal burden, if municipal revenues continued to decrease. There was no lack of protests and endless lawsuits with Venice, mostly in the large communities, where the local oligarchies were strongest, as, for example, in Martinengo and Romano or in the big villages in the mountains (Pederzani 1992, 431–40).

Venice's new financial requirements and the control over local finances gradually made the fiscal system of the province of Bergamo more uniform to the rest of the *Terraferma*. During the sixteenth century, like all other provinces, Bergamo contributed to the increase in state expenses and although it was granted larger sums for the fortifications or the local officials' wages, it was, at the same time, heavily burdened by military

---

[26] On the birth of the territorial fiscal bodies (the so-called *corpi territoriali*) on the *Terraferma*, see Borelli (1983), Zamperetti (1987), Pederzani (1992), Rossini (1994), Favaretto (1998) and Maifreda (2002). For a comparison with the 'Congregations of the *Contado*' existing in the State of Milan, see the recent summary in Colombo (2008).

billets and by corvées (Pezzolo 1998, 64–9). The convergence towards
the level of fiscal pressure common on the *Terraferma* was consolidated in
the early decades of the seventeenth century, when the revenue from the
Bergamo province reached the average for the whole state, and in some
phases even surpassed it (Pezzolo 2000, 217–20).

Verona

Verona came under Venetian rule in 1405 after a turbulent period that in
a few decades led first to the fall of the della Scala dynasty (1387), then to
the advent of the Visconti (1387–1404) and finally to a brief rule of the
Carrara (1404–05). Officially, also in this case Venice adopted a cautious
approach, recognizing the various rights of the city, confirmed in the
statutes of 1450–51. These rights also concerned taxation and involved
administrative autonomy in managing tax collection and in promulgating
the *estimi*. This does not mean that with the coming to power of the
Republic there were no disputes and bargaining also on account of the
reassessment of the administration and consequently of taxation
(Varanini 1980). However, local traditions were respected. This applied
both to the norms listed in the city statutes of the thirteenth century and
confirmed by a Ducal Bull of 1414 (Lanaro 1982b, 194) and to their
practical application. The oldest extant city *estimo* dates back to 1407, but
there exists a territorial *estimo* from 1396 which was kept updated until the
mid-fifteenth century,[27] suggesting that until the reforms of the seventeenth century the Veronese tradition of *estimi* survived unharmed and
intact despite repeated changes of rulers (Tagliaferri 1966, 11–24).

In this time frame the city of Verona enjoyed considerable administrative autonomy both for itself and for most of the territory, and any
intervention by Venice was more a formal authorization than any real
form of restraint. This was the case, for example, in the disputes over the
threshold under which tax exemptions were applied. During the fifteenth
and sixteenth centuries, these disputes pitted the patricians against the
rest of the inhabitants, with Venice acting as an impartial authority rather
than the ruler, in an attempt both to preserve the peace and to guarantee
its revenues. This approach changed, as in other provinces, only in the
second half of the sixteenth century and especially at the beginning of the
seventeenth century (Lanaro 1982b, 1992, 83–88).

In the seventeenth century, then, the Republic intervened to a considerable extent also in Verona, reviewing the way subjects were taxed and
standardizing the procedures of the *estimo*. The most important

---

[27] ASVr, Antico Estimo del Comune, f. 247.

innovations for the city *estimo* concerned the obligation to keep the documents once the coefficients had been transcribed on the survey, and to include the assets of the *clero* in the records. After many contrasts, the *estimo del clero* was completed in 1659 (Borelli 1986c, 384–85).

Regarding the organization of the *contado*, and referring only to the areas included in our study, from the early fifteenth century the important property owners of the city had had their sights on the Veronese lowlands and had gradually eroded the economic and political autonomy of the local communities, with a few exceptions, among them Legnago (Varanini 1996). The communities on the banks of Lake Garda, mainly given over to the commerce of grain and fish and the cultivation of trees on the hills beyond the Riviera, had seen, with the Venetian conquest, the growing militarization of their side of the lake, in an effort to control transit to the upper Adige valley and the Brenner Pass, which meant that most of the trade was moved to the Brescia side of the lake. Finally, the Valpolicella, which with the Valpantena occupied the low mountains near the city of Verona, had obtained considerable administrative independence already under the rule of the della Scala. Its villages had the right to choose their own *vicario*[28] from among the citizens of Verona and enjoyed a special fiscal system with regard to the duties on salt, wine and livestock and the payment of direct taxes (*gravezze*). The land in the Valpolicella was not particularly fertile, but the conditions of the climate and the soil had encouraged the cultivation of cereals and mulberries, attracting, as in the lowlands and on the hills around Lake Garda, the great property owners from the cities. These had considerably increased in number since the Middle Ages and especially since the crisis in manufacturing in the late sixteenth century (Lanaro 1991a; Maifreda 2002, 19–31). It was thanks to these property owners from the city that some of the most outstanding villas, characteristic of the *Terraferma* in the seventeenth and eighteenth centuries, were built (Borelli 1986b; Gullino 1994).

As happened in the rest of the *Terraferma*, also in Verona the communities of the *contado* began to feel the need to organize themselves into an institution – the 'Territory' (*Territorio*) – which could further their ambitions, especially in the matter of taxes. Formally recognized by the Senate in 1493, the Territory of Verona was followed shortly after by the institution of the Territory of Vicenza, while later on similar institutions were created in eastern Lombardy, too. The originality of the Veronese

---

[28] The *vicario* played an important role in the administration of justice and in the control of administration in all the communities in his jurisdiction. Most of the *vicari* of the Veronese *contado* were directly nominated by the city council, but did not cover all the territory, as there were several private *vicariati*, both laymen and clergy, and some were directly employed by the fiscal chamber of Verona (Varanini 1980; Maifreda 2002).

Territory was that it did not at first represent all the communities of the *contado*. On the contrary, its claims were lodged not against the city of Verona, but rather the privileged rural communities. It was only from the middle of the sixteenth century that the Territory of Verona freed itself from the control of the city, officially by the capitularies of 1572 and by continual reforms throughout the following century. In these decades, the tax levy increased throughout the Republic and the country people's demands and protests against the privileged citizens became more pronounced. In 1575 the Territory managed to obtain a reduction of 1,000 ducats from the 3,000 that it had to pay for the *dadia delle lanze* (Vigato 1989, 59). This was the period when Venice wished to increase its control over local measures for levying tributes. This objective was accomplished through the subsequent reform of the Territory promoted by Captain Geronimo Corner. The mentioned reforms of the *estimi* of the city are to be read in this context, like the aforementioned attempt of Venice to control the municipal budget, which was increasingly in dire straits. As Venice's demands increased and the emancipation of the Territory of Verona progressed, the greatest controversy between the country people and the citizens, apart from the drafting of the *estimi*, became that over the billeting and upkeep of troops stationed in the *contado* or in transit (Maifreda 2002, 72–103).[29]

Padua

Similarly to Verona, Padua and its territory were conquered by Venice in 1405, putting an end to a troubled period during which the area was contended by the powerful families Carrara and della Scala. In the province of Padua the allocation of taxes laid down by Venice was usually straightforward and was agreed between the fiscal bodies of the city, the *clero* and the territory. This relatively simple arrangement was possible because here, unlike in other provinces of the *Terraferma*, the city consistently kept its role as coordinator in fiscal matters over the *contado*, perhaps because there were few separated communities and lands[30] and because traditionally there had been no feudal jurisdictions of a certain size and duration. The key element was, on the contrary, a consolidated

---

[29] Another ongoing cause of conflict between the city and the Territory was the distribution of the expenses for the upkeep of the River Adige (Maifreda 2002, 112–16).

[30] The exception was the small *podestaria* of Castelbaldo which contributed to the payment of taxes, except for the *dadia delle lanze*, with half of its *estimi* and this was a cause of litigation within the fiscal body of the Territory (Vigato 1989, 55). For an exact picture of the centres in the area of Padua in the fifteenth and sixteenth centuries, see Favaretto (1998, 3–22).

urban tradition. The less important centres of the area which had come into being at the time of the communes (Cittadella, Piove di Sacco, Este, Monselice, Montagnana) had then been absorbed by Padua and only after the Venetian conquest had regained some autonomy, with the appointment of a *podestà*, nominated by Venice, and no longer a *vicario* sent by Padua (Camposampietro and Castelbaldo were added to the towns listed earlier). Officially, all these localities made up the *contado* of Padua, and the city, which with the introduction of the *podestà* system had lost some of its administrative power, especially in legal matters, maintained over these *vicarie* and *podestarie* a predominant role in questions of taxation. This does not mean there were no disputes between the city and the communities of the territory over the allocation of taxes (Favaretto 1998). But differently from elsewhere, the infighting did not prevent the city from continuing to organize the *estimi* throughout the territory, down to the level of individual taxpayers (i.e. households). Complications came from the outside, namely from the continual growth of Venetian property in the *contado* of Padua (Beltrami 1961; Ventura 1968; Gullino 1994; Varanini 1996). To that was added, as elsewhere, the purchase of estates in the *contado* by the citizens of Padua, then transferred to the city's *estimo*. This was why the *estimo* of each body differentiated among the 'non-exempt', the 'exempt' and the 'Venetians'. Listed in the first group were those who had to pay all forms of taxes, in the second those who benefitted from special privileges of exemption, while in the last were the Venetians who had to pay jointly with Padua only the *dadia delle lanze* and from the second half of the eighteenth century also the expenses for the upkeep of the River Adige (Vigato 1989, 45–47).

The territorial *estimi* were helpful when it came to allotting the total amount of the taxes among the fiscal bodies, but over time they were also utilized in the distribution and the collection of taxes among the registered taxpayers. The records had to be continually monitored for changes in ownership, which were registered in the so-called *Fia* books, and were the basis for the update of the individual quotas of the *estimi*. This required constant coordination between the chancelleries of the territorial bodies and those of the communities, who were responsible for the actual tax collection (Vigato 1989, 67–80).

The clergy and the religious institutions who, as in the rest of the *Terraferma*, were a separate body (*clero*), contributed only to a part of the payment of the *dadia delle lanze* (about 15% of the whole sum) and from 1424 their assets were assessed separately. Like other fiscal bodies they had to put up with their assets being handed over to the Venetians, who also controlled the episcopal see. Perhaps this was the reason why the *clero* of Padua was weaker than elsewhere, as the estimate of its assets was the responsibility of the city and this put it at a disadvantage in tax disputes with other fiscal bodies of the territory (Favaretto 1998, 27).

This seemingly linear procedure was not without various structural problems. One of these was the estimation of the Venetians' assets, which created various difficulties both on account of the quantity of the land owned and for the political and economic power of this type of landowners. The Venetians were always reluctant to be accountable for their property and to pay their dues. The problem worsened after 1575, as the people of the province of Padua (both citizens and country people) had to pay in advance to the local fiscal chamber the sums owed by the Venetians for the *dadia delle lanze*. The citizens of Padua tried to shift the fiscal burden onto the country people by transferring their property in the *contado* onto the town's *estimo*. Even though this practice had been forbidden since 1425, it was not stopped until the mid-sixteenth century, when in the broader framework of Venetian support of the territorial demands, the Territory of Padua managed to obtain significant advantages, starting from the renewal of the general *estimo* in 1585, which ten years later reduced the *dadia delle lanze* of the territory by 21%, to the detriment of the amount paid by the city (+12%) and by the *clero* (+9%). Also in this instance, the need both to guarantee tax collection and to contain the crisis of local finances prompted Venice's support of the demands of the rural communities. During the seventeenth century, however, the increase in fiscal pressure caused various communities to become indebted to the fiscal chamber (Vigato 1989, 52–67).

The Territory of Padua, emerging in the fifteenth century as an 'informal' institution and in the following century institutionalized, had tried to limit the privileges of the citizens of both Padua and of Venice. The Territory claimed that the citizens of Padua should contribute to corvées and military obligations. The gradual transformation of these obligations from personal taxes paid in the form of corvées to taxes paid almost only in cash allowed to oblige the citizens of Padua to contribute to these expenses. As elsewhere, the sixteenth century was the turning point, when thanks also to the support of Venice (in this case almost a suffocating embrace), the *contado* managed to establish a new dialectical relationship with the city. However, there was a substantial difference between the *podestarie* who reinforced their role and the *vicarie* who, on the contrary, forfeited part of their autonomy and were relegated to the fringes of the Territory institution (Favaretto 1998, 149–205, 203–33).

Vicenza

The acquisition of Vicenza by the Republic (1404) entailed a rearrangement of the territory, which seemed reminiscent of the division into different *vicarie* promoted by the della Scala (1322). However, by confirming the *podestà* of Lonigo and Marostica and the self-government of the seven communities of the Asiago plateau, it in fact conceded considerable power to the city in the administration of its *contado*. The city was granted the privilege of appointing the *vicari*.[31] In this context it is hardly surprising that specific fiscal privileges were granted to the citizens of Vicenza, above all with regard to their possessions in the territory (Zamperetti 1981). The situation was reversed in the second half of the sixteenth century, when in Vicenza, as in the other provinces of the *Terraferma*, Venice lent its support to the demands of the country people for a new distribution of direct taxes (*dadia della lanze* and the *sussidio*), facilitating the registration in the rural *estimo* of the assets acquired in the *contado* by the citizens, thus obliging them to contribute in full to local taxes (Knapton 1981b, 389).

The most obvious example of the support given by Venice to territorial demands is perhaps the *balanzon*. This general *estimo* of the entire province of Vicenza, which aimed to give an accurate indication of the capacity of the various bodies to pay their dues, was introduced in the same year that the transfer of city property to the urban *estimi* was formally forbidden (1564). Other measures were decreed at the beginning of the seventeenth century with the object of involving citizens progressively more in the payment of taxes for the assets owned in the *contado* (Knapton 1984). Also in this case, Venice aimed to rebalance taxes in order to be able to increase revenues and above all to cope with increasing military expenses. As elsewhere, the situation of local finances had now become precarious and between the 1620s and 1640s various measures were taken to rein in local finances and to monitor a fair tax distribution within the single communities. An equitable division of taxes within the community and a correct administration of local finances were of particular importance to Venice in this area, where, in April 1655, the revolt of Arzignano broke out. This caused considerable alarm in the Republic as a result of the violence which marked it with fires, assaults on the castle and on the pawnshop (*camera dei pegni*) and the concern that the revolt might spread to neighbouring villages. In a few weeks the revolt was put down firmly by the authorities sent in by Venice, and despite the exceptional nature of the malcontent, even in the case of Arzignano, the Republic

---

[31] For the procedure used in nominating the *vicario* of Arzignano and the administrative setup of the Chiampo Valley, inherited from the Visconti, see Preto (1981, 41).

tried to stem the revolt by issuing 'Orders of good government', a set of rules covering the administration of finances and local municipal assets, with the purpose of containing conflicts and the usurpation of such assets (Tagliaferri 1978).

Despite these measures, it was Venice itself, owing to the rise in public expenditure following the War of Candia, which was the cause of the increase in the tax burden and the local financial crisis. Venice attempted to remedy the situation also with the sale of the so-called *beni comunali*, assets owned by the state but usually managed by the municipalities. In actual fact, the communities in the area of Vicenza were only minimally affected by this, because only a minimal part of the state property granted to them was sold off. However, in the same years, calls for corvées increased across the province (Pezzolo 1982, 385–93).

1.4   Sources and the Database

The analysis of fiscal systems in use in different provinces has shown how the growing influence of Venice's political power did not immediately lead to complete administrative uniformity across the Republic. Between the fifteenth and sixteenth centuries many cities on the *Terraferma* were still able by themselves to organize the collection of tributes levied by the state on the basis of local norms introduced for the purpose of developing and renewing the *estimi*. Only the exponential increase in military expenditure in the sixteenth and above all in the seventeenth century induced Venice to impose overall norms governing the distribution of taxes and, more generally, for controlling local finance, which often led to the standardization of the norms for establishing *estimi*, at least within the same province.

The methods of assessment of the *estimi* were not the same in all the cities of the *Terraferma*. The system in Verona differed from that in Treviso, but was the same as that in Padua and Vicenza. In Treviso, the *estimo* of each *podestaria* was divided into four fiscal bodies: citizens, the inhabitants of the territory, the *clero* and foreigners. In other provinces the division was among three bodies (the city, the territory and the *clero*, but no provision was made for foreigners). This entailed a more class-based system, because all the inhabitants of the city were listed on the city's *estimo*, while the inhabitants of the communities of the *contado* were on the *estimo* of the territory (Grubb 1982; Scherman 2009, 2013). Significant differences are also found in the compilation of the *estimo*, which in Treviso was carried out by a commission that directly evaluated the assets in loco (Cavazzana Romanelli and Orlando 2006), while in other cities the *polizze*, that is, the original declarations, were first completed by those listed on the property registers and only subsequently checked (Maifreda 2009, 91–92). For example, the compilation of the *estimi* in the rural communities in the territory of Verona was regulated by the 1450 city statutes which indicated in detail the procedure to be adopted in the election of the appraisers (Rossini 1993, 1994). The basic objective was to involve the councils of the community and a reasonable number of inhabitants to guarantee adequate participation and an efficient control over the procedure. At the same time cross-checks were envisaged in an attempt to avoid genuine or deliberate errors. The same system, on a larger scale, was practiced in the city of Verona, where the city council had to appoint the various compilers of the *estimo*. The process was often slowed down or invalidated by the local elite because it was not in their interests (Maifreda 2009, 92–93). Furthermore, even when a new *estimo* was formally correct, they tried to make the allocation of the fiscal onus unfair, for example by lowering the minimum thresholds of the tax exemption (Lanaro 1982a). The calculations used by the *estimi* in the province of Verona were aligned in the early decades of the seventeenth century in an attempt by Venice to standardize procedures throughout the *Terraferma* (Chilese 2002; Maifreda 2002).

As a consequence of this heterogeneity in rules and practices, the availability as well as the quality of the sources is not everywhere the same. However, even taking into consideration the gaps in some of the series of documents and the different methods of compilation, the *estimi* available for the single communities are broadly comparable and have some key characteristics in common. In fact, all the sources considered here can be included in the category of 'per property' *estimi* which include in the assessment real estate (land and houses) (Alfani 2015, 1062). From the Middle Ages the sums registered on the *estimi* were the capitalized income at a specific rate of the assets owned, and not the value of the assets themselves (Zangheri 1980; Borelli 1986a; Chilese 2002, XXVI). Additionally, it was not uncommon for a non-specific entry related to incomes from commercial activities or manufacturing to be added to the assets mentioned above (Vigato 1989, 68; Alfani and Caracausi 2009, 190 and no. 12),[32] which, however, was of very limited importance in defining the total amounts of the individual tax returns of the *estimo*.

---

[32] Although this determined an unusual characteristic compared to the classic definition of 'per property' *estimi*, it would be incorrect to include these sources in the category of the so-called per yield *estimi*, which also assessed capital, credits and other movables (Pini 1981). This was typical of some *estimi* on the *Terraferma* in the Middle Ages and more commonly in the Alpine communities, for example Clusone or the nearby Valtellina (Della Misericordia 2006, 146–48, 931–33). However, from the sixteenth century, in most cases (Padua, Bergamo and Treviso) records of movables (particularly of animals) and of capital were excluded, leaving only an entry of the income from

The situation in Verona was different again. It would seem that their *estimi* were among the most complete and complex, including real estate, movables and income from capital and work, from which various liabilities were deducted, among them even the presence in the household of people unfit to work (Tagliaferri 1966, 35). The custom of burning the preparatory documentation (the so-called *polizze*) after the total amounts had been registered in the *estimo*, makes it impossible to verify these norms at least until the end of the seventeenth century, when the compilation of the Veronese *estimi* change, distinguishing among the 'real' (real estate), the 'personal' (a tax levied on the number of able-bodied people in the household) and the ownership of domestic animals (Tagliaferri 1966; Maifreda 2002). This was similar to the situation in Vicenza (Grubb 1982, 152). Here only the 'real' *estimo* will be used, in line with other areas.

Our analysis covers most of the Venetian *Terraferma*, where the localities to study have been selected on the basis of the sources available, but also on their geographical position, their institutional role and the socioeconomic environment they represented. Our database includes some localities in four provinces: Bergamo, Padua, Verona and Vicenza, which for all of the period considered were subject to the Republic.

The series of the *estimi* of Bergamo, among the oldest available, begins in 1430, a few years after the devolution of the territory to Venice. The sources available cover the period 1430–1704.[33] As well as the city, the database includes an important locality in the *contado* of Bergamo, the community of Romano di Lombardia, situated on the plain about 25 kilometres from Bergamo. Romano was an important centre of the Bergamo plain, the seat of the *podestà* and the main city of the homonymous '*quadra*' (fiscal jurisdiction) on the boundary with the State of Milan. For its administrative position, as well as for its socio-economic and demographic importance, Romano can be considered an 'almost-city' (*quasi città*: Chittolini 1990). Another important community in the mountains of Bergamo is Clusone, the seat of the *podestà* and reference point for the entire Seriana Valley. The series of the *estimi* of Romano and Clusone is shorter than that of Bergamo, but is complete and covers an interesting period, because it includes two

---

manufacturing (for Treviso, Scherman 2009, 2013; for Bergamo, where these values were not so well documented, Gioia 2004; for Padua, Vigato 1989).

[33] BCBg, Archivio Storico del Comune di Bergamo-Sezione antico regime-Serie Estimi, 1.2.16-II (1430), 1.2.16–14 (1448), 1.2.16-XXI (1537), 1.2.16-XIII A and B (1555), ASBg, Estimo Veneto, ff. 1 and 2 (1610), 6 and 7 (1640), 11–14 (1704). Note that for some years, not all the *estimi* of the neighbourhoods (*vicinie*) have been kept.

major mortality crises (the plagues of 1575–77 and 1629–30).[34] Furthermore, until about 1636 the community of Clusone covered a jurisdiction which was larger than the present one, including also the territories of the communities of Oltressenda Alta, Piario, Villa d'Ogna and Rovetta (Oscar and Belotti 2000, 122). So up to that date, these localities were included in the *estimi* of Clusone, but as they were recorded separately, it was possible to treat them as autonomous series.[35]

For the province of Verona, we have a very long series of documents for the city (1409–1800) and some short, but geographically well-distributed series for the *contado*. In the case of the city of Verona we have incorporated in our analysis the data already published by Tagliaferri (1966) related to the *estimi* of the period 1409–1635. We added new sources to complete the series.[36] The *estimi* of Verona seem to be complete; in fact, they always include all the neighbourhoods (the *contrade*). In the second half of the seventeenth century some innovations in the assessment of the *estimi* were introduced, which led to the gradual exclusion of the poorest from the *estimo* compared to the consideration given to the declarations of wealthier citizens (Tagliaferri 1966, 38, no. 87).[37]

Some good, though short, series of *estimi* for the Territory of Verona are kept in the local State Archive and cover the period 1628–1750. These series begin with the seventeenth century in the context of the well-known contrasts between the city and the *contado*, and as a result of the role played by Venice in supporting the latter (Knapton 1984). The reform of the *estimi* in the area of Verona, encouraged by some of the rectors, was completed by Captain Giovanni Contarini and introduced new norms for the 'real' and 'personal' *estimi* to be applied in all the localities of the territory (Maifreda 2002, 81–83, 136). Unfortunately not all the *estimi* have the same characteristics and in various cases different units of measurement are adopted to indicate assets and liabilities, without any substantiated method of conversion. When deciding which communities to study we took these factors into consideration, privileging the sources which created fewer

---

[34] ASCRom, Estimi, unnumbered registers of 1552, 1605 and 1663. ASCClu, Estimi, ff. 108 (1579), 111 (1618), 112 (1624), 120 (166), 136 (1700).

[35] As in the *estimo* of 1579 some localities are registered in pairs, it is necessary to limit the series to the following communities or aggregations: (1) Clusone; (2) Rovetta; (3) Oltressenda Alta, Piario and Villa d'Ogna.

[36] ASVr, Antico Archivio del Comune, registers 249 (1409), 255 (1456), 260 (1502), 264 (1545), 270 (1605), 273 (1635) and Antichi Estimi Provvisori, registers 103 (1696) and 169–70 (1800). Herlihy (1973) also studied the *estimi* in the Veronese area, although only from a demographic perspective.

[37] With the acts of 27 February 1646 and of 20 December 1650, the city council altered the calculations of the *estimi* introducing also the exclusion of the destitute (the *miserabili*), with the result that the new *estimi* lost the 'universal' character of the previous ones (Tagliaferri 1966, 202; Lanaro 1982b; Chilese 2002, XVII–XXXVII).

technical problems. The second fundamental benchmark in making a choice is the different geographical locations of the communities. The database includes five communities of the Valpolicella, a hilly and mountainous zone to the north of Verona, two communities on the Veronese side of Lake Garda and another two on the plain. In each case the communities are medium to small in size with 30 to 200 households listed on the *estimi* and with a population of about 450 to 1,500 people (Table 1.2). The whole area was cultivated using traditional methods – cereals on the plain and grape vine and other fruit in Valpolicella, an area in which the wealthy families from the Veronese patriciate took a keen interest between the Middle Ages and the early modern period (Borelli 1974; Rossini 1982; Varanini 1987; Maifreda 2002).[38]

The most remarkable case, among those studied, is that of Padua, whose *estimi* have virtually unique characteristics. In Padua, from ancient times and until the decline of the *ancien régime*, the city organized the compilation of the *estimi* not only for its citizens, as in Bergamo or Verona, but for the entire *contado*. Actually, all the cities in Veneto had similar privileges, but it was only in Padua that they lasted until the eighteenth century. Consequently, the *estimi* of Padua include the communities of the *contado* with lists of single taxpayers and their *estimo* coefficients. Furthermore, in Padua the property of the Church and that of Venetian landowners of the territory (the so-called Veneti) were assessed using the same procedures, excluding assets bought before 1446.[39] For some years the same system of assessment was used to fix a price also on the assets of the exempt – and, as far as we know, this was the only case in Italy. All these categories of owners were listed in different *estimi* as they were not subject to the same taxation; however, the system for evaluating the assets – or rather the definition of the capitalized income of each asset (Borelli 1986a, 327) – was the same and so the coefficients are comparable with each other.[40] From the reform of 1560, the standard was to allocate a '*soldo d'estimo*' for every 100 lire of capitalized income (Vigato 1989, 71). In other words the *estimi* of Padua accurately describe the structure of the property throughout the territory without exception. Unfortunately the fifteenth century *estimi* in Padua have not all been kept and for this reason our analysis is focused on the sources

---

[38] ASVr, Antichi estimi provvisori, ff. 390 (Parona), 489 (Nogara), 469 (Visegna), 605 (Prun), 609 (Sant'Ambrogio), 616 (Ceredello), 626 (Rivalta), 646 (Garda), 662 (Peschiera).

[39] In Padua, unlike what happened in Verona, property belonging to the Venetians increased considerably during the early modern period. See Alfani and Caracausi (2009) as well as Section 3.5.

[40] On the *estimi* of Padua see Saviolo (1667), Vigato (1989), Favaretto (1998) and Alfani and Caracausi (2009).

Table 1.2 *Composition of the database*[41]

Community/ territory	Urban/ rural	Province	Sources used (year)	Population (year of reference between parentheses)
Arquà (Vicariato)	R	PD	1549; 1627; 1642; 1694	Of the whole contado: 116,075 (1548); 127,373 (1616); 87,393 (1634); 234,511 (1766)
Arzignano	R	VI	1449; 1500; 1549; 1602; 1650; 1696; 1756;	4,861 (1546); 4,000 (1645); 4,706 (1686); 4,994 (1742); 5,526 (1790)
Bergamo	U	BG	1430; 1448; 1537; 1555; 1610; 1640; 1704	5,886 (1430); 7,681 (1451); 15,111 (1499); 19,000 (1553); 18,000 (1610); 10,251 (1632); 20,000 (1668); 24,349 (1704)
Camposampietro (Podestaria)	R	PD	1549; 1627; 1642; 1694	Of the whole contado: 116,075 (1548); 127,373 (1616); 87,393 (1634); 234,511 (1766)
Castelbaldo (Podestaria)	R	PD	1549; 1627; 1642; 1694	Of the whole contado: 116,075 (1548); 127,373 (1616); 87,393 (1634); 234,511 (1766)
Ceredello (locality of Caprino Veronese)	R	VR	1628; 1639; 1690; 1752	Of Caprino Veronese: 3,006 (1616); 1,190 (1631); 3,031 (1710); 3,696 (1744)
Cittadella (Podestaria)	R	PD	1549; 1627; 1642; 1694	Of the whole contado: 116,075 (1548); 127,373 (1616); 87,393 (1634); 234,511 (1766)
Clusone	R	BG	1579; 1618; 1624; 1646; 1700	1,968 (1575); 1,710 (1666); 2,181 (1688); 2,210 (1708)
Conselve (Vicariato)	R	PD	1549; 1627; 1642; 1694	Of the whole contado: 116,075 (1548); 127,373

[41] For the estimates of the population of Bergamo: Belfanti (1995), 180, table 1, (years 1553, 1610, 1668, 1704) and Albini (1999), 240, table 7.a (years 1430, 1451, 1499 – the number of the households has been multiplied by 4.5 persons). For Romano: Saba (1995), 272, table b. For Clusone: Saba (1995), 243, tables 51 and 245, table 54; Oscar and Belotti (2000), 122. For the population of Verona: Tagliaferri (1966), 44–45, table 4, 54, table 10; of the Verona area: Donazzolo and Saibante (1926), 120 and appendix 2; of Padua: Beltrami (1961), appendix to chapter 1; Alfani and Caracausi (2009); Fornasin and Zannini (1999), table 1; of Arzignano: Povolo (1981), 142, table 1, 153, table IX, 158, table XII, 159, table XIII, 160, table XIV, 193, table XXXVII. For Vicenza: Beloch (1994), 13, 57, 446–50; Malanima (1998), 111. For Treviso: Beloch (1994), 13, 49, 421–24; Malanima (1998), 111.

Table 1.2 *(cont.)*

Community/ territory	Urban/ rural	Province	Sources used (year)	Population (year of reference between parentheses)
				(1616); 87,393 (1634); 234,511 (1766)
Este (Podestaria)	R	PD	1549; 1627; 1642; 1694	Of the whole contado: 116,075 (1548); 127,373 (1616); 87,393 (1634); 234,511 (1766)
Garda	R	VR	1628; 1670; 1709; 1750	501 (1616); 199 (1631); 560 (1710); 1,053 (1744)
Grosio	R	SO	1479; 1526; 1604; 1637; 1676_1711; 1730_1769; 1783_1801	Terziere superiore di Valtellina: 4,610 (fuochi, 1589); 20,484 (1599– 1603)
Mirano (Vicariato)	R	PD	1549; 1627; 1642; 1694	Of the whole contado: 116,075 (1548); 127,373 (1616); 87,393 (1634); 234,511 (1766)
Monselice (Podestaria)	R	PD	1549; 1627; 1642; 1694	Of the whole contado: 116,075 (1548); 127,373 (1616); 87,393 (1634); 234,511 (1766)
Montagnana (Podestaria)	R	PD	1549; 1627; 1642; 1694	Of the whole contado: 116,075 (1548); 127,373 (1616); 87,393 (1634); 234,511 (1766)
Nogara	R	VR	1628; 1639; 1709; 1752	1,422 (1616); 632 (1631); 1,300 (1710); 1,756 (1744)
Oriago (Vicariato)	R	PD	1549; 1627; 1642; 1694	Of the whole contado: 116,075 (1548); 127,373 (1616); 87,393 (1634); 234,511 (1766)
Padua	U	PD	1549; 1627; 1642; 1694	35,000 (1550); 34,770 (1615); 32,714 (1648); 40,795 (1766)
Parona	R	VR	1628; 1639; 1709; 1750	834 (1616); 372 (1631); 500 (1710); 1,005 (1744)
Peschiera del Garda	R	VR	1628; 1642; 1709; 1765	1,230 (1616); 498 (1631); 1,242 (1710); 1411 (1744)
Piove di Sacco (Podestaria)	R	PD	1549; 1627; 1642; 1694	Of the whole contado: 116,075 (1548); 127,373 (1616); 87,393 (1634); 234,511 (1766)
Prun (locality of Negrar)	R	VR	1627; 1639; 1709; 1750	939 (1616); 337 (1631); 1,102 (1710); 2,405 (1744)

Table 1.2 *(cont.)*

Community/ territory	Urban/ rural	Province	Sources used (year)	Population (year of reference between parentheses)
Rivalta (locality of Brentino Belluno)	R	VR	1628; 1638; 1709; 1752	Of Brentino: 451 (1616); 173 (1631); 494 (1710); 530 (1744)
Romano di Lombardia	R	BG	1522; 1605; 1663	2,108 (1559); 2,300 (1596); 1,673 (1632)
Sant'Ambrogio	R	VR	1628; 1670; 1709; 1753	1,122 (1616); 575 (1631); 960 (1710); 1,826 (1744)
Teolo (Vicariato)	R	PD	1549; 1627; 1642; 1694	Of the whole contado: 116,075 (1548); 127,373 (1616); 87,393 (1634); 234,511 (1766)
Treviso	U	TR	1448; 1486	8,000 (1400); 10,000 (1500); 12,000 (1550); 14,000 (1600); 10,000 (1628); 9,000 (1650); 10,000 (1750); 11,000 (1800)
Verona	U	VR	1409; 1456; 1502; 1545; 1605; 1635; 1696; 1800	20,100 (1409); 21,227 (1456); 41,071 (1502); 46,050 (1545); 57,706 (1605); 31,196 (1635); 35,075 (1692); 55,101 (1790)
Vicenza	U	VI	1453; 1505	19,000 (1400); 20,000 (1500); 21,000 (1550); 30,000 (1574); 32,000 (1628); 25,000 (1650); 26,000 (1700); 28,000 (1750); 29,000 (1800)
Visegna (locality of Salizzole)	R	VR	1628; 1670; 1709; 1751	Of Salizzole: 1,310 (1616); 1,136 (1631); 1,670 (1710); 2,536 (1744)

BG = Bergamo; PD = Padua; TR = Treviso; VI = Vicenza; VR = Verona.

produced between the sixteenth and eighteenth centuries, including all the different categories of owners.[42]

[42] ASPd, Estimi Miscellanea, f. 2 (1549), Estimo 1518, f. 382 (Venetians with the *contado* 1549), f. 379 (Venetians with the city 1549), f. 412 (exempts 1549), Estimo Miscellanea, f. 24 (1627), Estimo 1575, f. 170 (Venetians with the contado 1627), Estimo 1615, ff. 166–70 (*clero* 1627), Estimo Miscellanea, f. 24 (1642), Estimo 1668, ff. 415–20 (*contado* 1694), ff. 376–89 (city 1694), ff. 557–58 (*clero* 1694), f. 555 (Venetians with the city), f. 556 (Venetians with the *contado*). The *estimi* for the city for the years 1549, 1575, 1627 and 1642 were studied in Alfani and Caracausi (2009), from which the original data have been taken.

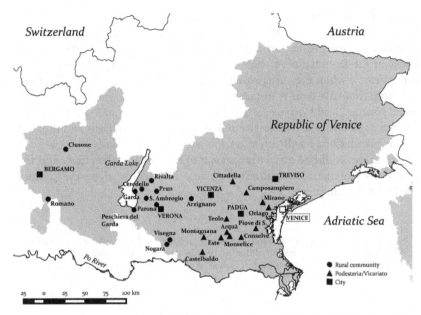

Figure 1.2 Communities in the database (political boundaries of the
Republic of Venice ca. 1560).
Notes: After the Peace of Cateau-Cambrésis (1559) which concluded the
Italian Wars, the boundaries of the Republic of Venice in Italy remained
basically unaltered until the end of the Republic in 1797.

Finally our database includes a series related to the territory of Vicenza,
the community of Arzignano, an important town located between
Vicenza and Verona, at the entrance to the Chiampo Valley. Seven *estimi*,
covering a relatively long period (1443–1756),[43] have been preserved for
this community, which consists of various localities with an overall population of between 500 and 1,000 households. Some published data are
available for the city of Vicenza and for Treviso (for the former only for the
quarter of S. Stefano), though, pertaining only to the second half of the
fifteenth century (Grubb 1982; Sherman 2009). Table 1.2 summarizes
the structure of the database. Figure 1.2 gives the location of each case
study.
    Although there are some differences between the sources available for
different communities and areas they should not be overstated.
Community per community, the *estimi* changed in time only marginally,

---

[43] Archivio di Stato di Vicenza (ASVi), *Estimi*, ff. 1061 (1443), 1065 (1500), 1074 (1547–
    49), 1085 (1602), 1094 (1650), 1103 (1696), 1105 (1718–56).

at least for the purposes of our study. Between communities, the differences can usually be greatly reduced, or removed entirely, by means of proper standardization of the data (for example by removing the propertyless in the few instances – such as the cities of Padua and Bergamo in some years – when they are present). This can be shown practically, both by comparing the results obtained from standardized and non-standardized sources, and from using the most detailed cases (such as that of the province of Padua) to demonstrate that adding the Venetians and the *clero* to the calculations hardly changes the overall picture (indeed, as we will argue, there would be good reasons *not* to include the Venetians and the *clero* in the calculations in the first place). This will be done throughout the following chapters.[44]

---

[44] See in particular Section 2.2 and Chapter 3 concerning the impact of including or excluding the propertyless on different distribution and inequality indicators, and Section 3.5 concerning the impact of including or excluding Venetians and *clero*.

2   The Rich and the Poor

The property tax records (*estimi*) of the *Terraferma*, especially those of some provinces like Padua, provide an exhaustive representation of different fiscal bodies. The very fact that different fiscal bodies existed, though, reminds us that the society of the Republic of Venice was a stratified and hierarchically ordered one. This chapter provides, first, an overview of the social stratification of the Republic, dedicating particular attention to the poor. Then, using the new archival data we have collected, we provide new measures of the prevalence and the relative position of the poor, as well as of the rich. The comparative analysis of the dynamics of the top and of the bottom of the wealth distribution is the starting point in the analysis of the long-term trends in economic inequality and of their determinants, which will be the focus of the rest of the book.

2.1   Social Stratification and Poverty: An Analysis of the Literature

The composition and the stratification of the society of the Republic of Venice during the late medieval and early modern period have attracted much research, especially regarding the relative position and the characteristics of the poor. In particular, poverty has been the object of a seminal book by Brian Pullan (1971), *Rich and Poor in Renaissance Venice*. Building on this, subsequent literature has paid particular attention to the late Middle Ages and to the beginning of the early modern period, as shown by David D'Andrea's (2013) recent synthesis. Regarding social stratification, pioneering works like that dedicated by Amedeo Tagliaferri (1966) to Verona were the starting point in a research program which originally focused mostly on fiscal sources (the *estimi*). Later, research on social stratification evolved towards the use of a greater variety of historical sources and a prosopographic approach, as exemplified by James Grubb's book, *Provincial Families of the Renaissance* (1996). In this section we provide a general overview based on the literature, which will later be integrated and expanded by making use of our own data.

A first point to underline is that, although highly stratified and hierarchic, as was the rule across preindustrial Europe, the society of the Republic might have been exceptionally stable, including from the political point of view. This is supposedly due to the existence of a vast range of charities, such as the confraternities called *scuole*, which were widespread in Venice as well as in the *Terraferma* and somehow bound the poor to the rich, also by reserving some important offices to the commoners (Pullan 1971). This relatively harmonious situation, however, was also to some degree a political myth – albeit one in which the Venetians themselves believed, often acting accordingly (Muir 1981; Grubb 1986; D'Andrea 2013).[1] Charitable initiatives were a typical prescription of the medieval and early modern political theory, as a well-governed and 'charitable' state was supposed to meet the favour of God. This was, in fact, a common theme in Venetian political thought: 'Venice's system of charity reflected its unique political history. ... Venetian nobles pursued welfare policies that would please God and secure the civic harmony of the well-ordered, Christian Republic, and the regulation of charitable activities was premised upon a basic principle: public manifestations of religious piety should serve the needs of the state' (D'Andrea 2013, 421).

Of course, the objective was not to pursue an egalitarian society, as social differences were considered a natural part of the order of a Christian state governed by social justice and by charity. In such a state, the rich had the moral obligation to provide the poor with relief from their sufferings, and this in a broad sense and not limited to their economic conditions (Grendi 1975, 621; Pullan 1978, 985–88 and 996–97; Woolf 1988, 11–20; Garbellotti 2013). In their turn, the poor were expected to pray for the salvation of the souls of their benefactors. Consequently, poverty was not to be eradicated, but the situation of the poor had to be made more tolerable by means of laws and charitable institutions (D'Andrea 2013, 421–24).

The perception of the poor, however, changed in time, as from the beginning of the early modern period, the Christian ideal of poverty as a model of a lifestyle (the poverty of Christ) was progressively replaced by distinctions and classifications which aimed to separate the truly needy from the false poor, the vagabonds and the beggars, who became the object of many restrictive laws (Gutton 1974; Mollat 1978; Pullan 1992; Geremek 1994; Jütte 1994). These distinctions had fundamental

---

[1] This was just one of many 'myths' informing Venetian politics and influencing its self-perception. For a recent synthesis, see Fusaro (2015, 10–16).

importance in times of crisis (famines, plagues, sieges, etc.) when vagabonds and beggars were expelled from the cities with decrees that also
involved other categories of the so-called 'useless mouths' (Alfani 2009c,
2013a, 23–27). Not by chance, the first 'poor laws' of Venice were
introduced in 1528–29, after severe harvest failures due to adverse
meteorological events in 1527 had triggered one of the main Italian
famines of the sixteenth century.[2] Rural dwellers flocked to the cities in
search of assistance, leading (in 1528) to temporary decrees of expulsion
of the foreign poor which were followed (in 1529) by a more organic
legislation aimed at contrasting the spread of beggary and of the
'unworthy' poor while at the same time providing help to the 'deserving'
poor[3] (Pullan 1971; D'Andrea 2013, 434–36). Of course, this did not
prevent the same problems faced in 1527–29 from occurring again in time
of severe crises. For example, vagabonds and beggars were expelled from
Padua and Verona during the 1575–77 plague (Preto 1978, 122). The
Venetian poor law of 1529, though, marks a significant change in attitudes, as 'it became possible, without in any way deforming the traditional doctrine of Christian charity, with its emphasis on voluntary and
spontaneous acts of compassion, to implement a series of repressive
measures aimed at the poor' (Geremek 1994, 136).

There was, however, a degree of ambivalence in the attitude towards
the poor as *after* a severe mortality crisis the city doors became open to all
those who could provide a fresh workforce – and often their numbers
counted members of precisely those categories that during the crisis
would have faced expulsion (Belfanti 1994; Garbellotti 2013, 39–44).
Especially in the cities, then, the composition of the lowest strata of the
society varied according to the moment (the economic and demographic
'conjuncture' in its cyclical development) as well as to the laws on the
poor and the foreigners. Some clarification is needed about the latter.
Residing and working in a city were not sufficient conditions to gain
access to charity and assistance, especially not in a lasting and stable
way. Only the rights of citizenship gave full access to the local welfare
and guaranteed protection in times of crisis, which is why obtaining
citizenship has to be considered a key component in the process of the
integration of immigrants (who often, but not always, originally belonged
to the poor) into the host community (Bellavitis 2001; Cerutti 2003,
2012; Tedoldi 2004; Alfani 2012, 2013d). The *privilegium civilitatis* (i.e.
the right of citizenship) or the *vicinitas* (a similar right which, especially in

---

[2] About this famine, see Alfani (2013a, 50–56); Alfani, Mocarelli and Strangio (2017).
[3] The 'deserving poor' included citizens reduced to poverty by personal misfortune or by
circumstance.

rural communities, gave access to commons and to some magistratures and political institutions) were key juridical institutions throughout the early modern period (Di Tullio 2014a, 1–3 and 44–45).

Citizenship was a crucial factor of stratification in the society of the Republic – or maybe it would be more proper to use the plural here, 'societies', as the prerogatives of citizens and more importantly, the procedures (formal and practical) to acquire citizenship varied slightly across communities. Indeed, the distinction to be made is not only between those who had full citizenship rights and all others – as we should further separate the 'quasi-citizens', i.e. those foreign in-comers who, as they had resided for some time in the city and as they possessed a house there and were subject to taxes, enjoyed certain rights (Tedoldi 2003. 2004; Barbot 2007), from those who did not have any of the prerogatives of citizens. This juridical distinction had great social relevance: not only because in time of scarcity or crisis the citizens and the quasi-citizens enjoyed protection and access to public help and resources to which other residents simply *had no right* (Alfani 2013a, 25–26), but also because the progressive integration into the local society and economy was a key component in the process slowly leading to the acquisition of full citizenship rights. In this sense, the status of quasi-citizen can be considered a step in a process which, however, was not always completed, and in some instances could even reverse. But we should be wary of proposing this as a rigid and immutable picture. Indeed, the procedures leading to the acquisition of citizenship evolved in time, surely in practice and maybe not as much looking at formal rules. This reflected local dynamics, as well broader changes in the economic and social context of the Republic (Zannini 1993; Fusaro 2007, 377–80). So, for example, obtaining the status of citizen became much easier after 1630 than it had been in earlier decades, as cities tried to fill in the gaps opened by the plague (for example, Tedoldi 2004, 57).

In the Republic as well as in the rest of northern Italy, the process of acquisition of citizenship seems to have been easier and ultimately more successful for those able to mobilize vast resources (and to acquire sizeable properties locally) and/or exercising a prestigious profession (notaries, lawyers, physicians, etc.) or at least one considered useful to the community, such as the artisans (Alfani 2013d).[4] Consequently,

---

[4] The case of the merchants might have been partly different, as it has been argued that from the mid-sixteenth century, the growing complexity of transactions as well as the different economic context made it easier for them to elude regulations limiting the economic activities of non-foreigners. This reduced their economic incentive to try to obtain the status of citizen – which of course could have been sought after for different reasons, including personal life choices (Fusaro 2007, 377–78).

wealth and personal skills interacted to some degree with juridical status, beyond acting as factors of socio-economic stratification on their own.

Full citizenship, however, did not guarantee full 'political' rights as, generally speaking, those were reserved to the patriciate – a group which indeed, was defined primarily by its political prerogatives as it had the monopoly of government also thanks to the hereditary character of many charges. In Venice, this had been guaranteed to the original families (the *cittadini originari*) ever since the first *serrata* (closure) of the *Maggior Consiglio* at the end of the thirteenth century – although with some adjustments throughout the early modern period and at least one moment of 'forced' (and temporary) opening in the late seventeenth century, when the title of patrician was put up for sale to finance the wars of Candia and Morea (Bellavitis 2013, 322). In time, a patriciate functionally similar to the Venetian one also developed in the cities of the *Terraferma*, at least if we define it as 'a restricted body of families monopolizing high municipal office, possessing great and honorable wealth, and eventually effecting "aristocratic transformation"' (Grubb 1996, 156 modelled on Lanaro 1991b). Although for a period the precise boundaries of the patriciate remained much more fluid in the provincial cities compared to Venice, by the end of the sixteenth century across the *Terraferma*, too, city councils had become formally closed and their seats were inherited within a well-defined group of original families which tended to constitute the upper level of the local society.

The patriciate tried to preserve its privileges against incumbents, usually coming from a group which we could call the 'bourgeoisie', composed of merchants, functionaries and professionals. This group enjoyed wealth, relationships and even a culture similar to that of the patriciate, but did not have its political role (Bellavitis 2013, 320–25). This of course could create problems. If we focus on the centre of the Republic (Venice), 'when the political elite no longer corresponded to the ruling class, a fissure developed within the state. The new economic elite did not have direct access to the centres of power, as only patricians could be elected to any council of state or executive position. The only avenues for influencing political action were lobbying and petitioning the government' (Fusaro 2015, 178).

A largely analogous situation was to be found, albeit with varying intensity, across the cities of the *Terraferma*. In Venice the bourgeois had access to the administrative offices of the *Scuole Grandi* (the most powerful confraternities), which helped to compensate for their frustrated political ambitions (D'Andrea 2013, 425). But maybe more importantly, throughout the *Terraferma* the incoming members of the local bourgeoisie enjoyed at least a relative ease of access to full citizenship rights, as already explained and more generally, opportunities for making it to the top were never entirely missing (as detailed in Section 2.4).

This kind of basic stratification was found in all the cities of the Venetian mainland. In the minor cities and towns, however, or more generally in those which did not have a clear mercantile vocation, the patriciate as a specific group tended to be absent or at least less influential, and to be incorporated in the ruling elite with feudal origins. In these places, the key distinction became one between just two groups: nobles and *popolo* (Ventura 1964; Borelli 1974; Berengo 1975; Tagliaferri 1984; Lanaro 1992, 21–24, 193–94; Grubb 1996, 156–84). Admittedly, across the *Terraferma* the distinction between patriciate and nobility (as well as the precise boundaries of the two groups) was not very precise. One reason for this was that the actual definition of who had to be considered 'noble' was much discussed, and ultimately depended greatly on local customs (Donati 1988). Another was that many patricians sought noble titles as a means of status recognition (Grubb 1996, 170).[5] Some examples will be provided in Section 2.4, where we will also examine further the composition of the upper strata of the society.

Here, something more needs to be said about the lowest levels of the social ladder, which comprised a large part of the overall population. Beyond the beggars and those who pursued extreme religious ideals (following Christ's model), a great many experienced a condition that can be defined as one of poverty. This included both the 'miserable', who did not own anything and were exempt from taxation, and those whom the tax collectors estimated to be taxable but only at the lowest possible level. These people had in common the characteristic of being unable to accumulate the resources needed to face a crisis. Large families and low salaries were the main determinants of this kind of poverty, which was further fuelled by the condition of indebtedness into which they were regularly forced. All this made poverty 'a potential process, before being an acquired status' (Fontaine 2013, 4, our translation). This is why charities included among their main activities, in the Republic of Venice as elsewhere in Italy, paying housing rents, providing young women with dowries, giving access to cheap credit and paying fees to free the indigents from jail. To these activities, which were aimed at preventing the less well-off from falling into a condition of what we would call today 'absolute poverty', we can add the action of the many institutions created to receive

[5] 'Nobility offered the one means by which a loosely defined patriciate could obtain status recognition ... and distinction from the unprivileged. In practice, however, definitions and criteria of nobility were nearly as imprecise as those of the patriciate itself. Theory did not offer much certainty – or, rather, different theories supported and denigrated a variety of claims' (Grubb 1996, 170).

and raise abandoned children. These institutions allowed families facing difficulties, for example, during a famine, to relieve themselves anonymously of the newborn they were unable to care for (Pullan 1978, 1020–25).

Wage workers were among those at greater risk of crossing the boundary between subsistence and absolute poverty, and indeed, they often did so, especially during severe crises such as plagues or famines. This was especially the case of the unskilled workers of the urban manufactories, who were usually paid low wages and who were subject to heavy consumption taxes. This situation was functional to the needs of the wealthiest strata of society, not only because they had an economic interest in keeping salaries low or in pushing the burden of taxation downwards on the social ladder, but also because of the aforementioned propensity to use charitable actions as a means to secure divine grace. Moreover, charity can also be understood as a means to secure social control, as it placed the poor and the needy in a condition of dependence and submission which would not have arisen if the same amounts had been corresponded to them in the form of higher wages (Pullan 1978, 1034–36; Cavallo 1995). However, during the early modern period the status of waged worker became less and less automatically coincident with that of poor. This is reflected in developments in theory and tracts and is apparent, for example, in the aforementioned growing precision in distinguishing different kinds of 'poor' with varying legitimacy to receive assistance (Pastore 2000, 189–92).

2.2 How Many Poor?

We could wonder whether the changes in the perception of the poor and in the laws regulating their presence and activities within cities really reflect long-term changes in their prevalence. However, the literature provides us with very little reliable information about how many they actually numbered. The information we have is not only sparse but has been produced with different methods and with recourse to varying, and sometimes arbitrary, concepts of 'poverty'. According to Pullan, in early modern Italy the 'structural poor', i.e. those who were constantly in need of help (for example, due to disease) as well as the beggars, were 4–8% of the population. If we add to these the 'conjunctural poor', i.e. those who received low and/or occasional salaries and had to avail themselves of public assistance in times of crisis, we cover about 20% of the population. Finally, if we also include in our calculations the 'non-indigent poor', a somewhat complex group (which included, for example, many small artisans) composed of those that easily *could* slide into absolute poverty, we reach a sizeable 50–70% of the total (Pullan 1978, 989). Although these figures constitute an important point of reference, they clearly also present us with the problem of where to set the bar of poverty.

We have some examples of how this problem has been assessed from earlier research on the Republic of Venice. Among the cities of the *Terraferma*, Verona stands out as having been the object of studies attempting not only to count the poor, but also to reconstruct their profile. This is due to the particularly detailed nature of its *estimi*, where almost everybody was recorded as it seems that even those entirely devoid of property were listed with a minimum value of just 5 *soldi* (and sometimes, even less: see Tagliaferri 1966, 33–37). By assuming those recorded in the 1558 *estimo* with a value of just 5 or 6 *soldi* as poor, Paola Lanaro managed to describe the composition of this category, which included the 'authorized' beggars, the diseased and the indigent assisted by public charity, many widows and the 'workers living with the simple use of their arms and who did not own any sort of goods' (Lanaro 1982a, 50). The latter category was the most complex, as it included not only members of the lowest groups of waged workers – labourers, skilled and unskilled workers in the local manufactories – but also small artisans and some of the lowliest merchants and public officers. Of course, other members of the same categories who owned some property were recorded with larger *estimo* values and are not counted among the 'poor' according to this fiscal definition. This is consistent with a view of the poor as those who, *even if* they had an occupation, did not own property and did not have savings, which made them and their families acutely subject to changes in their work conditions, to periods of crisis or simply to fluctuations in the local economy (Pullan 1978). Overall, the households recorded with minimum *estimo* values (5 *soldi*) in 1558 Verona were 40.15% of the total. To these we have to add 370 households (4% of the total) officially recognized by the sources as *pauperes* (poor), which raises the figure to almost 45%. Lanaro argues that we should include in the computation of the poor also the households estimated at 6 *soldi*, which include those who owned just the house where they lived (although there is some incertitude on the matter). These account for 14.7%, bringing the overall count to almost 59% (Lanaro 1982a, 51–55), close to Pullan's general estimates reported earlier. However, it seems that the condition of this last group, which at the very least was guaranteed shelter and did not have to pay rent for it, is altogether less fragile compared to the other 'poor'.

These figures for Verona depend strongly on the specificities of the local fiscal sources, and could not meaningfully be calculated for other cities or areas with different rules about the redaction of the *estimi*. There

Table 2.1 *The propertyless in Bergamo and Padua (%)*

Year	Bergamo	Padua	Contado of Padua
1537	3.4		
1555	6.9		
1575		3.0	
1610	10.0		
1627		10.2	3.1
1640	5.0		
1642			
1694		6.7	8.1
1704	5.4		

is, though, another possible definition of 'fiscal poor' which seems to be more homogeneous. We refer to the 'propertyless', i.e. those recorded in property tax records with a value of zero. These are important for two reasons. First, they provide us with a lower boundary to the number of the poor (as in many instances, also those declaring to own properties with very small value can be considered to be 'poor'). Second, their estimation is usually a requirement to assess the overall reliability of attempts to measure long-term trends in economic inequality – as unfortunately, in the vast majority of cases the propertyless were simply omitted from fiscal records. It is in this second perspective that they have been focused on in recent studies about other areas of Italy, from the Sabaudian State (Alfani 2015) to the Florentine State (Alfani and Ammannati 2017) and the Kingdom on Naples (Alfani and Sardone 2015).

In our database, the propertyless were recorded in two cities, Bergamo and Padua. Unfortunately, in neither case are the propertyless always present in the sources, but in Bergamo they were recorded in five years in the period 1537–1704, while in Padua they were recorded in just three years: 1575, 1627 and 1694. In the last two years, they were recorded also in the *contado*. From these sources, we can calculate the prevalence of the propertyless households, as summarized in Table 2.1.

The series of Bergamo, which is the most complete, shows an interesting trend, which we can divide into two phases of growth in the prevalence of the propertyless. The first runs from 1537 to 1610, a period during which the share of propertyless households trebles (from 3.4% to 10%). The second covers most of the seventeenth century, from 1640 to 1704, although the growth is less intense (from 5% to 5.4%) and what is more, the prevalence of propertyless households seems to move around levels much lower than those reached in the early seventeenth century. The two phases of growth are separated by a steep decline – as the figure for 1640 is exactly half that of 1610. This apparent puzzle has in fact an easy solution: the terrible 1630 plague, which killed about 35% of the overall population of northern Italy (Alfani 2013b, 411). In Bergamo, plague killed at least 38.1% of the inhabitants, while Padua fared even worse, with losses as high as 59.4% (Ulvioni 1989a; Alfani and Percoco 2018). The plague led to an overall spread of property as the consequence of inheritance but possibly even more importantly, it led to a parallel increase in working opportunities and in real wages on the one side, and in the amount of property being actually sold on the market at low prices on the other side. This is in accordance with a basic economic reasoning (Alfani and Murphy 2017), which is also supported empirically by a few case studies, like that of the city of Ivrea in Piedmont during the same plague (Alfani 2010b). In other words, it is reasonable to presume that, at least for a few decades after the epidemic, it became easier for the lower strata of the local society to acquire property and move upwards from their condition of propertyless. This process could only have been reinforced by the social connotation of early modern plagues, which tended to make more victims among the poor than among the rich (Slack 1985, Alfani 2009c, 2013a; Cohn 2010; Alfani and Murphy 2017).

As a matter of fact, the overall medium- and long-term distributive consequences of the 1630 plague are not as clear-cut as it might seem, and will be subject to an in-depth discussion in Chapter 3. However, from the point of view of the prevalence of the propertyless only, the plague is the obvious 'culprit' in explaining the sudden drop in a trend which, in Bergamo, was otherwise clearly orientated towards a long-term growth in the number of propertyless. Although the series of Padua is more sketchy, it follows the same trend, with growth in the prevalence of the propertyless in the pre-plague century (from 3% in 1575 to 10.2% in 1627) and a sharp decline afterwards as in 1694, the figure of 6.7% was still well below that of 1627. For the *contado*, unfortunately we have data for 1627 and 1694 only. Between the two dates, propertyless households increased from 3.1% in 1627 to 8.1% in 1694. However, such growth probably took place only from the 1640s or 1650s, as, looking at the estimates of relative poverty presented in the following, the situation seems to be about the same in 1627 and 1642. Also in the *contado*, then, the 1630 plague seems to have temporarily stopped the tendency for an increase in the prevalence of the rural propertyless. Additionally, between 1627 and 1694 the relative conditions of city and country changed drastically, as the propertyless moved from being much more prevalent in the city to being significantly more prevalent in the *contado*. This steep growth in the rural propertyless is coherent with what we know about the progressive erosion of small peasant ownership during the early modern period, as discussed in Chapter 4. For 1627 and 1694 we can also calculate the prevalence of the propertyless in the entire province of Padua, which were 6.9% and 7.4%, respectively. Overall, these figures are in the same range as those measured for other parts of northern Italy. For example, in Ivrea and Moncalieri in Piedmont in 1613, the propertyless households were 9.2% and 8.5% of the total, respectively (Alfani 2015, 1063–64). In the same region, a couple of centuries earlier (1393), propertyless households were 9.2% in the city of Turin and about the same in the village of Coni (Comba 1982, 28, 30). However, at least one study for the Republic of Venice, dedicated to the city of Treviso in 1434–48, reports much higher figures, ranging between 19% and 29% in 1434–48 (Scherman 2009, 175; 2013, 381). These measures, though, are not directly comparable with ours owing to differences in the sources used.

The time trend in the prevalence of the propertyless as recorded in the *estimi* can be considered a valuable proxy of the general dynamics in the spread of poverty – but as an estimate of the *number* of the poor, it can be considered an (imperfect) measure of absolute poverty only. This concept refers to households which have access to resources below a minimum level considered acceptable, either subsistence (a popular threshold is having access to the minimum amount of calories necessary to sustain human beings in good health over the long run, but also clothing, housing and basic levels of sanitation can be counted among the basic human needs) or a kind of socially acceptable minimum which can include a broader range of goods and services. However, both the historical literature on poverty and studies of poverty in contemporary societies agree that in order to truly account for all the households that can be considered poor, we have to set the bar at a lower level. The easiest way of doing this is to focus on relative poverty: a household is considered to be poor when it is placed at a level of income or wealth much below some significant point in the overall distribution. In other words, a household (or an individual) is classified as poor if it is too far from the prevailing conditions of a given society. Usually, the threshold is set at a given percent of the median value of the distribution (Ravallion, Datt and Walle 1991; Ravallion and Bidani 1994; Ravallion 2009; OECD 2013). Notice that the notion of relative poverty, as applied to contemporary societies, is sometimes criticized because (it is argued) it has to do more with inequality than with poverty in itself. However, in the perspective of this book this is not necessarily a limitation (indeed, our study of poverty will be followed by an analysis of inequality and *distribution* is one of our key underlying themes). Moreover, the possible limits of measures of relative poverty are more than compensated for by the relative ease with which they can be applied to our historical sources, as is shown in the text that follows.

As the exact values recorded in different *estimi* generally reflect local evaluation rules and cannot be easily converted into one another, we establish our property threshold as a certain percent of the median. This is the preferred solution also in studies of contemporary societies and in addition, as we will show, the median has the particularly welcome characteristic of being fairly robust to some distortions in the observed distribution, and particularly to the absence of the propertyless. We adopt a simple 'headcount' approach: a household is defined as poor simply if it is below the relative poverty line.[6] As we are aware of no other study of preindustrial societies in which relative poverty was measured systematically using a headcount approach applied to wealth, we resorted to research on contemporary societies. However, most studies do not provide clear indications on the matter, as they tend to focus on income or on an integrated income–wealth approach. A notable exception is a study by Azpitarte (2012) in which income-poverty and wealth (assets)-poverty lines are established independently, in order to distinguish between households which are characterized by an insufficient level of *both* income and wealth (the 'twice poor' households) from those 'whose incomes are above the poverty line but hold few assets, which makes them vulnerable if current income were to be reduced or disappeared entirely' (Azpitarte 2012, 47). The two concepts seem to correspond quite closely to Pullan's distinction between the 'structural poor' and the 'conjunctural poor' and consequently they suit our needs well. Following Azpitarte, we adopt a wealth-poverty line set at 13% of the median, which is about one-quarter of the most popular income-poverty line (50% of the median). As a robustness check, we also apply a 50% wealth-inequality line as well an intermediate line set at 25%. Notice that this method works well only when applied to sufficiently large distributions – otherwise the computation of the median risks producing unstable results which do not truly reflect historical processes. As a consequence, we applied it only to the cities of Bergamo, Padua and Verona, as well as to their entire *contadi* (as will be remembered from Chapter 1, for the *contado* of Padua our distributions cover the entire rural population, while for Verona they are built from a sample of nine rural communities).[7] The results are

---

[6] Formally, $P^{HC}(x) = \frac{1}{n} \sum_{i=1}^{n} 1_{x_i < \delta} = \frac{p}{n}$, with $1_{x_i < \delta} = 1$ for $x_i < \delta$ and $1_{x_i < \delta} = 0$ elsewhere, n being the number of households, p the number of poor households and δ the relative poverty line.

[7] Also note that for Verona, we report the measures calculated for 1700 to 1800 only, as for earlier dates the specificities of its distribution – with a large part of the population recorded at a minimum value of 5 *soldi* – do not allow us to measure relative poverty in a meaningful way.

Table 2.2 *The prevalence of the poor, 1450–1800 (%)*

	Cities			Rural areas	
	Bergamo	Padua	Verona	Padua (contado)	Verona (contado)
Poverty line = 13% of median					
1450	6.7 (1448)				
1500	8.3 (1537)				
1550	8.5 (1555)	11.7 (1575)		4.1 (1549)	
1600	11.4 (1610)	17.6 (1627)		7.3 (1627)	5.2
1650	10.6 (1640)	15.9 (1642)		7.1 (1642)	3.1
1700	13.0 (1704)	20.0 (1694)	13.4 (1696)	6.2 (1694)	1.9
1750					6.5
1800			11.8		
Poverty line = 25% of median					
1450	6.7 (1448)				
1500	18.6 (1537)				
1550	20.0 (1555)	21.1 (1575)		11.2 (1549)	
1600	21.6 (1610)	25.3 (1627)		14.5 (1627)	14.7
1650	23.1 (1640)	23.6 (1642)		14.6 (1642)	13.0
1700	21.9 (1704)	28.9 (1694)	25.8 (1696)	14.2 (1694)	11.1
1750					15.2
1800			21.5		
Poverty line = 50% of median					
1450	23.8 (1448)				
1500	35.6 (1537)				
1550	34.8 (1555)	34.1 (1575)		28.6 (1549)	
1600	34.6 (1610)	38.3 (1627)		30.7 (1627)	30.6
1650	36.5 (1640)	36.7 (1642)		29.1 (1642)	29.2
1700	34.9 (1704)	38.5 (1694)	37.3 (1696)	30.5 (1694)	26.2
1750					31.6
1800			35.2		

Notes: Measures organized around reference years when needed. The actual years are in parentheses. For the *contado* of Verona, the data related to each of the nine rural communities covered had slightly different dates so that only the reference year is reported (see Table 1.2 for further details about the exact dates for each community).

summarized in Table 2.2 (notice that the series of Bergamo and Padua have been standardized by removing the propertyless in the years when they were present).

Our measures of relative poverty confirm that the numbers of the poor grew during the early modern period. This conclusion is robust to changes in the poverty line. If we take as an example the city of Bergamo, we discover that around 1450 poor households were 6.7% of the total if we take a poverty line of 13% of the median. Their prevalence grew during the sixteenth century, reaching 11.4% at the beginning of the seventeenth century. The prevalence of the poor declined by the mid-seventeenth century (10.6%), but by the end of the century it had increased to 13%. This picture changes only marginally if we take a 25% or 50% poverty line – only the mid-seventeenth century decline disappears or is even replaced by some temporary growth as overall the prevalence of the poor seems to have stagnated during the entire century. A similar dynamic is found in Padua, where the trend does not change at all if we change the poverty line. In 1575 Padua, relative poverty involved 11.7%, 21.1% and 34.1% of the overall households if we take a poverty line of 13%, 25% or 50% of the median, respectively, and reached a maximum level at the time of the last observation (1694) of 20%, 28.9% and 38.5% depending on the poverty line. The only phase of interruption in an otherwise monotonic growth occurred in the mid-seventeenth century, presumably in connection with the 1630 plague. Also in the *contadi* of Padua and Verona we find signs that the plague temporarily arrested the tendency for relative poverty to increase – even though the overall picture remains one of a gradual increase in relative poverty throughout the early modern period (in the *contado* of Verona, the rise noticeable between 1700 and 1750 is particularly impressive).

Measures of relative poverty, then, broadly confirm the trend we identified looking at the more sparse information available for a possible indicator of absolute poverty, i.e. the prevalence of the propertyless (Table 2.1). We might wonder, though, whether measuring relative poverty on distributions which do not include what was, generally speaking, the poorest part of the population distorts the picture and generates an artificial trend. Consequently, we calculated relative poverty measures also on the entire distributions for the years and communities (Bergamo and Padua) for which we had information about the propertyless. In Figure 2.1, these new measures are compared to those which exclude the propertyless. For the sake of simplicity we report only the information related to the 25% of median poverty line.

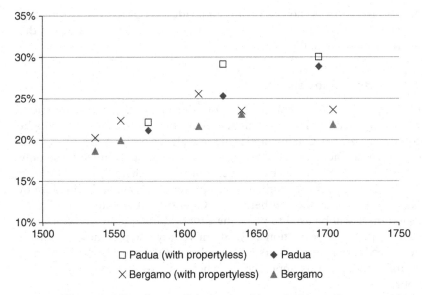

Figure 2.1 Prevalence of the poor, with and without the propertyless. (Bergamo and Padua,1500–1750. Poverty line = 25% of median value.)

The figure clearly shows that excluding the propertyless does not change the trend, which is always orientated towards a long-term growth in the prevalence of the poor (although most of such growth occurred before the 1630 plague). As was to be expected, if we include the propertyless in the distributions we get higher estimates of relative poverty. For example, in Bergamo in 1555, poor households are 20% of the total excluding the propertyless and 22.3% including them. The differences, however, are small owing to the resilience of the median to changes at the margin of the distribution. In some instances the two measures are virtually indistinguishable, like in Bergamo in 1640, when poor households are 23.1% of the total excluding the propertyless and 23.5% including them. Differences are always below 5 percentage points – the empirical maximum is found in Padua in 1627 and amounts to 4.8 percentage points (17.6% excluding the propertyless, 22.4% including them).

All the available information suggests that the number of the poor grew at the closing of the Middle Ages and during the early modern period. Although this is the first time that a systematic measurement of the prevalence of poverty in the Republic of Venice has been attempted, this is consistent with the impression coming from the general literature on poverty. This is, however, only one side of a process of divergence between different strata of the society that also involved the top of the distribution: that is, the rich.

2.3   How Many Rich?

If the poor became ever more numerous during the early modern period, what happened to the rich? This seems an obvious question, so it might come as a surprise that a study of the prevalence of the rich in European preindustrial societies has very rarely been attempted. Indeed, the only systematic study seems to be the recent article by Alfani (2017), covering some Italian states (Sabaudian State, Florentine State and Kingdom of Naples) as well as the southern Low Countries. The information published there will be used to place the case of the Republic of Venice in a broader picture (see Section 2.5). Alfani's study also provides us with the necessary parameters to pursue an analysis of the prevalence of the rich entirely similar, in its approach, to what has already been done for the poor.

In the case of the rich, it would be difficult to reason in absolute terms. Even for contemporary societies, proposed thresholds are significant mostly because of their ability to elicit the curiosity of the public – such as when 'billionaires' are singled out. However, there are no strong scientific reasons to argue that a billionaire is any different from those with, say, 10% less wealth – while in the case of poverty, it makes sense to distinguish those who are below a subsistence (or social subsistence) threshold, as being below the threshold implies a greater risk of death (or social exclusion). Consequently, for the rich the natural choice is to resort to a relative threshold, defined as a given multiplier of the median value, to measure their prevalence. Indeed, to do this we will make use of a 'headcount' index which is entirely analogous to that employed to study the poor – the main difference being that we'll focus on those 'above', and not 'below', the threshold or 'richness line'.[8]

As with the poverty line, setting the level of the richness line requires some caution. In studies of contemporary societies, the most common value for the richness line seems to be 200% of the median household income (Medeiros 2006; Peichl et al. 2010; Medeiros and Ferreira de Souza 2014). However, again similarly to what we have argued for the poverty line, we need to adjust the richness line to take into account that the information we have is about wealth, not income. In particular, we

---

[8] Formally, $R^{HC}(x) = \frac{1}{n} \sum_{i=1}^{n} 1_{x_i > \rho} = \frac{r}{n}$, with $1_{x_i > \rho} = 1$ for $x_i > \rho$ and $1_{x_i > \rho} = 0$ elsewhere, n being the number of households, r the number of poor households and ρ the relative richness line.

Table 2.3 *The prevalence of the rich, 1400–1800 (%)*

	Cities			Rural areas	
	Bergamo	Padua	Verona	Padua (contado)	Verona (contado)
Richness line = 1,000% of median					
1400	7.8 (1430)				
1450	7.3 (1448)				
1500	7.3 (1537)				
1550	10.9 (1555)	10.2 (1549)		4.3 (1549)	
1600	10.5 (1610)	16.9 (1627)		6.7 (1627)	5.2
1650	8.7 (1640)	15.7 (1642)		6.9 (1642)	6.3
1700	12.7 (1704)	14.2 (1694)	7.5 (1696)	8.7 (1694)	5.3
1750					7.0
1800			9.6 (1800)		
Richness line = 500% of median					
1400	17.0 (1430)				
1450	14.0 (1448)				
1500	17.7 (1537)				
1550	20.5 (1555)	20.2 (1549)		11.3 (1549)	
1600	20.1 (1610)	25.7 (1627)		13.6 (1627)	15.3
1650	19.6 (1640)	23.9 (1642)		13.7 (1642)	14.8
1700	23.0 (1704)	23.1 (1694)	15.0 (1696)	16.4 (1694)	12.4
1750					14.6
1800			18.9 (1800)		
Richness line = 200% of median					
1400	33.9 (1430)				
1450	30.6 (1448)				

Table 2.3 *(cont.)*

	Cities			Rural areas	
	Bergamo	Padua	Verona	Padua (contado)	Verona (contado)
1500	35.1 (1537)				
1550	36.0 (1555)	35.6 (1549)		28.5 (1549)	
1600	35.5 (1610)	38.8 (1627)		30.9 (1627)	33.1
1650	36.3 (1640)	37.2 (1642)		31.3 (1642)	31.9
1700	37.1 (1704)	38.1 (1694)	31.3 (1696)	32.0 (1694)	29.7
1750					31.7
1800			36.4 (1800)		

Notes: Measures organized around reference years when needed. The actual years are in parentheses. For the *contado* of Verona, the data related to each of the nine rural communities covered had slightly different dates so that only the reference year is reported (see Table 1.2 for further details about the exact dates for each community).

will follow Alfani (2017) and will use as our 'preferred' richness line 1,000% of the median. The resulting measures of the prevalence of the rich are shown in Table 2.3. As a robustness check, we include measures calculated using a 200% richness line as well as an intermediate value of 500%.

If we set at a relatively high level the bar of what constituted a rich household (one with more than ten times the wealth of the median household), we find that for example, in Bergamo around 1450 rich households were 7.3% of the total. Their prevalence increased from the mid-sixteenth century (10.9% in 1555; 10.5% in 1610), dropped after the 1630 plague to a level of 8.7% in 1640, then quickly recovered, peaking at 12.7% in 1704. Entirely comparable tendencies are to be found when lowering the richness line – although obviously, the figures increase as we are less selective towards who is to be counted among the rich. For example, in 1704 they are 23% of the total if we set the bar at five times the median, and 37.1% if we focus on those above two times the median (up from 14% and 30.6% in 1450, respectively).

Overall, the city of Padua follows the same trend as Bergamo, with an increase in the prevalence of the rich throughout the early modern period, although here the drop after the plague might have been more long-lasting. Focusing again on our preferred richness line (1,000%), around 1700 the rich were 14.2%, below the pre-plague figures (16.9% in 1627) but still much higher than the 10.2% observed in 1549. But we should also consider that the latest observation we have for Padua dates to 1694, ten years before that for Bergamo. This might contribute to determine the slight difference in the trends.

The information available for Verona hints at a continuing increase in the prevalence of the rich throughout the eighteenth century. However, there the rich were a significantly lower share of the total compared to both Padua and Bergamo: 7.5% in 1696, growing to 9.6% by 1800 but still far from the 13–14% share to be found elsewhere already around 1700, albeit not much less what was found, on average, in cities of other Italian areas, for example, the Sabaudian State (Alfani 2017, 332–33). Furthermore, the difference between Verona and the other cities of the Republic reduces as we lower the richness line (setting it at 200% of the median, we find that the rich were 31.3% in Verona around 1700, versus 37.1% and 38.1% in Bergamo and Padua, respectively).

In the country, the rich were less numerous than in the city. In the *contado* of Verona around 1700, they were 5.3% of the total (rising to 7% by 1750), versus 7.5% in the city. In the *contado* of Padua in 1549, they were just 4.3% instead of the 10.2% found in the city. This large difference of 5.9 percentage points increased further during the late sixteenth–early seventeenth century, then shrunk in the aftermath of the 1630 plague. This comes from a quicker recovery in the prevalence of the rich in the country than in the city: in the *contado* in 1694, the rich touched the maximum level of 8.7%, significantly higher than the 6.7% pre-plague. Notice that overall, it seems that the 1630 plague led to a reduction of the rich (whatever the richness line), especially in the cities. This was probably a consequence of patrimonial fragmentation after the wave of inheritances triggered by the epidemic itself (see Chapter 3 for a more detailed discussion of the distributive impact of mass mortality, and below for some additional information about inheritance practices in the Republic of Venice).

For the rich, as for the poor, we need confirmation that the trends that we detected are not driven by the absence of the poorest part of the population (the propertyless). Indeed, this is a relatively minor problem when focusing on the rich, as it has been shown empirically that head-count measures of their prevalence are very resilient to the absence of the propertyless (Alfani 2017). In the case of the Republic of Venice, we can make use of the sources of Bergamo and Padua, which for some years

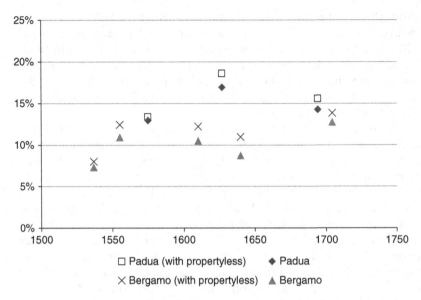

Figure 2.2 Prevalence of the rich, with and without the propertyless. (Bergamo and Padua, 1500–1750. Richness line = 1,000% of median value.)

include the propertyless, to estimate the consequences of their exclusion. This is done in Figure 2.2.

The figure clearly shows that when we can calculate them, measures of the prevalence of the rich including the propertyless are only slightly different from those excluding them. Indeed, for both cities the differences are always less that 2 percentage points, exception made for Bergamo in 1640 when adding the propertyless to the distributions means adding 2.2 percentage points to the estimate. The case of the Republic of Venice, then, also suggests that when we have to work with distributions in which the poorest part of the population is missing, the prevalence of the rich is a particularly reliable indicator of at least some aspects of the distributive situation of any given society.

2.4   Making It to the Top: Composition and Behaviour of the Rich

Who were these rich, whose numbers seem to have constantly increased throughout the early modern period? Most of the literature focusing on groups whose components would usually have to be considered rich according to our classification (being at least 10 times above the median wealth) did not provide an overview of *all* of the rich in the study area. Instead, much research was directed towards specific socio-economic groups defined primarily by characteristics other than wealth (field of activity, juridical status, membership of specific bodies or colleges, etc.). This would be the case for the merchants, the nobility or – more rarely – for those practicing specific 'liberal' professions. Their privileged access to resources was usually considered as a somewhat secondary feature or their status.

There are, however, a few studies of other northern Italian areas which provide useful elements for a comparison. For example, in the city of Ivrea in 1544, it was found that the richest individuals belonged to the urban elite composed of *gentillhomini* (gentlemen) and professionals (Alfani 2010a). For the same city, as well as for a sample of other cities of north-western Italy under Sabaudian rule, including the capital city of Turin, an exceptional source dated 1613 – a kind of census of the entire population, in which every head of household was recorded with his (or rarely, her) profession (Alfani and De Franco 2015) – provides a similar picture, as

[in Ivrea] among the rich [defined as those above the 1000% richness line] we find highly skilled professionals (lawyers and notaries; doctors and *speziali*, i.e. pharmacists) and high officials (the tax collector, the captain of the militia, etc.); merchants (especially of cloths and iron); and finally the '*gentillhomini*' or gentlemen, who belonged to the nobility. The richest household was that of a *referendario* of the Duke (an officer who received requests of justice or pleas to the Duke). ... In Susa, where information about occupations is relatively sparse, we know at least that the richest household was that of an '*oste*' (innkeeper) – although his very considerable wealth ... came also from his secondary activities as leaser of the properties of the priory of Susa and probably most importantly, as tax collector (he had the sub-tender for the *dacito*, an indirect tax on the transit of goods through the Susa valley, for which he employed directly two agents). The second richest was another individual holding an important office: the governor of the city ... The other components of the local rich for whom an occupation is declared include notaries, merchants and owners of the local tanning activities ... In Turin, the capital of the State, the presence among the very richest (say, the top 0.1% of the distribution) of high officials of the ducal court and of nobles is ... clear – and also clear is a marked difference in the extent of their wealth compared to that of the top rich of the secondary Sabaudian cities. (Alfani 2017, 337)

For communities of the Republic of Venice we have few, if any, sources as accurate as this one in providing us with information about the occupations of all heads of household. Surely this is not the case for the fiscal sources we focused on.[9] Although the older sources tend to be more

---

[9] Only in rare cases it is possible, at least in principle, to link the *estimo* entries to the preparatory documents (which are informative of occupations of household heads) used in the making of the *estimo* itself. This is what Tagliaferri (1966) did for Verona; see discussion in the text that follows.

informative in this respect, in general the early modern *estimi* only give us some hints about the presence among the rich of the nobility – as nobles can be identified from their honorific titles. So, for example, in Bergamo, among the richest ten household heads in 1555 we find three counts and a knight (*cavaliere*), in 1640 five counts and in 1704 four counts and a marquis. Around this final year, in Padua in 1694 we find a count, a marquis and a lesser noble (*nobile signor*) appearing among the ten richest households, and in Verona in 1694, two counts and a marquis. A century later in Verona (1800) high nobility made for the majority of the top ten richest, with five counts and a marquis. Some of these nobles owned enormous patrimonies, as in the case of the *Signor Conte* Francesco Grumello, the richest man in Bergamo in 1704, whose taxable wealth was eighty-five times the median (8,500%). It would be impossible, however, given the nature of the *estimi*, to use them for providing a deeper and more accurate analysis of a social group – the nobility – which was indeed very complex. And overall, these sources are quite reticent in providing us with systematic information about the components of the rich beyond the nobility, with the partial exception of some of those dating from the fifteenth century: see later for the cases of Verona and Treviso.

Some interesting information is provided by Pullan's (1971) classic study of the *Scuole Grandi* – institutions in which different components of the economic elite (nobility/patriciate and bourgeoisie) intermingled. Indeed, the main point to underline here (which was confirmed by many subsequent studies: see, for example, Cowan 2007), is that in Venice itself, and in the Republic at large, the boundaries between social groups which in other European areas were kept as separate as possible were much more blurred:

> Venetian society ... comprised two élites which, though legally distinct, discharged analogous economic, social and administrative functions. Patriciate and citizenry cannot be neatly classified as representing the feudal order and the bourgeoisie in early modern Venice. Venice offered no parallel to the social structure of Castile and France, where a 'nobility of the sword' ... contrasted with a 'nobility of the robe' or bureaucratic élite .... To a large extent, the citizens and the patriciate therefore derived their wealth from similar sources. (Pullan 1971, 105–6)

Although from the sixteenth and early seventeenth centuries patricians increased their investments in land, while at the same time citizens acquired a more prevalent role in industrial activity, the economic spheres of the two groups never came to be neatly separated. As argued by Pullan, this had social consequence and the strongest proof of this (relative) intermixing of the different components of the élite would be the comparatively high frequency of intermarriage. A list of 192 marriages between a patrician and a plebeian woman which occurred in Venice in 1600–34 reports the occupation of the fathers of most brides. Among these, numerous high officials and civil servants appear (government secretaries and notaries, accountants to public officers, etc.), along with professionals such as lawyers and physicians (Pullan 1971, 107). A more recent and broader study on the same topic, covering 484 marriages of Venetian patricians with 'outsider' brides (i.e. women who did not belong to the patriciate of Venice, although they might belong to the nobility of the *Terraferma* or of other states) during 1589–1699, found that 12% of the fathers were merchants, 11% were non-noble rentiers, 8% were lawyers (*avvocati*) or doctors of law (*dottori di leggi*), 7% were secretaries, 3% were notaries, 2% were doctors of medicine and another 2% were minor officials (Cowan 2007, 53). List of officers of the *Scuole*, such as that of the Guardians of the *Scuola* of San Giovanni in 1500–1650, also include information about their occupations. Again, we find numerous government secretaries, plus lawyers, notaries and physicians. Finally, merchants composed one of the largest group of Guardians (Pullan 1971, 109–10).

Beyond Venice, we have some information about the main cities of the mainland. In Verona, Tagliaferri (1966, 80–84) focused on those recorded in the *estimo* for a value of at least 7 *lire*, which the local legislation pointed out as affluent. These were mostly nobles, professionals and *milites*. The last group, which is specific to Verona, comprised noble families who had entered the highest strata of society in the late fourteenth to early fifteenth centuries, around the period when the city was conquered by Venice. In 1409, just fourteen families with at least 7 *lire* were qualified as *milites*, but they concentrated an enormous share of the property recorded in the *estimo*: 6,700 *soldi*, 5.8% of the total. A very large part of those with at least 7 *lire* were not recorded with a profession; hence they were simply big landowners, and most of them belonged to the nobility.[10] Other members of the local economic elite comprised professionals exercising the liberal arts, as usual: notaries, lawyers or doctors of law (*dottori di leggi*), physicists and doctors, as well as some key actors in the local productions, particularly the *drappieri*, who had the monopoly on the production and exchange of wool[11] (Tagliaferri 1966, 121–26, 139–47). From the seventeenth century, public officials involved with the

---

[10] These accounted for 56.9% of all the households with 7 or more lire, who collectively owned 16.5% of all the property included in the *estimo* (calculations on data from Tagliaferri 1966, 81).

[11] In 1409, 94 *drappieri* were recorded for an overall value of 5,722 *soldi* (4.9% of the total). Hence their average patrimony was a little over 60 *soldi*, or 3 *lire* (Tagliaferri 1966, 141). Only some of them exceeded the threshold of 7 *lire*.

local and the state institutions start to become more numerous, partly displacing notaries who were very prevalent at earlier dates. Also from the seventeenth century, the *drappieri* were replaced by the *mercatores* or 'merchants', who were involved in a larger number of sectors (especially silk) and had a more entrepreneurial approach (Tagliaferri 1966, 195).

Another interesting example is that of Treviso during 1448–86, thanks to the research on the composition of the rich conducted by Scherman (2009, 178). He ordered occupations by the size of the average patrimonies of their members. In 1448, the very top position was occupied by thirty textile entrepreneurs with an average patrimony of 5,515 *lire* (note that these *lire* are an entirely different unit of measurement from the Veronese *lire* used in the foregoing). The textile entrepreneurs were followed, at a distance, by 16 tanners (average patrimony of 3,781 *lire*), 76 notaries (3,100 *lire*) and 21 apothecaries (*speziali*, 3,078 *lire*). By 1486, textile entrepreneurs had further strengthened their position as just 18 of them, with their average patrimonies of 13,084 *lire*, outmatched, and by far, the growing fortunes of the notaries, although these were a much larger group counting 93 households owning on average 4,240 *lire*. They were followed by 36 clothiers (*merciai*, 2,659 *lire*) and by 33 tanners (2,301 *lire*). The richest households of all, though, do not appear in this list because their heads were not recorded with a specific occupation. In particular the Barisan family, which was the richest of Treviso both in 1448 and in 1486, in the two dates concentrated, respectively, 2.7% and 4.2% (41,084 *lire* and 178,496 *lire*) of all the properties recorded in the *estimo* (Scherman 2009, 175). The Barisan belonged to the local patriciate and regularly expressed members of the city council as well as occupying important positions in the local government.

The kind of information provided until now confirms that in the Republic of Venice, the rich belonged to basically the same socio-economic groups as in other northern Italian areas, such as the Sabaudian State. However, in many respects this information is unsatisfying. In the first place, it gives us only a few hints about how the composition of the rich changed in time. Given the specific characteristics of the society of the Republic, this might be a relatively minor issue (as the components of the socio-economic elite intermixed more than elsewhere); however, it is still a question that we would like to have answered, given the tendency for the prevalence of the rich to increase throughout the early modern period. As a matter of fact, we lack reliable studies of long-run changes in the composition of the economic elite not only for the Republic of Venice, but for all the ancient Italian states. In a way, the only systematic attempt to achieve this is that conducted by a group of Marxist economic historians in the 1960s and 1970s: the so-called Dal Pane School.

Members of the Dal Pane School intended to trace in time the rise in the share of wealth owned by a rising social 'class', the bourgeoisie. They argued that especially during the early modern period, the share of the bourgeoisie increased constantly. For example, in the territory of Ravenna in the northern Papal States (placed 50–60 km from the southern boundary of the Republic of Venice) it was 19% of the whole in 1569, 19.6% in 1612–14, 20.9% in 1659, 33.4% in 1731 and 42.5% in 1835 (Porisini 1963, 43–45), and a similar tendency to increase was also found elsewhere (see, for example, the case of Imola in Rotelli 1966, 115). However, these results were met with harsh criticism, because these authors defined 'bourgeois' property simply as that owned by non-noble households. But, as noticed in a particularly effective way by Marino Berengo (1970), also on the grounds of his deep knowledge of the society of the Republic of Venice, not only would this definition lead to include among the bourgeoisie small peasant landowners (who obviously *could not* meet the requirements of a functional definition of bourgeoisie), but also the data from the *estimi* do not allow us to distinguish the rise of the merchant élites from that of other specific bourgeois groups like professionals, civil servants and high officials, and great 'capitalistic' landowners: that is to say, the single components of the rich that here we would like to single out.

A more detailed account of the findings of the Dal Pane School and of the criticism it suffered is provided elsewhere (Alfani 2009b, 2014, 2017). Here we should point out that in other aspects this older research program was successful in establishing facts confirmed by later studies. This is the case for the resilience of the nobility as owner of *non-feudal* lands. For example, in Ravenna in 1835, nobles still owned 25.4% of the real estate (Porisini 1963, 43). This was the case also elsewhere in Europe, like in France, where the prevalence of the property of nobles increased during the first half of the nineteenth century, also thanks to new ennoblements under Napoleon, peaked at 29% of the total in 1847, and only later started to decline in parallel with the rising fortunes of financiers and industrialists (Piketty et al. 2006, 244–46).

Ennoblements remind us of a crucial fact: the nobility was never impermeable to the upward social mobility of other groups. Indeed, some of the components of the rich who showed the greatest dynamism in the late Middle Ages and at the beginning of the early modern period were keen to acquire a noble title, as this was seen as a further step up the social ladder. For the Republic of Venice, revealing examples are provided by Grubb's (1996, 156) study of Vicenza, like that of the Arnaldi family, who built their early fortunes during the fourteenth century on their professional skills as notaries. In the fifteenth century, Andrea

Arnaldi (himself a notary) was the first of his family to be elected to high office and consequently, gain access to the city government. Together with his brother Tommaso, he experienced a significant increase in his material wealth, so much so that in 1453 their patrimony belonged to the top 1% according to the local *estimi*. The brothers also became episcopal vassals. In the following generation, 'Gaspare II was elected to the leading civic magistracy and built a substantial palace in the new Renaissance style. Cousin Silvestro ... married into the old feudal nobility and found spouses for his children in the great house of the Thiene. Within a century, the Arnaldi had joined the local patriciate. ... After 1575 the Arnaldi were papal *cavalieri*, and traced their origins from the mythic Germanic warrior Arnaldus' (Grubb 1996, 156–57).

Other examples are provided by Alfani and Caracausi's (2009, 204–05) study of Padua. The Zambelli family, originally from Bergamo, moved to Padua in the mid-sixteenth century. In 1562, the joint patrimony of Gioanne Giacomo and Guaresco Zambelli was worth less than 3 *lire* – but already by 1615, Guaresco's sons owned collectively, in a *fraterna* (see later), about 95 *lire* or property, which assured them revenues in the order of 9,500 *ducati* and also made their household the third richest in the city after the Capodilista (Pio) and the Dal Relogio. By 1670, the Zambelli's patrimony had grown further, to more than 135 *lire*, and in the meantime (in the 1640s) the family had acquired the title of Venetians nobles – indeed, they had bought it, paying the enormous sum of 100,000 *ducati*. Finally, the city of Verona might have been a partial exception, as there incorporation of the newly rich mercantile families into the local nobility seems to have been much more difficult than elsewhere (Berengo 1975, 493–98; Grubb 1996, 160) – but not altogether impossible, as shown by the cases of the Ottolini and Zenobi families, originally from the Trentino area. These families acquired great wealth in Verona during the fifteenth and sixteenth centuries thanks to their merchant activities, but were excluded from the local councils until the mid-seventeenth century, when they acquired noble status by paying the aforementioned rate of 100,000 *ducati* (Knapton 1995, 480).

Again, however, these examples raise more questions than they answer – in this case, regarding the paths of mobility (upwards and downwards) followed by those households which, at any given point in time, we might qualify as 'rich'. But it would be impossible to answer such questions within a study of wealth distribution and inequality, such as this – as the information needed for a study of social mobility, as well as the techniques that should be employed, differ considerably. A proper analysis of the mobility of the rich (which could also allow for a deeper study of their composition) will have to be left to further research.[12] Such analysis should explore also paths for upward social mobility different from the acquisition of wealth through merchant activity (possibly followed by ennoblement), as also the army and the service of the state offered interesting opportunities to many citizens of the *Terraferma*, including to members of the lesser nobility. Indeed, public posts of the Republic such as those of *provveditori ai confini* ('supervisors of the boundaries'), *avvocati fiscali* (literally 'fiscal lawyers', charged with protecting the interests of the fiscal chambers) and jurists of various kinds, such as the *giudici assessori*, were much sought after and offered opportunities of advancement different from, albeit integrated with, those offered by the local institutions and governments. See, for example, the case of Ettore Ferramosca, a citizen of Vicenza, who was *giudice assessore* (as many of his family) in the late sixteenth century, became *provveditore ai confini* in the early seventeenth century and was created *cavaliere* ('knight') by the Republic, apart from acting repeatedly as ambassador of Vicenza in Venice to further his city's claims – with an intermixing of 'Republican' and 'local' posts, which was not at all uncommon (Knapton 1995, 483–84). The practice of tax farming[13] also offered interesting opportunities for economic advancement, from which many members, not only of the local bourgeoisie, but also (again) of the small nobility, profited. Nobles higher up the social ladder might still get involved indirectly in the tax farming business, by acting as guarantors as in the case of Altobello Averoldi, who belonged to one of the foremost noble families of Brescia and who during the 1570s acted as guarantor for the farmers of the duties on bread and on fodder (*biave*) (Pezzolo 1990, 172–74).

In this section dedicated to the rich, a final aspect needs to be clarified, which indeed is closely connected to both mobility and distribution: the way in which wealth, and particularly substantial patrimonies, was transferred from one generation to the other. Indeed, during the early modern period the main families of the Republic actively tried to preserve and when possible, to further concentrate their patrimonies as well as other key features of their socio-economic status such as posts in government institutions and public offices. The fierce pursuit of strategies of socio-economic reproduction, however, never resulted in absolute immobility for the society as a whole (Chauvard 2009) and as we have argued, the Venetian early modern society might well have been significantly more open compared to other parts of Italy or Europe (although we still lack

---

[12] Some additional reflections on social mobility among the elite of Venice – especially upward social mobility leading to acquiring the status of nobles – can be found in Cowan (2007).

[13] See Chapter 1, Section 1.3 for a general discussion of tax farming in the context of the Venetian fiscal system.

precise quantitative estimates of this possibly exceptional condition). Marriage strategies were totally coherent with this objective of socio-economic reproduction, as they were shaped in such a way as to avoid patrimonial dispersion among too many heirs, given that partible inheritance was the Republic's custom (Grubb 1996, 2–3; Chojnacki 2004).[14] More precisely, the Venetian inheritance system was egalitarian (partible) among male descendants, who were favoured over women regarding the transmission of real estate, although the richest dowries could also include lands and buildings. Dowries ensured that daughters received a substantial part of the family patrimony, but overall their share tended to be lower than that of their brothers. The husband had the right to manage the dowry for the duration of the marriage. However, in case of the husband's death, the dowry had to be given back to the woman, while if the woman died childless, half the dowry was returned to her family (Grubb 1996, 15–24; Chojnacki 2004; Lanaro 2012, 526; Bellavitis 2013, 328–29).

Regarding male inheritance, up until the mid-sixteenth century and across the *Terraferma*, wealthy families involved in industry and trade seem to have been quite keen on creating new branches, by division of the capital among all sons. Later this tended to change as the opportunities offered by international trade had begun to dwindle and the so-called 'return to the land' had begun (Beltrami 1961; Ventura 1964), a process also favoured by the interesting economic opportunities offered by substantial improvement in waterworks and the related wave of reclamations, leading to improvement in the quality and in the rent of much of the *Terraferma* lands (Ciriacono 1994). To reduce patrimonial dispersion, wealthy families tried to restrict as much as possible the number of marriages. Common, or more precisely 'undivided', property among brothers (*fraterna*) became frequent. In practice, brothers lived together, only one of them married, and the others designated his legitimate sons as their heirs. The *fraterna* became widespread among merchant families, and came to play a key role in the economic system of the Republic, with brothers involved in the management of the family company in a lasting way, together with their father, when he still lived (Lanaro 2003c; Chauvard 2005; Bellavitis 2013, 328–29, 335). However, the *fraterna* and the related marriage practices[15] – sometimes referred to as the 'limited marriage' system – also involved risks for the survival of the family (and consequently, of the company). Restricting marriage to just one son

---

[14] For a comparison with the Florentine State, see Molho (1994).

[15] Although the practice of limited marriage usually went together with the *fraterna*, this institution was also compatible with all brothers marrying, with all their wives' dowries being integrated into the capital of the *fraterna*. For example, see Bellavitis (2013, 335).

per generation seems to have determined an inordinately high rate of extinction of family lines: as it increased the risk that a whole cohort of brothers might not generate any son who survived until adulthood (Davis 1962; Hunecke 1997). In such a case, childless fathers willing to favour agnatic inheritance could designate as inheritors their brothers or nephews, or even the sons of the paternal uncles, but different choices were frequent (other relatives or friends, connected by marriage and/or affection) (Grubb 1996, 99–100). Beyond the *fraterna*, other institutions could also be used to ensure intergenerational patrimonial integrity, in particular the *fideicommissum*. Goods, usually real estate, that were the subject of a *fideicommissum* could not be sold, donated or diminished in any way, save in exceptional circumstances and could therefore be transmitted unaltered from one generation to the next (Lanaro 2000, 2012, 522–23; Leverotti 2005; Chauvard 2015).

Overall, this set of institutions and practices was successful in limiting the risk of excessive patrimonial fragmentation and final dispersion. Some of these were typical of Venice, especially the limited marriage system, while others are encountered also elsewhere. This is not only the case of the *fideicommissum*, but also of the practice of undivided inheritance among brothers (see, for example, the *in solido* inheritance practices widespread in Piedmont: Alfani 2010b). After all, different Italian societies were looking for solutions to the same problem: preserving the patrimony, which was instrumental to preserving the family (*familia, id est substantia*, as the celebrated fourteenth-century jurist Bartolus had declared), even in face of the most acute demographic and economic shocks, like those caused by plague and the related mass mortality. These aspects will be discussed further in Chapter 3.

2.5   The Prevalence of the Rich and the Poor in the Republic of Venice and Elsewhere in Italy: A Comparative Overview

The data presented in earlier sections, community per community and area per area, can be used to provide an impression of the prevalence of the rich and of the poor across the Republic's mainland as a whole, and can be usefully discussed within a broader, comparative framework. To do this, we will make use of distributions that are meant to represent the whole of this vast area. The characteristics of such representative distributions will be discussed in Chapter 3 (Section 3.6). However, the way in which they have been built from the community-level information available is explained in greater detail in the Appendix, to which the curious reader can refer immediately. For simplicity, here we will simply assume such distributions as valid, as well as the others that we employ for a comparison (related to the Sabaudian State and the Florentine State) and which have been obtained using the same methods.

The representative distributions we will focus on now refer to the urban and rural environments separately, and to the Republic (or more properly, the *Terraferma*) as a whole. We provide measures excluding the propertyless, which are more reliable as they are closer to the actual original information we had available in most cases. But we also present measures which include the propertyless, calculated from somewhat more hypothetical aggregate distributions (see Appendix A.4). The results are summarized in Table 2.4, where we compare directly measures of the prevalence of the poor and of the rich, using our preferred thresholds (poverty line set at 25% of median and richness line set at 1,000% of median).

Regarding the poor, the estimates related to the whole of the *Terraferma* confirm our main findings from the community-per-community analysis, particularly considering the tendency for their prevalence to grow in time. If we exclude the propertyless, the poor were 12.7% in 1500, increasing to a maximum of 19.4% around 1600. The 1630 plague temporarily rebalanced the society, as the poor declined to just 11.6% of the total around 1650. By 1750 they had gone back to the mid-sixteenth century levels, but at 16% they were still fewer than in the immediate pre-plague period. Hence the aggregate series stresses the redistributive impact of the plague compared to the information obtained for each specific community or area (compare to Table 2.2). If we include the propertyless, the figures change a bit (from 16.7% to 18.6% in 1550, from 11.6% to 13.7% in 1650) but the trend stays largely the same, exception made for an important point: at the end of the period for which we could build aggregate distributions, in 1750, the figures including the propertyless reach a peak (22.4%) which exceeds by 4 or 5 percentage points the pre-1630 levels. In other words, we get a less 'optimistic' picture, in the sense that in this scenario the Republic seems to have been much more poverty-ridden, during the eighteenth century and in comparison to earlier periods, than if we focus on the estimates excluding the propertyless. Another finding that is confirmed is that the poor were more prevalent in the city than in the country. This is always the case if we include the propertyless (for example, in 1700, the poor were 24.8% in the city, almost double the 13.6% found in the country) while if we exclude them, this is true only from ca. 1550. It should be noted that when we consider city and country separately, the poverty line is set at different levels for the two environments (as it is established relative to each distribution, and the median wealth in cities will be different from the country). Consequently, what these measures really tell us when we compare them is that the urban

Table 2.4 *The rich and the poor in the Republic of Venice (*Terraferma*), 1450–1750: the overall picture*

	Republic of Venice			Republic of Venice (propertyless included)		
	Cities	Country	Overall	Cities	Country	Overall
The poor (poverty line = 25% of median)						
1450	6.7					
1500	13.3	15.0	12.7	16.1	10.9	13.9
1550	20.0	13.3	16.7	24.1	11.5	18.6
1600	23.3	12.5	19.4	31.1	15.3	17.0
1650	26.7	10.0	11.6	30.8	11.5	13.7
1700	26.7	13.3	13.3	24.8	13.6	18.2
1750	30.0		16.0	25.2		22.4
The rich (richness line = 1,000% of median)						
1450	6.7					
1500	2.3	3.0	2.8	2.3	3.0	2.8
1550	6.7	3.7	5.1	6.3	3.6	5.0
1600	3.7	5.0	7.1	3.3	4.8	9.1
1650	5.3	6.3	7.3	6.3	7.4	7.1
1700	8.3	8.3	9.3	15.7	7.7	9.9
1750	10.0	7.5	12.0	9.3	6.9	11.1

Note: The measures excluding the propertyless are to be considered the more reliable (as the representative distribution including the propertyless required additional hypotheses to be made: see Appendix A.4 for details).

societies were more polarized (in terms of the distance of a large part of the lower social strata from the median) compared to the rural societies: which indeed is what we should expect. Also note that when city and country are analysed together, the fact of using a common poverty line does not necessarily lead to measures of an intermediate level compared to those calculated on the two environments separately.

Looking at the rich, we also find confirmation of their tendency to grow over time. From a low point of 2.8% in 1500 (measure excluding the propertyless), they grew to 7.3% by 1600, stagnated in the period following the 1630 plague, but already by 1700 they had exceeded the pre-plague levels reaching 9.3% and continued to grow, peaking at 12% in 1750. We find a similar trend if we look at the more hypothetical measures including the propertyless. During the early modern period, then, the overall picture was for a growing number of poor, and *at the same time* a growing number of rich. This phenomenon strongly suggests a process of social polarization, with the extremes of the distribution (the rich and the poor) growing ever more distant not only one from the other, but also from the middle of the distribution. This process involved other areas of Italy, too, as can be seen from Figure 2.3, where the Sabaudian State and the Florentine State are included for a comparison.

Regarding the rich, Figure 2.3b clearly shows a tendency, from 1500 in the Republic of Venice, from 1550 in the Sabaudian State and from 1600 in the Florentine State, for their prevalence to grow almost continuously right to the end of the period for which it has been possible to build representative distributions. From being no more than 3–5% at the end of the Middle Ages, already by 1600 the rich had increased significantly in the Republic of Venice (up to about 7%). By this date, other areas were still lagging behind, but by 1650 the Florentine State had already over-taken the Republic regarding the prevalence of the rich (9% vs. 7.3%). This might have been partly the result of a lighter impact of the 1630 plague in Tuscany compared to Veneto and Lombardy (which would be related to considerably inferior demographic losses: see Alfani 2013b), but the relative position of the two states had changed for good. The rich remained more prevalent in the Florentine State than in the Republic until 1750 at least, when those having wealth at least ten times above the median were 14% and 12% in the two states, respectively. In the

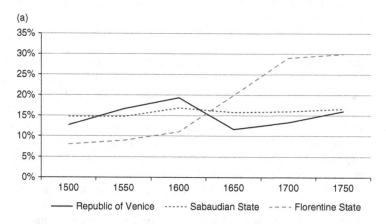

Figure 2.3 Long-term trends in the prevalence of the poor and the rich in central-northern Italy, 1500–1750 (propertyless excluded). (a) The poor (poverty line = 25% of median value). (b) The rich (richness line = 1,000% of median value).

(b)

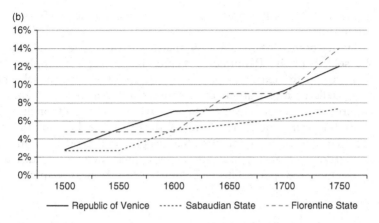

Figure 2.3 (cont.)

Sabaudian State, the process of growth in the number of the rich seems to have been at the same time slower and less intense. Here, although their prevalence grew monotonically from 1550, still around 1750 the rich were no more than 7.3% of the overall population (they would reach 10% in 1800: see Alfani 2017, 332).

Indeed, the society of the Sabaudian State seems to have been affected less by the overall process of polarization that we detected across Italy, as also looking at the poor (Figure 2.3a) we find there less tendency for their numbers to grow in time. In fact, the case of the Sabaudian State is very close to that of the Republic of Venice, as in both states the poor seem to have been, by 1750, not much more numerous than at around 1500 (but remember what has been noted in the foregoing regarding the apparent impact of the inclusion of the propertyless in an analysis of the poor). In the case of the Republic, however, it is the plague in 1630 that apparently displaced to a lower level what continued to be a path orientated towards growth: if we consider separately the periods 1500 to 1600 and 1650 to 1750, the growth was monotonic. This is also true for the Sabaudian State, although these variations during the seventeenth century are minimal (again possibly as a consequence of a lower demographic impact of the plague than in the Republic – albeit larger than in the Florentine State). The case of the Florentine State differs from the others not only because the plague does not arrest the growth in the prevalence of the poor, but also because the final intensity of the whole process is much greater: here, by 1750 the number of poor seems to have grown to 30% of the overall population, compared to 15–16% in the other states.[16]

To this point, our comparative analysis of the degree of polarization of the society of the Republic of Venice is still very incomplete. While focusing on the extremes of the wealth distribution (the rich and the poor) tells us much about the relative condition that was enjoyed, or suffered, by different strata of the society, we also need to include in the analysis its other components: that is, the rest of the distribution. Indeed, the quantitative reconstructions that we provided here are no more than an introduction to a systematic analysis of inequality and distribution across time and space. This is the objective of the next chapter.

[16] Possibly these relatively high figures for the Florentine State are at least partly to be explained with the spread of the *mezzadria* (sharecropping) system in Tuscany.

3   Economic Inequality in the Long Run

The study of long-term tendencies in preindustrial economic inequality is a fairly new field and indeed, until now only a few areas of Europe have been explored systematically. As a consequence, any new information provided holds much promise to change our understanding of what were possibly pan-European dynamics. The aim of this chapter is to provide a systematic and thorough analysis of economic inequality in the Republic of Venice (*Terraferma*). After some preliminary clarification about the nature of the information we use and the meaning of our measures, we begin by analysing each community separately, paying particular attention to possible differences between city and country. This also offers us the opportunity to build upon the analyses presented in Chapter 2, completing our reconstruction of the long-term processes of socio-economic polarization by focusing on the share of the overall wealth owned by the top rich and on other indicators.

The abundant information available will also allow us to explore systematically the possible redistributive consequences of the main mortality crises (plagues) that occurred in the period we cover, especially those of the late sixteenth and early seventeenth centuries. Another specific question that we intend to answer, is the impact on the property structures of the *Terraferma* (and potentially, on redistribution and inequality measures) of the spread of property of religious institutions and of the Venetian citizens who increasingly looked at land not only as a direct source of providing food and other products, but also as a means to diversify their investments and to acquire social recognition. We analyse the impact of Venetians' and church property by using the exceptionally detailed *estimi* of the province of Padua. Finally, we compare the overall inequality trends across the Republic with those of other Italian areas – the final step before attempting to place our case into an even broader picture, in Chapter 4.

3.1   Some Preliminary Clarifications on Data and Measures

The information provided by the *estimi* allows us to explore in detail the level and the trends in economic inequality across a large part of the Republic of Venice. More precisely, it allows us to measure wealth inequality, not income inequality. Indeed, the *estimi* in use in this part of Italy belong to the (vastly prevalent) 'per property' category, i.e. they include real estate (lands and buildings). However, real estate was not listed in the *estimi* with its market value, but at a value which corresponded to the capitalized income which could be obtained from such assets (Zangheri 1980; Borelli 1986a). This issue is discussed in greater detail in Chapter 1, Section 1.4. This characteristic of the *estimi* of the *Terraferma* is also to be found in the sources available for other areas which have been the object of studies of long-term trends in inequality, like Tuscany (Alfani and Ammannati 2017). It does not change in any way the ability of the sources to reflect correctly the distribution of wealth (under the reasonable assumption that the income that could be generated by assets was proportional to their market value). Indeed, there is a consolidated historiographic tradition that has assimilated the 'capitalized income' recorded by the medieval and early modern property tax records to wealth (Herlihy 1978; Herlihy and Klapisch-Zuber 1985). After all, as clearly shown by Peter Lindert in his analyses conducted on the 1527 Florentine *catasto*, although it is theoretically possible to use the same information also to provide acceptable proxies of income inequality, a number of hypotheses need to be made and the underlying distributions have to be transformed accordingly, mostly by adding estimates of labour income to the evaluations of capital income provided directly by the sources.[1]

Although it is important to make it clear that the measures presented in the following refer to wealth, and not income, inequality, we might also wonder whether in fact they also tell us something about the latter. On the grounds of both the general literature on contemporary societies (Davies and Shorrocks 2000) and of some studies of preindustrial Europe (Alfani and Ryckbosch 2016) we know that the *levels* of wealth inequality will almost invariably be higher than those of income inequality – hence at most, measures of wealth inequality could be considered upper-boundary estimates of income inequality. However, regarding the *trends*, 'for pre-industrial societies in which most households earned their living from agriculture, wealth inequality is a good proxy of income inequality. The ownership of land was of great importance in defining how the total product was distributed and overall, it is very unlikely that, in agrarian pre-industrial societies, income and wealth inequality could move in different directions' (Alfani 2015, 1062). The same point

---

[1] Private communication between Peter Linder and Guido Alfani, as well as Milanovic, Lindert and Williamson (2011, 269).

has been made by many recent studies (Lindert 1991, 215; 2014, 8; Alfani 2010a; Alfani and Ryckbosch 2016; Alfani and Ammannati 2017) and consequently we will assume that our measures of wealth inequality also tell us something about (the trends of) income inequality.[2]

The *estimi* provide us with information about the property owned by entire households, as declared by the household head and as verified by the local authorities. Consequently here we use household wealth distributions, not individual distributions. The household is also the standard unit of measurement of wealth inequality used for contemporary societies (OECD 2013, 46–54). Also analogously to studies of contemporary societies, our distributions do not generally include all the properties of religious institutions – a task that would in any case have proved impossible, either because much of the church property was exempt from taxation *ab antiquo* and hence never recorded in the local *estimo*,[3] or because the (taxable) property of clergy and religious institutions was recorded in special *estimi*, often referred to as *estimi del clero*, which proved impossible to include in this study. The exception is the province of Padua, where at least for some dates we could collect complete information about all owners. Another exceptional feature of the sources available for this area is that they allow to study the spread of the property of Venetian citizens in the *Terraferma* (as pointed out in Chapter 1, the Venetians were subject to a different fiscal authority, and hence their properties were not always registered in the same *estimo* as those of the local residents).

A more serious problem is the absence from most of our sources of the propertyless, i.e. those who resided in a given community but did not own any property to be recorded in the *estimo*. This category of individuals, who as a whole can be considered to include a sizeable part of the poor, has already been discussed in detail in Chapter 2. Here it will suffice to note that albeit the absence of the propertyless from the *estimi* is a common problem faced also by studies on other areas (Alfani 2015; Alfani and Ammannati 2017), the Republic of Venice does in fact stand apart because a relatively large number of sources are exceptional in including them in their lists. Consequently, although our basic measures of inequality have been standardized excluding from the distributions the propertyless if they were present (in order to truly compare like with like across space and time), whenever possible we also provide measures including them. These will

---

[2] This will be especially relevant in the next chapter, where inequality trends in the Republic of Venice are compared to those of the Low Countries, for which we have information about the income distribution only.

[3] On the implications of this, which is a common problem with Italian property tax records, see Alfani (2010a, 2013c).

serve both as a robustness check, and to expand our understanding of the actual distributive situation.

The basic inequality measure that we use is the Gini index, which is by far the statistical instrument most commonly employed for studying concentration of income or wealth. The Gini is calculated using the formula:

$$G = \frac{2}{n-1} \sum_{i=1}^{n-1} (F_i - Q_i)$$

where (in our case) n is the number of declarants/households; i is the position of each individual in the ranking sorted by increasing wealth; the sum goes from 1 to $n-1$; F_i is equal to i/n; Q_i is the sum of wealth of all individuals between position 1 and i divided by the total wealth of all individuals (in other words, $F_i - Q_i$ is the difference between the share of the population up to position i in the wealth distribution moving from bottom to top and their share of the overall wealth). In this formula, the Gini index is standardized to vary between the value of 0, which corresponds to perfect equality (when each household has the same wealth, $F_i - Q_i$ is equal to 0 for every i), and 1, which corresponds to perfect inequality (one household owns everything). The index can be represented graphically by the Lorenz curve, examples of which will be provided in Section 3.4.

The Gini index is the best instrument we have to 'summarize' the level of inequality in a given society. However, the same index value can correspond to different distributions. For this reason, it is important to couple it with simple instruments which will allow us to keep in check important changes in specific parts of the distribution. To achieve this, we use common percentiles, for example, the share of wealth owned by the top 5% of the population, the deciles (such as D1, i.e. the share of wealth owned by the poorest 10% of the population, or D10, i.e. the share of wealth owned by the richest 10%[4]), and the interdecile shares. The latter are defined as the average income of a given percentile over another (OECD 2011, 80–81). So, for example, S10/S1 is the ratio between the average wealth of a household belonging to the richest 10% of the population compared to the average wealth of a household belonging to the poorest 10%. As interdecile shares can be easily calculated as the ratio of one decile over another, for simplicity we will use a notation of the kind D10/D1.[5]

---

[4] When referring to deciles, we adopt the notation used by the WIID – World Income Inequality Database-managed by the United Nations, www.wider.unu.edu/project/wiid-world-income-inequality-database .

[5] In fact, the relationship between interdecile shares and deciles is expressed by the following formula:

$$\frac{S_x}{S_y} = \frac{S_x * n}{S_y * n} = \frac{D_x}{D_y}$$

3.2   Inequality in City and Country

How unequal were the urban and rural communities of the Republic of Venice? This question can be understood in two different ways. First, how large were the disparities among the inhabitants of each community, taken separately? Second, how large was the distance between the average wealth of urban and rural communities? We aim to answer both of these questions, starting with the first.

Table 3.1 presents information about wealth inequality in five cities of the *Terraferma* (Bergamo, Padua, Treviso, Verona and Vicenza) as well as in the rural areas. For the sake of simplicity, we present measures related to the whole of the *contadi* of Padua and Verona, plus those for some communities in the territory of Bergamo and for Arzignano in that of Vicenza. To ease comparisons between communities, measures have been clustered around reference years (fifty-year breakpoints from 1300 to 1800). However, we also report the actual years in parentheses.

A striking result that can be easily inferred from the table is that overall and both in urban and rural communities, during the early modern period inequality tended to grow over time. Everywhere the highest Gini value is the one placed at the end of the series, with two exceptions: Padua, where around 1700 a Gini of 0.799 is slightly lower than that reported for the mid-seventeenth century (0.81) albeit much higher than those related to earlier epochs (0.744 in 1550), and some communities in the rural areas surrounding Bergamo. Here, for Rovetta and the cluster of small communities including Piario, Oltressenda and Villa d'Ogna we have available only information for two dates, 1550 and 1600. Between those two years the Gini indexes are found to decline. However, the opposite happens in nearby Clusone, where inequality grows from 0.739 in 1550 to 0.751 in 1600 – although it declines thereafter, to 0.742 in 1650 and more significantly, to the lowest recorded level of 0.659 in 1700. The significance of the findings for this relatively small community of about 2,000 inhabitants, though, should not be overstated as they seem to depend on local dynamics. Indeed, in another rural community in the territory of Bergamo, Romano, the tendency is clearly orientated towards inequality growth and more importantly, in the *contadi* of Padua and Verona, which include many communities, as

where S_x/S_y is the interdecile share, S_x and S_y are the shares of wealth owned by the average household of deciles x and y, respectively; n is the number of households per each decile (which is constant through deciles by definition, as each of them includes 10% of all households); D_x and D_y are the shares of wealth owned overall by deciles x and y.

Table 3.1 *Wealth inequality, 1400–1800 (Gini indexes)*

Year	Cities					Rural areas						
	Bergamo	Padua	Treviso	Verona	Vicenza	Padua (contado)	Verona (contado)	Arzignano (Vicenza)	Chusone (Bergamo)	Romano (Bergamo)	Rovetta (Bergamo)	Piario and others (BG)
1400	0.674 (1430)			0.566 (1409)								
1450	0.697 (1448)		0.654 (1448)	0.606 (1456)	0.61 (1453)			0.486 (1449)				
1500	0.72 (1537)		0.694 (1486)	0.545 (1502)	0.579 (1505)			0.533 (1500)		0.694 (1522)		
1550	0.747 (1555)	0.744 (1549)		0.565 (1545)		0.669 (1549)		0.55 (1549)	0.739 (1579)		0.664 (1579)	0.702 (1579)
1600	0.723 (1610)	0.788 (1627)		0.482 (1575)		0.728 (1605)	0.651	0.687 (1602)	0.751 (1618)	0.741 (1605)	0.622 (1618)	0.673 (1618)
1650	0.715 (1640)	0.81 (1642)		0.547 (1635)		0.727 (1642)	0.684	0.738 (1650)	0.742 (1646)	0.762 (1663)		
1700	0.764 (1704)	0.799 (1694)		0.717 (1696)		0.747 (1694)	0.66	0.762 (1696)	0.659			
1750							0.763	0.768 (1756)				
1800				0.74								

Notes: Measures organized around reference years when needed. The actual years are in parentheses. For the *contado* of Verona, the data related to each of the nine rural communities covered had slightly different dates so that only the reference year is reported (see Table 1.2 for further details about the exact dates for each community). The measures for the community of Piario in the territory of Bergamo (BG) also include the communities of Oltressenda and Villa d'Ogna.
Sources: EINITE database for all communities and areas, excepted Treviso (Scherman 2009) and Vicenza (Grubb 1982).

well as in the community of Arzignano in the territory of Vicenza we find significant inequality growth. For example in the *contado* of Padua, by 1700 the Gini index had reached 0.747, well above the 0.669 reported for 1550.

These conclusions are confirmed if we look at the single components of the *contadi* (nine communities for the *contado* of Verona and twelve *podesterie* or *vicarie* for that of Padua).[6] In the *contado* of Padua, by comparing the earliest date (1550) to the latest (1700) we find inequality growth in eleven out of twelve *podesterie/vicarie*, the exception being Cittadella.[7] In the *contado* of Verona, where the earliest date available is 1600 and the latest 1750, between them we find inequality growth in seven communities out of nine. So overall, by taking the earlier and the latest observations available, we find signs of a tendency for inequality to grow in 86% of the subareas that we can distinguish in the *contadi* of Padua and Verona (eighteen out of twenty-one).

The tendency for wealth inequality to grow during the early modern period is also clear if we look at the cities. Focusing on dates for which we have relatively abundant data, we find that around 1700 in Bergamo, Padua and Verona inequality was much higher that at 1550, having increased by 0.017 Gini points in Bergamo, by 0.055 in Padua and by 0.152 in Verona. Inequality increase in the city of Verona is particularly striking, especially considering that it seems to have continued in the following century (in 1800, Verona's Gini of 0.74 was another 0.023 point larger than the 0.717 reported for 1700).

If we focus on the earliest information we have available, we find that in the late Middle Ages the situation was much more mixed. In fifteenth-century Bergamo inequality was already orientated towards growth, as revealed by a Gini increasing from 0.674 in 1400, to 0.697 in 1450 and finally to 0.72 in 1500. A similar dynamic is to be found in Treviso, where it grew from 0.654 in 1450 to 0.694 in 1500. In Vicenza, for which we have information only for the same dates as for Treviso, we find an opposite tendency with the Gini declining from 0.61 in 1450 to 0.579 in 1500. Finally in Verona we find significant inequality increase from 1400 to 1450 (from 0.566 to 0.606), but this is followed by an even more significant inequality decline in the following fifty years (down to 0.545 in 1500) and

---

[6] Each *podesteria* and *vicaria* included a few communities. See Chapter 1 for details.
[7] In Cittadella, the Gini was 0.78 in 1550, 0.737 in 1600, 0.743 in 1650 and 0.701 in 1694. In the eight communities for which inequality increase is to be found, the overall inequality growth was often very significant, for example in Oriago, where it amounted to 0.207 Gini points (from 0.539 in 1550 to 0.746 in 1700); in Monselice, where it amounted to 0.142 Gini points (from 0.545 to 0.687); or in Piove di Sacco, where it amounted to 0.134 Gini points (from 0.634 to 0.768).

indeed, the overall tendency for Verona was orientated towards inequality decline up until 1600 when the minimum Gini value of 0.482 is recorded.[8] This tendency, as we have seen, was entirely upturned in the two following centuries (although Verona remained significantly more 'egalitarian' than either Bergamo or Padua).

The more mixed tendencies found for the late Middle Ages (and even, for Verona, for part of the sixteenth century) are not surprising if placed in a comparative perspective. Indeed, thanks to studies of those areas of Italy, such as the Sabaudian State or the Florentine State, for which information is available from the fourteenth century, we know that the Black Death epidemic affecting Italy in 1348 is the only event, in the entire period 1300–1800, that was capable of triggering a lasting phase of inequality decline (Alfani 2015; Alfani and Ammannati 2017). To the west of the Republic of Venice, in the region of Piedmont then part of the Sabaudian State, inequality declined from the Black Death up until circa 1450. In Tuscany to the south-west, inequality recovery began already from ca. 1400. In the Republic of Venice, overall a clear phase of inequality increase seems to begin from ca. 1500 only. We have no explanation for these small differences, which, however, should not be overstated (see also the comparisons in Section 3.6).

Figure 3.1 provides a graphical representation of these trends, clearly confirming the impression that the overall tendency was for inequality to increase and that this tendency only became stronger and more generalized in time. Additionally, the graphical comparison between cities (Figure 3.1a) and rural areas (Figure 3.1b) suggests that this phenomenon was even more marked in the country than in the city. The time series for the rural community of Arzignano in the territory of Vicenza, which is the longest we have, is particularly impressive, as it shows a monotonic inequality growth throughout three centuries, leading to a very considerable overall increase in inequality measured by a Gini index rising from 0.486 at 1450 to 0.768 at 1750.

---

[8] Tagliaferri provided an explanation of this phenomenon – which he identified only partially, by an analysis of *estimo* 'classes' over time and without providing proper measures of overall inequality. He focused on demography, arguing that in the periods 1450–1500 and 1550–1600, a progressive levelling of the *estimo* values, especially of those placed at the bottom of the distribution, resulted from intense demographic growth which had inflationary consequences on the labour market (Tagliaferri 1966, 70–72). This explanation, however, fails to fully convince for many reasons. In particular, it is not clear why demographic growth had these consequences in Verona, but not elsewhere – especially considering that demographic growth has often been seen as a factor promoting the growth, not the decline, of inequality. See Chapter 4 for a discussion of this point.

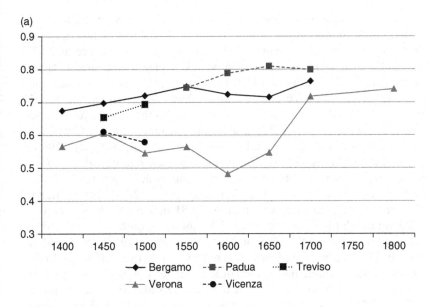

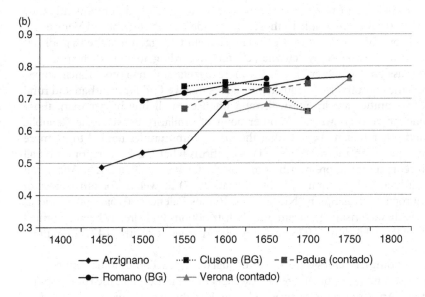

Figure 3.1 Long-term trends in economic inequality. (Gini indexes of wealth concentration. Propertyless excluded.) (a) Cities. (b) Rural communities.

Notes: Measures organized around reference years when needed (see Table 3.1 for details, including about the sources used).

The significance of our inequality measures can be better understood by placing them in a comparative perspective. In the three centuries from 1400 to 1700, we find urban inequality growing from a range of 0.57–0.68 to 0.72–0.80. In rural communities, the range was seemingly larger to begin with (0.53–0.69 at 1450) but converged towards a much narrower range of 0.66–0.76 by 1700, again showing a considerable growth in inequality levels. These values are in line with those to be found elsewhere. For example in the Sabaudian State, around 1400 the Gini index equalled 0.546 in Cherasco and 0.663 in Moncalieri, rising by 1700 to 0.796 and 0.657, respectively. In the Piedmontese countryside, the Gini was equal to 0.633 in 1450 Vigone, growing to 0.733 by 1700. At the same date, it equalled 0.579 in Cumiana (Alfani 2015, 1069). In the Florentine State, the Gini was equal to 0.481 in a city such as Arezzo in 1400 but much higher in Prato in 1450 (0.683). In both cities, by 1700 it had grown to exceed the level of 0.8 (0.81 in Arezzo in 1700; 0.831 in Prato in 1750). Lower inequality was to be found in the rural areas. In the *contado* of San Gimignano the Gini index equalled 0.499 in 1400, while in the *contado* of Florence it reached 0.57 at the same date then rising to 0.737 by 1700 (Alfani and Ammannati 2017, 11–13). All the measures reported for the Sabaudian State and the Florentine State refer to inequality in ownership of real estate (propertyless excluded) and consequently they are entirely comparable to those we provide for the Republic of Venice.

From this comparison, we find no element to suggest that the Republic of Venice, a supposedly 'charitable' state according to public rhetoric (see discussion in Chapter 2), was any more 'egalitarian' than other Italian states. On the contrary, the inequality measures that we find for its urban and rural communities are in line with, and often even slightly higher than, those encountered elsewhere. Another point of similarity between the Republic and other Italian areas, is that the urban communities tended to be more unequal than the rural ones. This confirms what has been reported by all recent studies of preindustrial inequality, for Italy (Alfani 2015; Alfani and Sardone 2015; Alfani and Ammannati 2017) as well as for other areas of Europe such as Spain (Nicolini and Ramos Palencia 2016a, 760). Indeed, this characteristic of ancient wealth distributions had already been identified by David Herlihy (1978) in his pioneering work on the 1427 Florentine *catasto*.

Finding that cities were more unequal than rural communities brings us to our second question: Were city dwellers much richer than the rural population? An easy way to answer this is look at the average wealth declared by each household. However, as the units of measurement (the local *lire*) used in each *estimo* are not easily convertible one into another[9] it is not quite so simple. In fact, the only area for which such a comparison can be easily accomplished is that of Padua. Here, in 1549 the average urban household owned 703 *denari* of property, much more than the 94 *denari* of the average rural household. The ratio did not change much by 1627 (680 vs. 88 *denari*) and reduced slightly in the following period, mostly as a consequence of the declining size of the average urban patrimony. The average wealth of owners inscribed in the urban *estimo* was 546 in 1642 and 773 in 1694, versus 88 and 109 found for owners of the *contado* at the same dates. Overall the average urban patrimony remained between 6.4 and 7.7 times as large as the average rural patrimony throughout the period. However, Padua was the wealthiest city of all those included in this study, so it might be that elsewhere in the *Terraferma* urban households had a somewhat reduced advantage over rural households. On the grounds of some simple calculations discussed in Appendix A3, we can estimate that on average across the *Terraferma*, urban owners were between five and six times as wealthy as rural owners. This is greater than what was found elsewhere, but the difference seems to be due to two factors: the comparatively large size of the main cities of the Republic, and the differences in the time periods considered. In particular in the case of Tuscany in 1427 (which is surely that researched more thoroughly, by subsequent generations of scholars) owners residing in medium-sized cities such as Arezzo, Pistoia and Pisa were 2.2 to 2.7 times as rich as those of the rural villages and 5 to 6 times as rich as those residing in sparsely populated areas – but if we look at the capital city of Florence, its residents were 8.5 times as rich as those of rural villages and 19.5 times as rich as those of the sparsely populated areas (own calculations from data in Herlihy 1978, 136–39). An overall estimate for the whole of the Florentine State has recently been proposed, according to which urban owners would be 3.4 times as wealthy as rural owners in 1450, then progressively improving their relative position until becoming 4.8 times as wealthy as rural owners by 1750 (Alfani and Ryckbosch 2016, appendix D): not very far, then, from the ratio of 7.1 which we find for 1694, the residual difference being probably due to the aforementioned difference in the size of the main cities of the two states.[10]

These findings, albeit illustrative of a real (and well-known) difference between the relative wealth of city and country, a difference which the

[9] This is also because, generally speaking, these *lire* were units of measurement used exclusively for the purpose of redacting the *estimo* and of distributing proportionally the fiscal burden: see further discussion in Chapter 1.

[10] Note that, as again was found for Tuscany, the tendency is for the average wealth of urban households to grow with the size of the city. On this matter, see Herlihy (1978); Herlihy and Klapisch-Zuber (1985); Alfani and Ryckbosch (2016, appendix); and Alfani and Ammannati (2017).

rules about citizenship and residence helped to enroot throughout the medieval and early modern period, are not very informative if we wonder about their significance in distributive terms. Indeed, as inequality tended to be higher in the city than in the country, on principle it is possible that while the average urban owner was richer, the median owner (i.e. the owner placed exactly in-between the poorest and the richest halves of the population) was less well-off in the city than in the country. Generally speaking this was not the case, and surely it was not in Padua and its territory – even though the differences between city and country are considerably smaller. In 1549, the median owner of the city declared a wealth of 163 *denari*, 4.7 times the 35 *denari* declared by the median owner of the *contado*. In 1694, the ratio was a slightly lower one of 4.5 (125 to 28). This suggests that a large part (and not just a few lucky individuals) of the city inhabitants were richer than the rural dwellers.

We might also wonder what happens to our distributions (and to our estimates of inequality levels) when we place together the urban and the rural population. At least in the province of Padua, where (1) much of the wealth distribution of the city was placed at a higher position compared to the country, (2) the ratio of urban to rural wealth seems to have been exceptionally high and (3) the urban population was a relatively large share of the overall population of the province, the net result is that the overall distribution for the whole province is more unequal compared to those of city and country taken separately. This can be clearly seen in Figure 3.2 for the years 1549, 1627, 1642 and 1694, i.e. in all the years when we have information about the *contado* (notice that for the city of Padua, the observation for 1627, when the Gini equalled to 0.819, was not reported in Table 3.1 and in Figure 3.1 as it was redundant). Indeed, the fact that the overall distribution is more unequal than its single components seems to have been a characteristic of the Republic as a whole (see Figure A4 in Appendix A4), not always to be encountered elsewhere. For example, in the Sabaudian State, the overall distribution lies in-between those representative of city and country separately (Alfani 2015).

We still need to address a crucial question. Up to now, we have standardized our distributions by removing the propertyless, in the few instances when they were recorded along the owners. Given that the propertyless were by definition those placed at the very bottom of the distribution (with a value of zero), their absence distorts systematically our inequality measures towards lower-than-real levels. In this sense, the Gini indexes of wealth inequality that we have presented so far are to be considered lower-bound estimates of the actual inequality. We would like to know, though, how great we can expect the inherent distortion to be

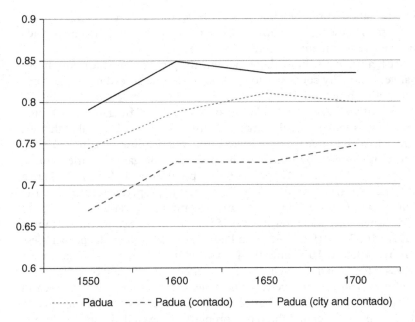

Figure 3.2 Economic inequality in city and country: the case of Padua, 1550–1700 (Gini indexes of wealth concentration).
Sources: EINITE database.

and even more importantly, whether the absence of the propertyless changed the trend (from growing to declining, or vice versa).

Regarding the trends, a first point to make is that the general literature on poverty suggests that across Italy, the prevalence of the poor grew during the early modern period (Pullan 1978; Woolf 1988). This view is also confirmed by the analyses that we conducted in Chapter 2, the only possible exception being the decades immediately following the 1630 plague which saw a decline in the prevalence of both the propertyless and the relative poor. Consequently, we expect that if we included some estimate of them in our sample, some of our key findings would probably be strengthened: in particular, the long phase of rising inequality which characterized the early modern period. As will be seen when discussing the aggregate estimates for the entire Republic of Venice, this is exactly what we obtain if we try to factor in the prevalence of the propertyless over time.

However, we also have further direct evidence of the fact that including the propertyless does not change our conclusions about the inequality trends. In particular, the sources for the cities of Bergamo and Padua are exceptional because, for some years at least, they also record the propertyless, thus allowing comparison of the Gini indexes obtained by including or excluding them, as seen in Figure 3.3.

The figure clearly shows that by adding the propertyless, the trends never change: inequality continues to grow or to decline according to the community and the period. If anything, adding the propertyless accentuates the trends that we have already identified. The cases of Bergamo and Padua also allow us to measure the degree of distortion towards equality that we suffer when excluding the propertyless from our distributions. Indeed, such distortion seems to be somewhat limited, as in Bergamo it varies from a minimum of 0.8% in 1640 (or 0.006 Gini points, from 0.715 to 0.721) to a maximum of 4.1% in 1610 (when adding the propertyless increases the Gini from 0.723 to 0.753). In Padua, the minimum variation is 0.8% in 1575 (when Gini increases from 0.788 to 0.794), while the maximum is 2.3% in 1627 (0.819 to 0.838). In Padua's *contado*, where the propertyless were recorded in 1627 and 1694 only, adding them to the distribution increases the Gini index by 1.1% (from 0.728 to 0.736) and by 2.5% (from 0.747 to 0.766), respectively.[11] The general conclusion is that, at least in the specific setting of the *Terraferma*, the measures of wealth inequality which can be generally obtained (propertyless excluded) are surely distorted towards greater-than-real equality – but are nevertheless very close to the real inequality levels.

3.3   The Happy Few: Wealth Concentration and Socio-economic Polarization

The analysis of economic inequality as measured by the Gini index provided an overview of the general trends. However, synthetic measures such as the Gini are not informative of all relevant changes in the distribution. Indeed, even an almost unchanging Gini can hide significant developments, while the same changes over time in the index value could be due to very different phenomena, not necessarily affecting the same portion of the distribution. To solve this problem, and to get a better understanding of general long-term dynamics, a deeper analysis is necessary. The easiest way of doing this is to focus on relevant quantiles. A particularly popular measure is the share of wealth owned by the top of

---

[11] For Treviso during the fifteenth century, Scherman (2009, 184) reports a considerably larger distortion in the Gini indexes, resulting from a much larger prevalence of the propertyless. For example, in 1448, adding the propertyless leads to a 16.8% increase in the Gini (from 0.654 to 0.764). However, as discussed in Chapter 2, Scherman's measures of the propertyless are not entirely comparable with our own owing to differences in the sources used.

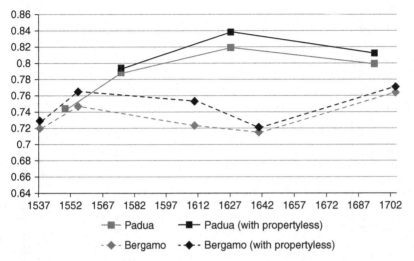

Figure 3.3 Wealth inequality, with and without the propertyless (Bergamo and Padua, 1537–1704).
Sources: EINITE database.

the distribution – the richest part of the population. A useful feature of the share of the top rich is that it tends to be closely correlated with overall inequality (as measured for example with the Gini index). This is an empirical regularity described for contemporary societies by many authors (Atkinson et al. 2011; Alvaredo et al. 2013; Piketty 2014; Roine and Waldenström 2015) and also usually found in preindustrial societies (Alfani 2015, 2017; Alfani and Sardone 2015; Alfani and Ryckbosch 2016) – but it is not a statistical necessity and indeed, as discussed below, in the Republic of Venice we find some interesting instances of Gini indexes and top shares moving (temporarily) in opposite directions. In Table 3.2 we present the share of the top 5% and 10% rich for all the cities and rural communities for which we have information, organized according to the same criteria discussed earlier for Table 3.1.

The table clearly shows that wealth ownership was extremely polarized. The share owned by the top 5% rich touched an empirical maximum of 62.5% in the rural community of Arzignano in 1700. In the cities, the maximum recorded value was found in Padua in 1650 (52.9%). The same communities maintain this unpleasant record when looking at the share of the top 10%, which equalled 71.8% in Arzignano in 1700 and 70.2% in Padua in 1650. These high levels are the consequence of a long-term process. In cities, the share of the richest 5% moved from a range of 36.6–39.1% in 1400 to a much higher one of 40.8–50.6% in 1700. In the

Table 3.2 *The share of the top 5% and 10% rich, 1400–1800*

	Bergamo	Padua	Treviso	Verona	Vicenza	Padua (contado)	Verona (contado)	Arzignano (Vicenza)	Clusone (Bergamo)	Romano (Bergamo)	Rovetta (Bergamo)	Piario and others (BG)
Share of top 5%												
1400	39.1			36.6								
1450	40.3		n.a.	38.9	40.8			20.2				
1500	43.0		n.a.	41.1	40.2			30.1		44.6		
1550	44.9	46.4		42.6		41.4		32.0	44.7		31.6	47.6
1600	39.6	50.9		39.3		48.3	34.4	45.2	45.5	46.4	31.3	41.0
1650	39.0	52.9		42.1		47.8	38.7	57.2	49.1	51.5		
1700	45.5	50.6		40.8		48.3	38.5	62.5	41.2			
1750								61.2				
1800				43.8			53.6					
Share of top 10%												
1400	54.5			49.4								
1450	56.4		49.3	53.7	51.0			33.2				
1500	57.4		55.6	54.4	53.5			42.3		57.9		
1550	60.7	61.7		55.6		55.2		43.2	60.6		51.3	58.7
1600	57.0	67.4		49.3		62.4	49.5	60.4	63.6	61.6	44.1	56.1
1650	55.2	70.2		53.8		62.1	54.4	68.4	62.9	67.0		
1700	63.0	68.2		58.0		63.9	53.4	71.8	53.1			
1750							67.1	71.0				
1800				60.2								

Notes: Measures organized around reference years when needed. See Table 3.1 for actual years and for additional details about the information provided. For Treviso, measures of the share of the top 5% are not available.

Sources: EINITE database for all communities and areas, except Treviso (Scherman 2009) and Vicenza (Grubb 1982).

country, in 1500 the range was 30.1–44.6%, growing to 41.2–62.5% in 1700. In the same years, the share of the richest 10% grew from a range of 49.4–54.5% in 1400 to one of 58–68.2% in cities, and from 30.1–44.6% to 53.1–71.8% in the rural areas. This growth-orientated tendency is particularly impressive in Arzignano, which moves from being characterized by relatively very low concentration at the top (just 33.2% of the overall property went to the richest 10% in 1450, about 20 percentage points less than what was found in other communities – all cities – at the same date), to becoming the place where the upper crust stood out more clearly from all others, as the top 10% owned 71.8% of all the property recorded in the local *estimi* in 1700, and slightly less (71%) in 1750.

More generally, the tendency for wealth to become more concentrated during the early modern period is even clearer when looking at the share of the richest than at overall inequality measures like the Gini indexes, as can easily be seen by comparing Figure 3.4 to Figure 3.1. Indeed, even in Verona, where the Gini index had been declining overall from 1450 until 1600, we find an almost monotonic increase of the share of the top 5% or 10% rich throughout the period, an exception made for a temporary slump between 1550 and 1600.

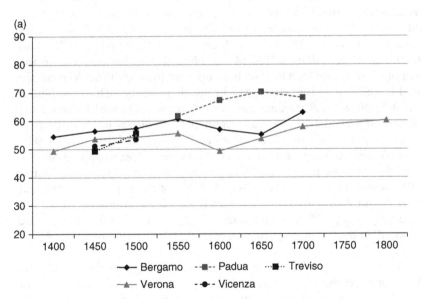

Figure 3.4 Share of wealth owned by 10% top rich. (a) Cities. (b) Rural communities.

(b)

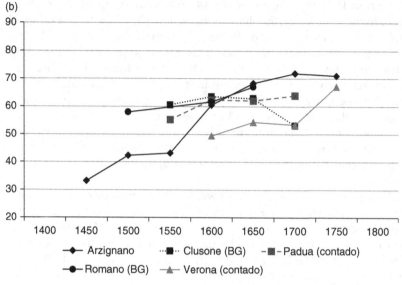

Figure 3.4 (cont.)

Yet again, the measures described for communities of the Republic of Venice are in line with those found for other Italian areas. For example, in cities of the Sabaudian State, the top 10% rich owned 50.9% of the overall wealth in 1400, 51.2% in 1500, 54.4% in 1600, 65.6% in 1700 and 68.9% in 1800 (Alfani 2017, 341–3. Note that in the only city of the Republic of Venice for which we have information after 1700, Verona, we find traces of a continued growth in the share of the rich in the period 1700–1800, too). Regarding rural areas, in the *contado* of Florence the richest 10% owned 43.9% of all wealth in 1400, 40.7% in 1500, 48.76% in 1600 and 60.5% in 1700 (Alfani and Ammannati 2017, 1093–94). Outside Italy, in the Spanish rural communities of Cervera and Reus, the growth over time in the share of the richest was less intense, as the top 10% owned, respectively, 48.2% and 39.7% of all property in 1500, and 48.1% and 43.7% in 1700 (Cervera is the rare community where the share of the top 10% declined during 1500–1700 – but it became more 'normal' in the following period, as by 1800 it had grown to 52%) (Alfani 2017, 342–43).

Per se, the growth in the share of the top rich suggests that wealth was becoming ever more concentrated at the top – and, one might be tempted to say, 'in the hands of the few'. But was it really a small minority, that which experienced such a significant increase in its relative position? The question is more subtle than it might seem, as technically, an increase in the share of, say, the top 5% households as a whole might result from a large increase in just a few patrimonies while the others might remain stable or even decline a little. Indeed, if we recall the findings from our earlier analysis of the prevalence of the rich (Sections 2.3 and 2.5), it is worth noting that the richest group (composed, in our definition, of those whose patrimony was ten times or more as large as the median) was growing in size. Across the entire Republic of Venice (city and country together), those with a patrimony worth at least ten times the median were 2.8% in 1500, 7.1% in 1600 and 9.3% in 1700. In other words, throughout the early modern period the rich were becoming *at the same time* more numerous and more distanced from the other strata of the society regarding their average wealth. This suggests an intense process of economic polarization within the society of the Republic. To analyse it more comprehensively, we will make recourse to interdecile shares.

In Table 3.3, three particularly significant indicators are presented: D10/D1, which is the ratio between the top and the bottom deciles of the distribution; D10/D5, which compares the richest to the middle ranks of society; and finally D5/D1, useful to compare the relative position of the middling groups with the poorest part of the population. Note that for technical reasons, the city of Vicenza could not be included in the analysis while Verona could be included from 1700 only.[12]

The analysis of the interdecile shares clearly shows that during the early modern period, the share of wealth of the top 10% rose both in comparison to the bottom, and to the middle of the distribution. Indeed, it rose compared to *all* other deciles, including the next richest D9 and D8 – but it is considerably more marked when one considers the lower socio-economic strata. In Bergamo, the city for which we have the earliest usable data, the top 10% rich were on average 72.7 times as rich as the bottom 10% in 1400, 198.1 times as rich in 1500, 316.8 times as rich in 1600 and 572.4 times as rich in 1700. But this is dwarfed by Padua, where the same interdecile shares equalled to 612.4 in 1600 and to an astounding 1704.8 in 1700. At the same time, the top was also growing more distant from the middle of the distribution. If we look at the D10/D5 interdecile share, in Bergamo it grew steadily from 20.9 in 1400, to 24.7 in 1500, 26.9 in 1600 and 39.4 in 1700. A similar increase also occurred in Padua and all other areas, both urban and rural. For example, in the *contado* of Padua, the 10% richest households were on average 16.7 times as rich as those belonging to

---

[12] The reason for this is that for Vicenza and for Verona before 1700 we had to reconstruct a distribution from the simplified wealth classes published by Grubb (1982) and by Tagliaferri (1966). Such classes tend to aggregate considerably the poorest levels of society, making it difficult or altogether impossible to identify correctly the shares of the first wealth deciles.

Table 3.3 *Economic polarization in the Republic of Venice (Terraferma), 1400–1800: interdecile shares*

a. Cities

Year	Bergamo			Padua			Treviso			Verona		
	D10/D1	D10/D5	D5/D1	D10/D1	D10/D5	D5/D1	D10/D1	D10/D5	D5/D1	D10/D1	D10/D5	D5/D1
1400	72.7	20.9	3.5				129.8	16.1	8.1			
1450	235.0	21.7	10.8									
1500	198.1	24.7	8.0				198.6	20.3	9.8			
1550	319.7	33.2	9.6	199.0	32.8	6.1						
1600	316.8	26.9	11.8	612.4	45.8	13.4						
1650	345.1	25.8	13.4	1002.6	63.8	15.7						
1700	572.4	39.4	14.5	1704.8	55.4	30.8				276.3	22.9	12.0
1750												
1800										334.4	30.1	11.1

b. Rural communities

	Padua (contado)			Verona (contado)			Arzignano (Vicenza)			Clusone (Bergamo)			Romano (Bergamo)			Rovetta (Bergamo)			Piario and others (Bergamo)		
	D10/D1	D10/D5	D5/D1	D10/D1	D10/D5	D5/D1	D10/D1	D10/D5	D5/D1	D10/D1	D10/D5	D5/D1	D10/D1	D10/D5	D5/D1	D10/D1	D10/D5	D5/D1	D10/D1	D10/D5	D5/D1
1400																					
1450							30.8	5.5	5.6												
1500							35.5	7.5	4.7												
1550	95.2	16.7	5.7				40.4	7.8	5.2	201.9	30.4	6.6	111.3	20.2	5.5	82.7	18.9	4.4	101.3	19.9	5.1
1600	208.0	25.0	8.3	120.7	15.3	7.9	59.2	21.7	2.7	254.2	31.9	8.0	280.1	28.8	9.7	84.7	13.4	6.3	114.4	15.3	7.5
1650	200.3	24.8	8.1	113.3	19.2	5.9	61.1	28.9	2.1	190.5	29.1	6.5	291.2	33.8	8.6						
1700	236.7	29.6	8.0	93.7	16.0	5.9	79.8	34.2	2.3	161.0	11.5	14.0									
1750				248.6	32.1	7.7	107.5	34.1	3.2												

Notes: Measures organized around reference years when needed. See Table 3.1 for actual years and for additional details about the information provided.

Sources: EINITE database for all communities and areas, exception made for Treviso for which we used data from Scherman (2009).

the fifth decile in 1550, 25 times in 1600, 24.8 times in 1650 and 29.6 times in 1700.

The enormous growth in the share of wealth owned by the top compared to all other groups is just a part of the story. Not only were the top rich leaving all behind, but the poorest strata were also distancing themselves from those above, as shown by the D5/D1 interdecile share. In Bergamo around 1400, those belonging to the fifth decile were 3.5 times as rich as the bottom 10%. In 1500 this figure had grown to 8, then it increased further, reaching 11.8 in 1600 and 14.5 in 1700. In that year, Verona showed a similar situation (D5/D1 of 12) while in Padua the middling ranks were significantly more distant from the bottom (30.8). Something similar was happening in the rural areas, albeit admittedly on a smaller scale.

Overall, interdecile shares give the impression of a society which in time was becoming ever more polarized: with *both* the top and the bottom of the wealth distribution distancing themselves from one another, as well as from the middling groups. This suggests that, on the one side, the richest part of the population was acquiring ever more distinctive characteristics over the rest (while at the same time growing in numbers), maybe contributing to compromise the inclusiveness of a merchant Republic which, at least according to a sizeable part of the literature (see Section 2.4), had long granted its people relatively easy paths for upward social mobility (but we lack, to this date, reliable quantitative measures of the actual degree of mobility over time). On the other side, the poorest part of the population seems to have found itself in an evermore disadvantaged and dependent position – as in relative terms, their situation was worsening compared to that of a very sizeable part of the population, and not only to the rich. The only temporary contrast to this process seems to have been provided by the plague – but whether the epidemic produced this effect through 'benign' forces (i.e. through a partial redistribution of the riches) or through 'malign' ones (by killing the poor more than the rich) is a question that will be answered in the next section.

3.4   Plague, Inheritance and Inequality

The distributive consequences of the main plagues have been the object of a recent surge of interest, following by many decades David Herlihy's pioneering studies on the Black Death of 1348 (Herlihy 1967, 1968). Although this terrible epidemic (the worst ever to affect Europe, having killed 35–60% of its entire population: Alfani and Murphy 2017, 316–18) has been for some years at the centre of the attention of economic historians, earlier works focused mostly on the way in which it affected labour markets and real wages (Munro 2003; Cohn 2007; Pamuk 2007; Campbell 2010). The possible impact that the Black Death had on economic inequality, however, was not specifically assessed by this literature, notwithstanding the interesting hypothesis put forward by Herlihy on the grounds of limited evidence concerning a couple of rural villages in the Tuscan countryside. According to Herlihy, in the medium and long term the Black Death would have determined a marked increase in inequality over the pre-plague period, mostly due to the damage that it caused to the urban and rural middle class, which resulted in increasing polarization between a few extremely wealthy owners and a mass of poor entirely, or almost entirely, devoid of property. Inheritance systems and managerial factors both contributed to this process (Herlihy 1967, 190–91).

However, recent research on two deeply different regions of Italy, Tuscany – the same area covered by Herlihy – and Piedmont, suggested that the Black Death *did not* lead to an increase in inequality but on the contrary, it triggered a long phase of declining inequality which continued until ca. 1400–1450 (Alfani 2015; Alfani and Ammannati 2017). This is also confirmed by some in-progress work on the region Emilia-Romagna, as well as, beyond Italy, some parts of southern France (Alfani and Murphy 2017, 333–34). Inequality decline after the Black Death is entirely consistent with the widely held idea that it had increased real wages across Europe, allowing a larger part of the population to gain access to property in a moment when decent land had become particularly abundant (in per capita terms) due to the demographic catastrophe. Additionally, the reanalysis of Herlihy's case studies conducted by Alfani and Ammannati has led to the conclusion that the inequality growth that he thought to detect from what data was available at the time, was in fact an optical illusion caused by inadequate standardization of information collected from non-homogeneous sources.[13] Indeed, if such standardization is applied correctly, we find inequality decline in every community (Tuscan or other) for which pre- and post–Black Death information is available (Alfani and Ammannati 2017; Alfani and Murphy 2017). Also using EINITE's information, Walter Scheidel (2017) generalized this view by arguing that the Black Death is one of the few large-scale, civilization-shaking catastrophes that seem to have had an inequality-reducing impact, from the fall of the Roman Empire (possibly epidemic-induced) to World War II.

Unfortunately, the time series of inequality measures which we reconstructed for the Republic of Venice do not cover the Black Death and the

---

[13] Unfortunately, the same problem is also present in an otherwise praiseworthy book by Daniel Curtis (2014; see Alfani 2016b for comments).

immediately post–Black Death periods. Also in this area, however, during the fifteenth century we find mixed tendencies which could realistically be the late and final consequences of a process of large-scale redistribution triggered by the Black Death, as argued in Section 3.2. Here we will focus on events for which we have more direct evidence. In fact, during the early modern period the Republic of Venice was struck particularly severely by the plague of 1575–77, which was the worst epidemic of the sixteenth century (Beltrami 1954; Preto 1978; Cohn 2009; Stevens Crawshaw 2012; Alfani 2013a), then by the 1629–30 plague, which was even worse – indeed, it was probably the worst ever to strike northern Italy after the Black Death, as well as the last one[14] to affect it (Cipolla 1981; Alfani 2010d, 2013b; Alfani and Melegaro 2010; Alfani and Percoco 2018). The exceptional severity with which these two events affected the Republic of Venice is clear by looking at the urban mortality rates collected in Table 3.4.

As the table clearly shows, urban mortality rates in both plague waves could be extremely high, in 1629–30 even exceeding the 50% threshold. Focusing on the cities included in our database, mortality rates were 344 per thousand in 1575–77 and 594 per thousand in 1629–30 in Padua, while in Verona they amounted to 200 per thousand and 615 per thousand, respectively. Bergamo was almost unaffected by the 1575–77 plague, but paid a heavy toll in 1629–30 (381 per thousand). During that plague in fact all our cities fared worse than Venice, where the mortality rate stopped at 'just' 330 per thousand. Although the seventeenth-century plague was characterized by higher average mortality rates than even the worst sixteenth-century epidemic, the main difference lies elsewhere and in particular in what has been called the 'territorial pervasiveness' of the two plagues, that is their ability to spread not only to the main cities but also to rural areas, affecting even small villages. From this point of view, while the 1575–77 plague was a 'typical' mostly urban late medieval or early modern plague, the 1629–30 plague was a Black Death–like event considering both overall mortality and its ability to spread pervasively in the countryside (Alfani 2010d, 2013b). According to a recent estimate, in the whole of northern Italy the 1629–30 plague would have killed 30–35% of the overall population, while the probability that a community was spared would have been (excluding the region

---

[14] With one exception: plague outbreaks occurred until the early eighteenth century in the north-eastern extremity of present-day Italy, in the territories of Gorizia and in Carniola which bordered the Republic of Venice and, during the early modern period, were under Habsburg rule (Železnik 2015). Additionally, plague coming from the bordering Ottoman Empire periodically affected the non-Italian domains of the Republic of Venice on the other side of the Adriatic Sea. For example, in the Venetian-controlled city of Split in Dalmatia, plague outbreaks occurred in 1690, 1731–32, 1763–64 and 1784. However, the health authorities of the Republic were very effective in preventing the infection from spreading to the Italian mainland (Andreozzi 2015).

Table 3.4 *Urban mortality rates in the Republic of Venice during the 1575–77 and 1629–30 plagues (mortality rates per thousand)*

	1575–77	1629–30
Bergamo	(almost unaffected)	381
Brescia	444	458
Capo d'Istria	(no information)	385
Chioggia	286	433
Crema	220	481
Padua	344	594
Treviso	(not affected)	157
Udine[a]	(not affected)	100
Venice	265	330
Verona	200	615
Vicenza	79	375

[a] Udine was not affected in 1575–77, but it was struck by the plague which in 1598 spread to Friuli while sparing other areas of the Republic of Venice. In that year, the city suffered a mortality rate of 246 per thousand. Additionally in 1630, while according to some the city was affected by the plague (Beloch 1994, 419), others argue instead that it was spared, and that the extra mortality is due to the famine which in 1629 affected Friuli in a particularly severe way (Ulvioni 1989b; Fornasin 2001).
Sources: Alfani (2013a), 91 for 1575–77; Alfani (2013b) and Alfani and Percoco (2018) for 1629–30.

of Liguria) just 5% for cities and 7% for rural communities (Alfani 2013c, 418, 420). These figures would definitely be higher if calculated for the Republic of Venice only, as seemingly here the probability of being spared was lower (indeed, the point estimate is zero for both cities and rural villages) and possibly the old estimate of a 40% overall mortality in the Republic proposed by Beltrami (1961) is quite close to the mark. Regarding 1575–77, an estimate (probably a bit too high) places overall mortality in the Republic at almost 25% (Preto 1980, 124).

The distributive consequences of these extremely severe mortality crises have never been the object of specific studies for the Republic of Venice, and indeed they have rarely been explored for any other area – the exception being, to some degree, the region of Piedmont in the Sabaudian state, as discussed later. We will focus on the 1629–30 plague, because for that of 1575–77 we lack couples of *estimi* positioned close enough to either side of the event to allow for a meaningful analysis of its direct consequences. This is also because a first conclusion that comes strongly from the available data is that the 1630 plague (and *a fortiori* that of 1575–77) *did not* trigger a phase of sustained inequality decline on the same scale as the Black Death. Indeed, if we look at the data presented in Tables 3.1 and 3.2, we do not find an even temporary generalized process of inequality decline – although the signs that the plague did have some sort of distributive impact are plentiful (to clarify: the plague *obviously* had a large-scale distributive impact, for the simple reason that it killed an inordinately high number of owners – but what we want to determine is whether it also caused a shift in inequality levels, and in which direction). In Bergamo between 1610 and 1640, the Gini index declined from 0.723 to 0.715. The decline is much larger if we include the propertyless, as the Gini index is found to decline from 0.751 to 0.729. In Padua between 1627 and 1642, the Gini (propertyless excluded) reduced very slightly, from 0.819 to 0.81. In the *contado* of Padua between the same dates, the level of inequality did not change. Instead in the city and in the *contado* of Verona, where, however, the pre- and post-plague sources are more distant in time, we find an increase rather than a decline in inequality. If we factor in the analyses that we conducted on the share of the top rich, as well as on interdecile shares, the evidence that the 1630 plague did at least slow down a long-term process of inequality increase becomes stronger. This being said, overall the process is small scale compared to that found in the aftermath of the Black Death (in Tuscany, in the city of Prato the Gini equalled 0.703 in 1325 and just 0.591 in 1372. In the village of Poggibonsi, it was 0.55 in 1338 and 0.474 in 1357. Alfani and Ammannati 2017, 1081–82).

There are two reasons why it proves relatively difficult to detect the distributive impact of the 1630 plague. One is technical: if the impact of the plague was short term, then we need to use pre- and post-plague *estimi* very close to the event (because the overall tendency was for inequality to increase in the early seventeenth century, and because the inequality-reducing consequences of the plague might have evaporated quickly). The second has to do with the empirical finding that even the worst plague after the Black Death had a vastly inferior impact on inequality levels (indeed, explaining why this happened is quite crucial if we are to understand correctly *how* inequality could grow so much during the early modern period). Debating the first point is a preliminary step in assessing correctly the second.

The city of Bergamo is the one for which we have the best information available, also because the sources closer to the plague include the propertyless. A first aspect to clarify is whether the plague affected some parts of the distribution more than others. A visual inspection of the entire distribution is useful, and can be accomplished by tracing the Lorenz curves related to the

(a)

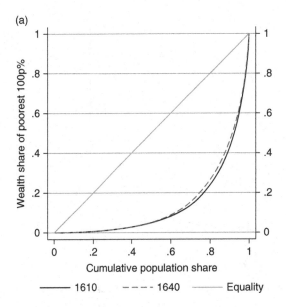

Figure 3.5 Wealth distribution in Bergamo, before and after the 1630 plague (Lorenz curves). (a) Propertyless excluded. (b) Propertyless included.

Notes: Lorenz curves have been drawn using the glcurve Stata package.

immediately pre- and post-plague situation (the inequality declines if the curve gets closer to the 45-degree line – the 'equality' line).[15]

From Figure 3.5a, we notice that the post-plague distribution 'dominates' the pre-plague one, meaning that it is placed entirely to the left of the pre-plague one and closer to the equality line. However, the graph also suggests that the parts of the distribution which profited most from the plague are the middle and middle-high ranks, approximately from the 6th to the 8th decile. Comparing the two years, we find that the share of the 6th decile grew by 7.1%, that of the 7th by 14.7%, and that of the 8th by 4.8%. The bordering deciles (5th and 9th) grew only marginally, while the poorest four deciles did not profit at all. The worst hit (at least in terms of wealth ownership) were the top 10% rich, who experienced a worsening of their relative position. These changes should not be overstated, as an increase by 14.7% for the 7th decile means that they gained just an

---

[15] Note that the Lorenz curve is directly connected to the Gini index, as the Gini can be understood as the area between the Lorenz curve and the equality line. If a Lorenz curve perfectly overlaps the equality line, the value of the Gini calculated on the same distribution is zero.

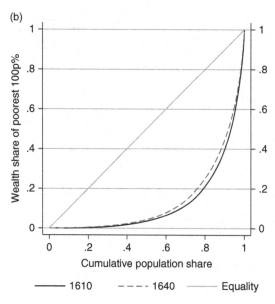

Figure 3.5 (cont.)

extra 0.81% of the overall wealth recorded in the *estimo*. However, it is interesting to note that the poorest part of the population *did not* profit significantly (if at all) from this overall 'egalitarian' trend.

We might wonder whether the picture changes when including the propertyless (Figure 3.5b). Visual inspection confirms dominance, and a further closing of the Lorenz curve towards the equality line, which is coherent with the reported larger decline in the Gini values when including the propertyless. Figure 3.5b also suggests that the largest increases in access to resources occurred, again, at the middle of the distribution and indeed, this time it is the 8th decile that profits most, acquiring an extra 1.1% of the overall wealth (+11.6%). The 7th decile follows, with an extra 0.9% which in relative terms represents an ever larger acquisition (+17.4%). However, when the propertyless are included in the series, *all* deciles seem to get something, bar the 10th. The richest part of the population is found to lose 3.4% of the overall wealth of the city to the various advantage of all other groups (although the rich maintained their grip on an inordinately high share of the overall wealth: 56.5% in 1640, down from 60% in 1610). In addition, if we look at relative increases, it is the poorest of all that seem to profit more, as the first two deciles together managed to almost double their share of the overall wealth (+ 95% –

although this increase led the poorest 20% of the population to control just 0.4% of all the property of the city).

We might think, then, that even though it caused terrible human consequences, at least regarding its distributive impact the 1629–30 plague was overall 'benign'. Unfortunately, this was probably not the case. In Bergamo, the prevalence of the propertyless declined from 10.2% in 1610 to 5.1% in 1640. While this halving in the propertyless is partly the direct consequence of some of them acquiring property (either by inheritance or by buying some morsels of real estate in a post-plague market characterized by dropping prices of land and housing[16]), many more were simply eliminated by the plague. Indeed, it is a well-known fact that from the fifteenth century, plague had acquired a social connotation affecting much more the poor than the rich, also because of the different urban environments where they lived (Slack 1985; Carmichael 1986; Alfani 2009c; 2013a, 103–07; Cohn 2010; Alfani and Murphy 2017). Even if the 1629–30 plague was exceptional because it proved able to kill a large part of the socio-economic elite, for example in Venice, where 17% of the members of the Great Council died (Pullan 1992, 111), this does not mean that the poor were not affected more severely (the aforementioned figure, albeit very high, is about half the overall mortality of 33% reported for the entire population of Venice).

Whether benign or malign in character, plague-induced redistribution was able to stifle, at least for some years, the tendency for inequality to grow. Indeed, there are reasons to think that 1640 or 1642 are dates too far from the epidemic to allow its immediate impact to be measured correctly. In the city of Ivrea in Piedmont, which is the only one for which yearly measures of economic inequality have been proposed for much of the seventeenth century (covering 1620–74), it was found that plague caused an immediate significant drop in inequality, from 0.672 in 1628 to about 0.65 in 1629–30 (−3.3%) which, however, had been entirely compensated for, over and above, by 1632 when the reported Gini is 0.692. This was mostly the consequence of immigration to the city of relatively poor rural dwellers, who profited from the opportunities to acquire property in an inflated market. At the same time, on the other side of the distribution, a few rich individuals were building enormous patrimonies. They were also profiting from the willingness to sell of members of the local elite who decided to move to the burgeoning capital city of Turin, equally affected by the plague and receptive to immigration (Alfani 2010a, 2010b). Similar processes of large-scale, post-plague migration are also known for cities in

---

[16] For example, in Milan, not far from the Republic's boundaries, as late as 1656 the *Collegio degli Ingegneri ed Architetti* (the College of Engineers and Architects) complained that house values were still 25% below the pre-plague levels (Sella 2010, 127).

the Republic of Venice, for example Padua, which seems to have been particularly successful in attracting new inhabitants, among them many skilled workers, thus limiting the damage caused by the plague both to its population and to its economy (Alfani and Caracausi 2009).

Migration is a crucial factor in understanding how the recovery of the pre-plague level could have been so quick – but it does not explain why the immediate decline in inequality caused by the epidemic was so limited. Again in the case of Ivrea,

> the egalitarian effect of the plague was limited by the fact that in the majority of cases two or more heirs inherited together (*in solido*), postponing a division or even renouncing the division of property in order to preserve patrimonial integrity. Especially in the case of the largest patrimonies, by the end of the sixteenth and the beginning of the seventeenth centuries many Italian families chose to establish a *fideicommissum* (similar to a trust) in order to prevent the dispersal of wealth and thus preserve the economic power and prestige of the dynasty. (Alfani 2010b, 67–68)

As will be recalled from our discussion of inheritance practices in Chapter 2, the richest families of the Republic of Venice behaved in exactly the same way. The *fraterna* system had consequences analogous to the practice of *in solido* inheritance found in Piedmont, as it prevented division of patrimonies among many surviving brothers if their father was killed by plague. Again analogously to Piedmont and other areas of Italy and Europe, the *fideicommissum* (which excluded sizeable patrimonies from the standard rule of partible inheritance) had been spreading in the Republic in the centuries following the Black Death (Lanaro 2000, 2012; Leverotti 2007; Chauvard 2015, 855). Indeed, this process can be understood as one of adaption by human societies faced with the deep change in the biological environment brought forward by the return of plague to Europe in 1347–48[17] (Alfani 2010b). In other words, institutions such as the *fideicommissum* and the *fraterna*, while they made patrimonies more resilient to large-scale mortality crises, also entrenched wealth inequality.

There is a lesson here about how we should consider the connection between resilience and inequality. Some recent literature has argued, maybe somewhat optimistically, that low inequality favours resilience to crises of various kinds (Curtis 2014). But if we focus on certain characteristics of a society, such as its property structures, the conclusion we draw from the, still admittedly limited, information we have about the

---

[17] Plague had disappeared from Europe after the series of outbreaks which affected the continent and the broader Mediterranean area from 540 to ca. 750, also known collectively as 'Justinian's Plague' (Little 2007; Alfani and Murphy 2017, 316–19).

distributive impact of plagues and other mortality crises is that higher societal resilience to shocks determines lower inequality decline in the immediate aftermath of the crisis – and also allows for reaching even higher inequality levels shortly afterwards, for example as a consequence of migration. While the two notions are not directly at odds, surely the evidence for the Republic of Venice suggests that, in the early modern period, correlation between inequality levels and social resilience might have a positive, and not a negative, sign (with more resilient societies being more unequal). However, more research is surely needed to clarify this aspect.

Another factor to consider when trying to understand why the main plagues of the early modern period did not manage to cause long-lasting inequality decline is that neither did they produce the same positive consequences as the Black Death in terms of increases in real wages and improved living standards (Alfani and Murphy 2017). Indeed, the time series of real wages that we have available for northern Italian cities do not provide any sign of an increase in real wages after the epidemic. On the contrary, it has been shown that the 1629–30 plague was able to displace the Italian urban populations (and economies) to a lower growth path, and this also because the plague affected Italy at the worst possible moment, when their manufactories were dealing with increasing competition from Northern European countries, themselves relatively spared by plague during the seventeenth century (Alfani 2013b; Alfani and Percoco 2018). Consequently, the opportunities for the lower strata of the population to finally gain access to property were much reduced compared to the aftermath of the Black Death. This is why the overall tendency for inequality to grow was briefly slowed down by the plague, but not arrested – and an opportunity for a more equitable, albeit painful, rebalancing of social disparities was mostly wasted. This is another reason why the overall very negative consequences of the 1629–30 catastrophe for northern Italian countries in general, and for the Republic of Venice in particular, should be strongly reaffirmed.

3.5   Citizens, Church and the Venetians in Padua and Its Province

In the institutional framework of the Republic of Venice, the citizens of the capital city were accorded a special status. As seen in Chapter 1, this was reflected in the fiscal system, as the Venetians's properties were under the jurisdiction of the Council of Ten and the Senate and the collection of taxes on their properties was supervised by a specific authority, the *X Savi alle Decime*, and not by the local fiscal chambers (Beltrami 1961, 58).

However, the Venetians had to contribute to at least some locally imposed tributes, and in particular to the *Dadia delle Lanze*, a tribute initially imposed in 1417 on the province of Padua and subsequently extended to most of the *Terraferma*, including on the provinces of Treviso, Verona and Vicenza (Maifreda 2002, 66). In some areas, and especially those closer to Venice like Padua, the Venetian property tended to expand considerably during the early modern period. Its growth was the most intense during the sixteenth century (Gullino 1994, 876)[18] and according to the estimates provided by Beltrami (1961, 60–61, 141), by 1636 across the territories east of the Mincio River (hence excluding the provinces of Bergamo and Brescia) Venetians owned 11.7% of all surfaces usable for agriculture. But this figure hides a very varied situation, as the Venetian penetration was considerably higher in the eastern provinces of Padua, where they owned 38.2% of the agrarian surfaces, of Treviso (19.2%) and in the Polesine area (27.4%), compared to the western part of Veneto, where their properties amounted to less than 5% of all surfaces (3.7% in the province of Vicenza; 3% in that of Verona) or to Friuli where they just exceeded that threshold (5.2%). West of the Mincio River, in the provinces of Bergamo and Brescia in Lombardy, the penetration of Venetian property was even lower. In the *Terraferma* to the east of the Mincio, Venetian landownership continued to increase during the early modern period. It was 12.9% of the total agrarian surfaces in 1665, 14.7% in 1682, 15.9% in 1722 and finally, by the last observation we have (the *catastatico* of 1740, which was the first, and the last, attempt to estimate the properties of most provinces of the Republic according to homogeneous criteria) it had almost doubled the 1636 level, peaking at 20.2% of the total (Beltrami 1961, 112–15, 122–23, 141).

The spread of Venetian property creates two kinds of problem. First, it is at the root of unbalances in the fiscal system and of contrasts between the socio-economic elite of the provinces and of the *Dominante* (at least in the areas more intensely affected by the process). This aspect is discussed in Chapter 1. A second problem, though, is to assess the impact on local inequality of the presence of Venetian owners. In most instances, Venetians are simply invisible in our sources: a common enough problem in studies of long-term inequality on states where the citizens of the capital city enjoyed special fiscal treatment (see Alfani and Ammannati

---

[18] Gullino (1994, 992) analysed the properties owned in the *Terraferma* by the Venetian citizens residing in three of the six *sestieri* in which the city was divided (S. Marco, Cannaregio and S. Croce), comparing the situation in 1537 and in 1661. During that period, the lands that the Venetian citizens owned in the *Terraferma* more than doubled (+150%). The process invested mostly the three provinces closer to the capital: Padua (+86%), Treviso (+153%) and Polesine (+240%).

2017 for the case of the Florentine State). However, in most of the provinces included in this study Venetian property was very limited and its impact can be supposed to be negligible. Padua is the obvious exception – but luckily enough, for three years (1627, 1642 and 1694) we were able to collect information about the property of the Venetians, recorded in a specific section of the *estimi* of the city and of the territory.[19]

For the same years, we could also collect information from Padua's *estimo* of the *clero* (literally 'clergy', but the records mostly refer to the properties of religious institutions). The difficulty of including church property in a study of preindustrial distribution has already been discussed (Section 3.1). In many instances we simply have no sources, for example in Bergamo. However, we know that in most areas of the Republic the property of the *clero* was always very limited, for example in the province of Verona, where in 1740 it amounted to no more than 6% of the surfaces included in the *catastatico* (Maifreda 2002, 17), slightly less than the 8% average for all the *Terraferma* to the east of the Mincio (Beltrami 1961, 135). If we calculate the latter estimate on the agrarian surfaces and not, as Beltrami did, on the surfaces included in the *catastatico*, the overall share of the *clero* turns out to be just 5.1%. Yet again, most of this property was concentrated in the areas closer to Venice. A very sizeable part of it was in the province of Padua, where it amounted to 12.7% of all agrarian surfaces (9.1% and 2.8% in the provinces of Treviso and Verona, respectively, and just 2% in Friuli). The majority (63.3%) of church property was owned by monasteries, especially those of Venice and the Dogado. For example, in the territory of Padua, the monasteries of St. Giorgio Maggiore of Venice and that of St. Giustina of Padua owned enormous patrimonies – and indeed, they figured among the main landowners of the entire state (Beltrami 1961, 135–36).

As with the property of the Venetians, also in the case of church property our main concern is with the province of Padua, where it was more prevalent, although its extent remained relatively stable in time. We calculated that the property recorded in the *estimi del clero* was 25.1% of the total in 1627, 26.8% in 1642, then slightly declined to 22.3% in 1694. Instead, in the same period the property of the Venetians grew constantly: from 12.7% of the total in 1627, to 14.0% in 1642 and finally to 23.6% in

[19] There are some residual problems, which are relatively minor given the purposes of this study. Two, however, are worth mentioning. First of all, the records of the property of the Venetians do not include the real estate they might have acquired before 1446 (Vigato 1989, 51; Alfani and Caracausi 2009, 189). Second, the transfers of property from Paduans to Venetians, and vice versa, were not always duly and promptly recorded (Beltrami 1961; Ventura 1968; Gullino 1985, 1994). For a more general discussion of problems in using Padua's *estimi* in a study of distribution, see Alfani and Caracausi (2009).

1694. This trend is entirely analogous to that reported in the foregoing for the *Terraferma* as a whole (note that Beltrami's estimates refer to agrarian surfaces, while ours refer to *estimo* values). The significant increase in the penetration of Venetian property in the second half of the seventeenth century, into the province of Padua as in other areas of the Republic, is connected to the sale of a large part of the properties of the communities, on which the Republic claimed the *dominium eminens* even though they had been given as 'concession' to the communities, to contribute to the financing of the War of Candia (1645–69). The sale of these properties represented an excellent opportunity to invest for wealthy Venetians and for some of the local economic elites, to the detriment of the peasants and more generally, of the poorest part of the population (Beltrami 1961, 64–77).

The central question we wish to answer here, is whether excluding the properties of the Venetians and of the Church produces a significant distortion in our inequality measures: either in their levels, or (which would be an even greater problem) in their trends. However, before looking at the data, we should make it clear that arguably, a good reason to *exclude* both Venetians and *clero* from our measures is that we are interested in providing a picture of wealth inequality among the house-holds residing in the province. Because the Venetians were not residents, and the religious institutions were not households, it is not at all a given that, were they always available, they should be included in the calcula-tions. This being said, the overall concentration of wealth throughout the province (or more properly, the concentration of the real estate existing within the province itself) is also interesting. Therefore, we need to know whether omitting Venetians and *clero* changes significantly the picture that we can reconstruct. This is not the case, as can be seen from the data summarized in Table 3.5.

One of the first things to consider, when assessing the impact of including or excluding specific portions of the overall distribution in the calculation of inequality measures, is how such portions differ from the rest. Some hints come from average wealth. As seen from Table 3.5, if we take the properties of city and country households together, the average wealth varied between a minimum of 346.5 *denari* in 1642, and a max-imum of 475.5 *denari* in 1694. It might come as a surprise that in the same dates, the average wealth of the Venetians was much lower: 178.8 and 254.8 *denari*, respectively. But it should be pointed out that this is calcu-lated on the property owned by Venetians in the province of Padua only, hence excluding their possessions in other parts of the *Terraferma*, in Venice itself, and elsewhere. The Venetians were also a relatively 'egali-tarian' group (again referring only to their possessions within the

Table 3.5 *Inequality in the province of Padua, 1627–1694*

	City	Contado	City and Contado together	Venetians	Church (clero)	All	All, including the propertyless
Gini index							
1627	0.819	0.728	0.849	0.665	0.793	0.835	0.843
1642	0.810	0.727	0.835	0.678	0.777	0.823	
1694	0.799	0.747	0.835	0.757	0.793	0.823	0.830
Share of richest 10%							
1627	71.3	62.4	77.9	53.7	72.2	75.6	76.5
1642	70.2	62.1	75.8	55.1	70.9	73.8	
1694	68.2	63.9	75.0	66.3	72.9	74.1	74.8
Average wealth per owner (in denari)							
1627	660.5	88.0	387.8	173.9	1431.7	398.4	379.2
1642	545.5	87.5	346.5	178.8	1422.2	372.9	
1694	773.4	109.0	475.5	254.8	1185.2	444.1	426.4

Sources: EINITE database.

boundaries of the province), as the Gini index calculated for them is always much lower than that related to the residents of city and country. For example in 1627, the Gini is equal to 0.665 among the Venetians, and to 0.849 among the households of the city and the *contado*. Another inequality indicator, the share owned by the top 10%, tells a similar story. If we look at the *clero* the situation is different as, in their case, the average wealth is considerably greater than that of the households of city and *contado*, varying from a minimum of 1,185.2 *denari* in 1694 to a maximum of 1,431.7 *denari* in 1627. But clergy and religious institutions were still more 'egalitarian' among themselves than the households of residents, albeit less so than the Venetians.

If we look at inequality among the Venetians, and inequality among the *clero*, we find a tendency towards growth for the first, and substantial stability for the second. But more interesting is what happens when we add them to the distribution. Indeed, the inequality measures calculated on the overall distribution (including city, *contado*, Venetians and *clero*) are very similar to those calculated on city and *contado* only. The Gini for the overall distribution was 0.835 in 1627 and 0.823 in both 1642 and 1694, compared to 0.849 in 1627 and 0.835 in the other dates when Venetians and *clero* are excluded. The share of the top 10% was, for the overall distribution, 75.6%, 73.8% and 74.1% in 1627, 1642 and 1694, respectively, compared to 77.9%, 75.8% and 75.0% if we exclude Venetians and *clero*. The conclusion is that not accounting for the presence of Venetian and Church property determines no more than a minimal distortion in our inequality measures, which affects only the levels and not the trend. Interestingly, this slight distortion is towards inequality, implying that were we interested in distribution of all property (and not, as we primarily are, in the distribution of *household* property) we would have to consider our measures as upper-bound estimates. Indeed, even when we include the propertyless the measures calculated on the overall distribution are lower than those related to city and *contado* only, propertyless excluded; for example, in 1694 the Gini index is 0.830 versus 0.835. Our conclusion is that, as even in the province most affected by the penetration of both Venetian and church property the impact on basic inequality measures of including or excluding such property is minimal, we can be confident that our inability to observe systematically the Venetians and the *clero* does not affect in any way the validity of our reconstructions.

3.6   Economic Inequality across the Republic of Venice and Italy

The analyses conducted up to this point on each community or area taken separately need to be integrated into a more encompassing picture, able to represent the long-term development in wealth inequality in the Republic of Venice (*Terraferma*) as a whole as well as to provide a basis for a comparison with those other ancient Italian states for which similar reconstructions are available. To do this, we resort to a method which has been introduced by Alfani (2015) in his study of the Sabaudian State, and has later been applied to the Florentine State as well as to some non-Italian areas, and particularly the southern Low Countries (Alfani and Ryckbosch 2016). This method allows us to generate regional measures of inequality by aggregation of local/communal data. First, we construct separate urban and rural inequality series, and then we weigh both based on the urbanization rate in each region and time period, using a procedure similar in principle to that described by Milanovic (2005) for calculating 'weighted international inequality'. The final result is a distribution representative of a broader area, which can then be explored per se and which can be subjected to statistical analysis exactly as any other distribution: for example to evaluate the prevalence of the poor and of the rich, as done in Chapter 2 (Section 2.5).

A detailed and step-by-step description of the procedures used and of the hypotheses and assumptions that we had to make is provided in the Appendix. Here it will suffice to clarify that the most reliable reconstruction we provide does not take into account the propertyless – as only rarely were they mentioned by our sources. However, thanks to the exceptional data available for Bergamo and for Padua (together with its *contado*), we were also able to produce distributions that do include an estimate of the overall presence of the propertyless in time, albeit from 1500 only. In Table 3.6 we present key inequality measures, for the cities and the rural areas as well as for the whole territory, including or not the propertyless. For the fifteenth century, we were able to generate a representative distribution for the cities only (as for the rural areas, we have pre-1500 information just for the community of Arzignano). Another issue is that our estimates do not include the capital city of Venice which, due to its fiscal privileges, was not subject to the *estimo* system. This is a common problem, usually encountered in studies of this kind (the reconstruction available for the Sabaudian State does not include Turin, and that for the Florentine State does not include Florence). In the case of the Republic of Venice, however, given its relatively large population and the considerable size of many of its provincial cities, this is a minor problem as including Venice would have a limited impact on the overall measures of inequality. Indeed, we demonstrate this in Appendix A.4, where we discuss a very tentative reconstruction which does include the capital city. Here we focus on the more reliable reconstructions, which are also those more directly comparable to the others available.

The Gini indexes presented in Table 3.6 reflect well what was found by looking at single cities or rural communities. From 1500, economic inequality rose almost monotonically in cities, and monotonically in rural areas as well as across the Republic as a whole.[20] If we focus on the estimates for the whole of the Republic, we find a Gini increasing from 0.687 in 1500, to 0.760 in 1600, 0.797 in 1700 and finally 0.820 in 1750. The general trend does not change if we factor in the propertyless, as the Gini indexes, propertyless included, evolve from 0.692 in 1500, to 0.771 in 1600, 0.812 in 1700 and finally 0.834 in 1750. However, the series including the propertyless shows more clearly the (limited) 'egalitarian' consequences of the 1630 plague, as from 1600 to 1650 the monotonic growth in inequality slows down considerably. Both including and excluding the propertyless, inequality is always higher if measured across the Republic, than on cities and rural areas separately: which reflects a high urban–rural differential in average wealth (see Section 3.2).

---

[20] The urban series shows some decline in both the Gini index and the share of the top 10% from 1700 to 1750, but this seems to be simply the result of the fact that for 1750 we had information about Verona only, which throughout the early modern period was significantly more 'egalitarian' than all other cities in our database (compare with the data in Table 3.1).

Table 3.6 *Economic inequality in the Republic of Venice (*Terraferma*), 1400–1750: the overall picture*

	Republic of Venice			Republic of Venice (propertyless included)		
	Cities	Country	Overall	Cities	Country	Overall
Gini index						
1400	0.632					
1450	0.647					
1500	0.627	0.629	0.687	0.639	0.633	0.692
1550	0.711	0.649	0.734	0.726	0.655	0.74
1600	0.702	0.694	0.760	0.733	0.703	0.771
1650	0.729	0.727	0.770	0.744	0.732	0.776
1700	0.774	0.730	0.797	0.788	0.750	0.812
1750	0.733	0.771	0.820	0.750	0.789	0.834
Share of the top 10%						
1400	51.6					
1450	53.8					
1500	55.1	50.8	56.8	55.6	50.8	57.1
1550	60.3	52.3	63.1	61.8	52.9	63.5
1600	59.1	57.5	64.0	61.2	57.9	64.9
1650	62.0	62.8	67.0	63.4	63.3	67.4
1700	64.0	63.4	71.1	65.4	64.5	72.5
1750	59.3	69.5	74.8	61.1	70.7	76.1

Note: The measures excluding the propertyless are to be considered the more reliable (as the representative distribution including the propertyless required additional hypotheses to be made: see the Appendix A.4 for details).

The trends in the share of the top 10% reflect almost perfectly those of the Gini index. Across the Republic, the richest decile owned 56.8% of all the wealth in 1500. By 1750, their share had grown considerably, to 74.8%. If we include the propertyless, the share of the top 10% is even larger at the two dates, amounting to 57.1% and 76.1%, respectively. The trends and levels in both the Gini indexes and in the share of the top 10% are similar to what was found elsewhere in central-northern Italy, as shown by Figure 3.6. Indeed, as will be discussed in the next chapter, the same tendency for inequality to grow during the early modern period is to be found across Europe.

The growing disparities between different components of the society, reflected by the Gini index, were mostly due to a concentration of larger and larger shares of the overall wealth in very few hands, as a comparison between Figure 3.6a and Figure 3.6b clearly shows that what happens at the top determines the whole trend. However, this is only a part (albeit

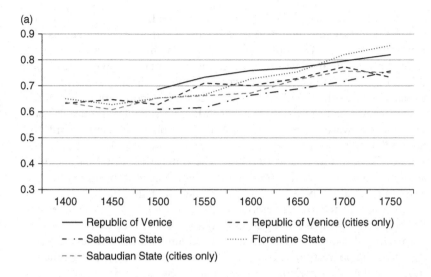

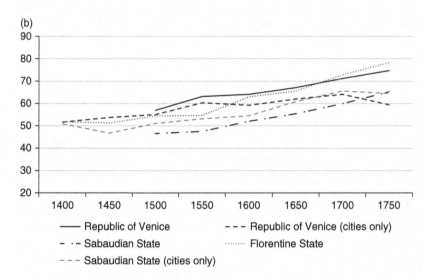

Figure 3.6 Long-term trends in economic inequality in central-northern Italy, 1450–1750 (propertyless excluded). (a) Gini indexes. (b) Share of top 10%.

possibly the most important one) of a more general process, which saw the bottom of the distribution growing ever more distant not only from the top, but also from the middle ranks of society. In Chapter 2, we argued for this by showing that during the early modern period, across the Republic the prevalence of *both* the rich and the poor was increasing (rich and poor defined with respect to the median of the overall distribution). To confirm this point, here we resort to another common indicator: the share of wealth owned by the richest half of the population, compared to the poorest half. The trends in this indicator, shown in Figure 3.7, are oriented towards growth in both the Republic of Venice and the Sabaudian State, which suggests an overall growing polarization in the wealth distribution. In the Republic, the only brief period of respite is again connected to the 1630 plague, which is not observed in the Sabaudian State – possibly due to the fact that this part of Italy was much less affected by the epidemic than the Republic of Venice (see Section 3.5, as well as Alfani 2013b; Alfani and Percoco 2018).

In 1500, the richest 50% owners owned almost twelve times as much wealth as the poorest 50%. By 1750, they owned more than thirty times as much. In the same period, in the Sabaudian State the richest half of the population moved from owning eight times as much as the bottom half, to nineteen times as much. The process continued in the second half of the eighteenth century, so that in the Sabaudian State, after three centuries

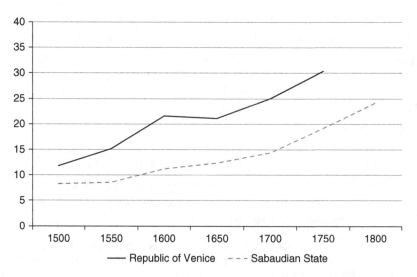

Figure 3.7 Social and economic polarization in the Republic of Venice (*Terraferma*) and in the Sabaudian State, 1500–1800. (Share of top 50% over share of bottom 50%. Propertyless excluded.)

during which socio-economic polarization increased without respite, the richest 50% came to own twenty-four times as much wealth as the poorest 50%. Compared to the Sabaudian State, the Republic's society seems to have been significantly more polarized throughout the period. Indeed, if we look at both Figures 3.6 and 3.7, there are no grounds whatsoever to argue that the Republic of Venice was more 'egalitarian' than the other Italian states for which we have information – on the contrary, only the Florentine State came to be slightly more unequal, and this only from the eighteenth century. In 1750, the Gini index was 0.856 in the Florentine State, 0.820 in the Republic of Venice and 0.758 in Piedmont. But two centuries earlier (1550), the Republic was leading the inequality ranking, with a Gini of 0.734 compared to 0.666 in the Florentine State and 0.617 in the Sabaudian State. A higher wealth inequality does not necessarily mean that a greater part of the population had inferior access to resources (including mere subsistence) compared to other areas, as we should also take into account the welfare system (this will be done in the next chapter). However, quite clearly the picture we get from our measurements of inequality requires deeper reflection as to whether the Republic of Venice could really be considered a relatively 'charitable', hence also relatively inclusive, state, as Venetian political thought (and maybe part of the historical literature as well) would have us believe.

The meaning of our wealth inequality figures can be better understood by comparing them with the estimates of the share of the richest 10% recently proposed by Piketty (2014, 336–50) for some areas of Europe and the United States, which cover the period 1810–2010. For 1810, close to the end of the period studied here, Piketty suggested that in Western Europe (including France, Sweden and the United Kingdom) on average the share of the top 10% was slightly above 80%: significantly more than in the United States were it was slightly below 60%. During the nineteenth century, the share of the richest 10% continued to increase, reaching an all-time maximum in 1910 when they owned about 90% of the overall wealth in Europe, and 80% in the United States.

These estimates have been produced from fiscal assessments of patrimonies used for calculating taxes on estates – the kind of information which can be considered roughly comparable to that used to study inequality in pre-industrial Italy (Alfani 2017). Importantly, our measures for the Republic of Venice in 1750 (the last date we have available) are very close to Piketty's for 1810: 74.8%. If we factor in the propertyless (as Piketty did) we get even closer, at 76.1%. If we make the reasonable assumption that inequality continued to grow in the second half of the eighteenth century, it can be easily seen that by 1810, the share of the top 10% in the Republic would fit almost perfectly Piketty's European average. The same can also be said for the Florentine State, while the Sabaudian State would be placed at a slightly lower level (as there, we have an estimate of 69.1% for 1800, propertyless excluded. Alfani 2015, 2017). We can also conclude that the long phase of inequality increase, which according to Piketty and some others would characterize the period from ca. 1800 until 1914 (the eve of World War I), was nothing but the final phase of a much longer period of almost monotonic inequality increase. This began around 1450–1500, as soon as a (shorter) cycle of inequality reduction and subsequent stagnation, triggered by the fifteenth-century Black Death, had ended. Identifying correctly a process, and measuring its intensity and cadence in time, is a necessary step towards understanding its nature as well as its causes – which is the objective of the next chapter.

4 Taxation, Redistribution and Inequality

In the Republic of Venice, inequality was found to grow continuously during the early modern period. This is not surprising per se, as the *Terraferma* was simply participating in a process which was also involving other parts of central-northern Italy – indeed, as we argue in this chapter, this was probably a pan-European process, whose causes have been explored by much recent research and are the object of intense debate. The case of the Republic of Venice allows us to make an important contribution to such debate, as for the first time we are in a position to explore in detail what is surely a major factor (and probably, at least during the early modern period, the main one) promoting inequality growth across the whole continent: the rise of the fiscal-military state. We will begin by discussing different views about the causes of preindustrial inequality growth, before focusing on the role played by institutions and in particular by the evolution of fiscal systems (thus connecting the general reconstruction of the development of the Venetian fiscal system provided in Chapter 1 with the analysis of inequality trends pursued in Chapters 2 and 3). This will also allow us to explore different aspects of the Venetian institutions and society, and particularly the degree to which this supposedly 'charitable' state was really working to reduce disparities, help the needy and build a relatively harmonious society.

4.1 The Debate on the Causes of Long-Term Inequality Growth across Preindustrial Europe

In a seminal article on Holland, where economic inequality was shown to have been growing continuously from 1514 to 1740 (thereafter stagnating or growing slowly, until 1808), Jan Luiten Van Zanden (1995) argued that preindustrial inequality growth was even 'over-explained' by economic growth. This interpretation was grounded in the specific context of the Dutch Republic, one of the most economically dynamic areas of early modern Europe – and indeed, the seventeenth century is often labelled the Dutch 'Golden Age' (Prak 2005). Recently, a similar view was expressed by Bas Van Bavel, who connected inequality increase in this part of Europe to the development of market economies, which might have led to growth in inequality of both income and wealth through increases in the efficient scale of trade and production; growing opportunities for financial dealing and speculation; and growing investment opportunities (favouring the elites) in landed property and in shares of the public debt (Van Bavel 2016, 192–93).

When Van Zanden published his pioneering research, no other European state or region had been the object of a large-scale attempt to reconstruct inequality trends. The situation has now changed, as for a range of European ancient states (most of them Italian) we have information about long-term inequality trends – which has made the question of causation much more difficult to answer, given that inequality growth was found also in periods of economic stagnation or decline.[1] In Figure 4.1, the trend in economic inequality in the Republic of Venice is compared to that of the Dutch Republic (Holland) as well as to that of the southern Low Countries (nowadays Belgium). For Italy, we include the case of the Kingdom of Naples (region Apulia only) in the south, as well the already discussed cases of the Florentine State in the centre and of the Sabaudian State in the northwest. The measures refer to wealth inequality for Italy and to income inequality for the Low Countries; hence the trends, not the levels, should be compared (as, in the past as today, wealth tends to be more concentrated than income). However, as discussed in Chapter 3 (Section 3.1), it is very unlikely that in preindustrial societies wealth and income inequality might have moved in different directions in the medium and long run.

Looking at the figure, a simple conclusion seems obvious: that in all the areas considered, inequality has grown monotonically during the whole of the early modern period. But if we take into account the history of each of these six states, it is easy to detect phases of economic stagnation or even

---

[1] The recent important book by Van Bavel (2016) does include a comparison to other western European areas, and particularly central-northern Italy, but it focuses on periods characterized by economic growth and quick development of market economies: the late Middle Ages (1000–1500) for Italy, while for the Low Countries the early modern period is included in the analysis, too (1100–1800). Hence Van Bavel is surely right in his claim that 'a strong link appears to exist between the rise of dominance of factor markets and the growth of wealth inequality. This link is at least suggested by the chronology of the two developments, in which the one (rising inequality) followed the other (dominance of factor markets) in all cases investigated' (Van Bavel 2016, 261) – but this kind of argument could not explain inequality growth in areas and periods characterized by economic stagnation and sometimes even markets breakdown. Hence it presents all the limitations implicit in attempts at explaining preindustrial inequality growth with economic growth, as discussed in the following.

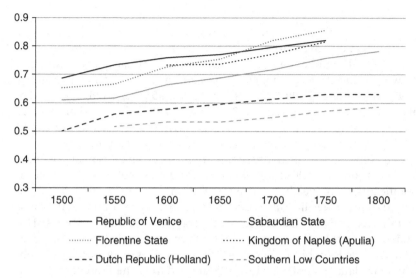

Figure 4.1 Long-term trends in economic inequality in Italy and the Low Countries, 1500–1800 (Gini indexes).
*Notes:*The series refer to wealth inequality for the Italian states, and to income inequality for the Dutch Republic and the southern Low Countries.
Sources: EINITE database for Italy and the southern Low Countries; Van Zanden (1995) for the Dutch Republic (Holland).

decline in 1500–1800. In particular, the Florentine State had been set on a path of decline since at least the first decades of the seventeenth century (Malanima 1982; Ammannati 2009; Alfani and Ammannati 2017); the Kingdom of Naples is usually considered a stagnant economy from about the same period or since even earlier (Galasso 1994); even the Sabaudian State, which was the only real rising star in early modern Italy, faced a difficult phase of economic stagnation from the early seventeenth century which lasted until the 1670s or 1680s (Barbero 2008; Alfani 2015, 1086–87). Regarding the Republic of Venice, as shall be recalled from the Introduction, the last chances of maintaining a central position in the European economy were finally lost in the mid-seventeenth century, as a consequence of the damage wrought by the plague of 1629–30 and by the War of Candia of 1645–69 (Alfani and Percoco 2018), which stretched to the limit the economic possibilities of the state and caused irreparable damage to its finances. Also in Northern Europe, the history of the southern Low Countries, which after the Dutch Revolt of 1566–85 had remained under Spanish rule, is one of economic decline during most of the seventeenth century. Only from the mid-eighteenth century would economic growth resume in this European area (Alfani and Ryckbosch 2015, 8; Ryckbosch 2016). So of all the states included in Figure 4.1, only the Dutch Republic was really characterized by sustained economic growth during the early modern period and until ca. 1750 (Van Zanden 1993), and interestingly, Van Zanden (1995, 653) reported a Gini index of income inequality fixed at 0.63 between 1732 and 1808. This general picture is confirmed if we compare the current estimates of per capita GDP in central-northern Italy, in the southern Low Countries and in the Dutch Republic, as for the first two areas the estimates are almost perfectly flat during 1500–1800, while the Dutch Republic seems to have significantly improved its per capita GDP (mostly before 1650, if we take the GDP estimates literally – which we probably should not). Also note that the currently available series for central-northern Italy, elaborated by Malanima (2011), does not seem to incorporate much data specifically related to the Republic of Venice – although it does incorporate relatively abundant data from the Sabaudian State and from the Florentine State.

Figure 4.2 also recalls the general picture of the Little Divergence, i.e. the process leading north-western Europe to experience quicker economic development compared to the rest of the continent (Allen 2001; Malanima 2013; Fouquet and Broadberry 2015). Different views exist about the causes of the Little Divergence – the opening of the Atlantic sea routes, human capital formation, institutional change, epidemiological factors . . . – as well as about the moment when it started, although almost all scholars would place it in-between the early sixteenth and the early seventeenth centuries. Seen from the perspective of Southern Europe and more precisely of central-northern Italy, which was its most advanced part, the Little Divergence is also the process leading to the loss of a position of centrality in the European economy, to the advantage of the most dynamic areas of north-western Europe – beginning with the Low Countries (Braudel 1984). But if we look at the two extremes of the Little Divergence (central-northern Italy and the Low Countries/Dutch Republic) in Figure 4.1, we find absolutely no signs of divergence: instead, we find a sort of 'Little Convergence' in inequality trends (Alfani and Ryckbosch 2015, 2016). This view is also confirmed by looking at some still-provisional results for central Spain, where again inequality growth has been detected even in phases of economic stagnation or decline (Fernández and Santiago-Caballero 2013). Indeed, until now the only European area where we have solid evidence of a correlation between early modern economic stagnation and (income) inequality decline is Portugal (Reis 2017), but this might prove to be just the exception that confirms the rule.

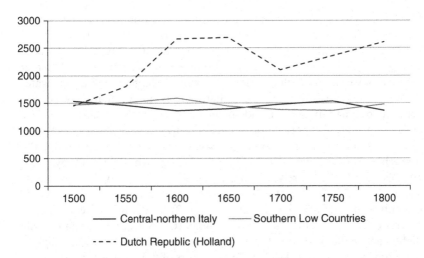

Figure 4.2 Estimates of per capita GDP in Italy and the Low Countries, 1500–1800 (in 1990 Geary-Khamis dollars PPP).
Sources: Clio-Infra database (www.clio-infra.eu/Indicators/GDPperCa pita.html consulted July 2018) for central-northern Italy, southern Low Countries and Dutch Republic (see Bolt and Van Zanden 2014 for details about the project).

It should be clear by now that we could not take economic growth as the standard explanation for the steady increase in economic inequality found in all but one of the European areas for which we have information about preindustrial inequality trends. Consequently, we need to explore different possible causal factors. Before doing that, though, we need to clarify a crucial point in the debate on economic growth as the possible source of inequality growth in the past: assuming that inequality growth is the consequence of economic growth leads us to characterize changes in distribution of this kind as somewhat 'benign', as they could be understood as a side-effect of increasing prosperity. Indeed, this view is shared by many economists, from Simon Kuznets (1955) to Angus Deaton (2013). The other potentially inequality-promoting factors that we will discuss will be found to be progressively less 'benign'.

Of all the possible explanations of long-term inequality growth, a relatively large family has to do with demography. In particular, many earlier studies have argued that population growth was associated with inequality growth, especially in cities (Herlihy 1978; Van Zanden 1995; Alfani 2010a, 2015; Ryckbosch 2016). The point here is not that cities were more unequal than villages, and larger cities than smaller cities – a finding which seems to be fairly well established in the literature (see for a synthesis Alfani and Ammannati 2017, 1084–85). It is instead the ability of population growth in a specific setting (a community urban or rural, or a broader aggregate such as a region or state) to promote inequality growth within that setting that we should evaluate. If we start with the larger possible aggregates – entire states – it is easy to notice that there is no automatic connection between population growth and inequality growth. For example, in the Sabaudian State the population stagnated during the seventeenth century (the 900,000 inhabitants reported for Savoy Piedmont– thus excluding the 'French' part of the state – in 1612 had indeed grown to 950,000 by 1700, but this was almost entirely due to the acquisition of the city of Alba with its territory in 1631: Alfani 2015, 1086) and something similar happened in the Florentine State (Breschi and Malanima 2002). In the Republic, the population of Venice and the *Terraferma* around 1650 was, at 1.5 million, only slightly above that of 1500 (1.4 million: Zannini 2010, 144). Some population growth had occurred during the first part of the sixteenth century, but from ca. 1550 and for about a century, overall the Italian territories of the Republic were characterized by demographic stagnation, as can be seen in Figure 4.3. Only from the second half of the seventeenth century, after the sharp population drop caused by the 1629–30 plague, do we find constant demographic growth – whereas inequality had been growing monotonically since at least 1500. Population change seems to be a better predictor of inequality change in the Low Countries, especially in the Dutch Republic,

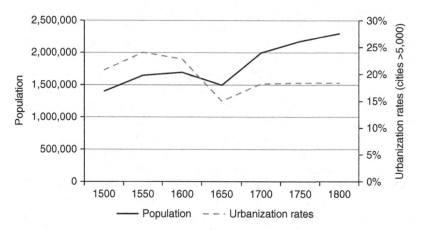

Figure 4.3 Population and urbanization rates in the Republic of Venice (Italian territories only), 1450–1800.
Sources: See Appendix, Table A.3.

where population growth was constant during 1500–1800, although it might have stagnated in the first half of the eighteenth century (De Vries and Van der Woude 1997, 49–51; Paping 2014, 8–9). In the southern Low Countries, overall population growth is associated to inequality growth from ca. 1600, but the sixteenth century was a period of demographic stagnation (Malanima 2009, 9), which did not prevent inequality growth.

To this general picture we can add that in Southern Europe the huge demographic catastrophes caused by the seventeenth-century plagues failed to cause significant inequality decline – indeed, the trends in Figure 4.1 are monotonic. The fourteenth-century Black Death certainly did reduce inequality, but this was the result of its broader consequences on the land and labour market, mediated through a specific institutional setting in which a key role was played by the presence of un-mitigated partible inheritance systems (as discussed in Section 3.4). More generally, it is not obvious why population change at the level of broader aggregates should affect inequality. One possibility is that this happens because demographic growth is positively correlated with economic growth – but this would simply lead us back to the criticism of economic growth as the cause of inequality growth and indeed, demographic growth seems to be an overall better explanatory factor of inequality change than economic growth. Another possibility is that demographic growth is one of the causes of the waves of 'proletarianization' that affected early modern Europe. The trigger, in this case, would be population pressure on resources, which might explain why in the context of early modern Europe, only population growth, and not population decline, is positively correlated to inequality.

The reasons why demographic factors were able to shape inequality trends are more easily observed on a smaller scale: that of single communities, and in particular of cities. Indeed, as early modern cities had a negative natural change (i.e. more individuals died in the city than were born there), growth in urban populations was possible exclusively through significant immigration from rural areas. Some micro-studies have shown how immigration acted as a kind of perpetual generator of inequality for cities, a process which became more intense after severe mortality crises, and – importantly – one which could occur even in the absence of significant economic growth, for example simply because physical space to live in had opened within the city walls following a mortality crisis (Alfani 2010a, 2010b), as well as in the absence of growth in urban population/urbanization rates, as would be the case of a severe epidemic affecting cities but sparing rural communities. We have provided some hints at dynamics of this kind also for the Republic of Venice (Section 3.4). It has also been pointed out that the impact of emigration on inequality in rural areas is less clear, and that urban–rural interaction should possibly be the object of specific studies, as – at least in principle – emigration towards cities of surplus population could leave rural inequality unchanged, or even increase it (Alfani 2009a). The microanalyses needed to assess this issue properly are still too few to allow for any generalization, but the aforementioned mechanisms are exemplary of how demographic factors could have affected inequality change per se, and not through their possible influence on economic growth or proletarianization. This being said, the evidence of community-level demographic growth actually explaining inequality growth at the *local* level is currently inconclusive. In his econometric study of inequality in cities of the southern Low Countries covering ca. 1500–1900, Ryckbosch (2016) reported a low significance of population as a predictor of inequality. In a broader econometric study of inequality in communities of the Florentine State during 1300–1800, Alfani and Ammannati (2017, 1095–98) found that the correlation is not at all significant as a predictor of inequality – at least if we control for whether a community is a city or not. In other words, in the specific context of the Florentine State from the late Middle Ages to the early modern period, although cities were more unequal than rural communities possibly also due to their much greater population as well as to other factors such as the concentration of specific institutions and magistracies and of the related high-skills, high-pay jobs, if we consider cities and rural communities separately population change does not explain inequality change.

The last, and in some regards the most important, demographic factor which has been considered a possible determinant of inequality change is urbanization. One reason for this is that, again, urbanization rates are considered good indicators of economic growth (see e.g. Acemoglu et al. 2005; Alfani 2013b), while having some advantages over other indicators: they are easier to measure with actual direct archival data (while estimates of per capita GDP tend to be, unavoidably, highly speculative), and they are often available at a regional and subregional level. In Table 4.1 we present urbanization rates for all the six states included in Figure 4.1.

Again, when looking at urbanization rates, we discover an absence of correlation with inequality change.[2] In Italy, we find urbanization decline in the seventeenth- and eighteenth-century Florentine State as well as in the seventeenth-century Sabaudian State and the Kingdom of Naples (Apulia only). In the Republic of Venice, urbanization rates peaked at

---

[2] A broad study of the determinants of income inequality, measured from social tables, in past societies found the correlation between urbanization and inequality to be positive, but not statistically significant (Milanovic 2016b).

Table 4.1 *Urbanization rates in Italy and the Low Countries, 1500–1800 (cities >5,000 inhabitants)*

	Republic of Venice (Italian territories)	Sabaudian State (Piedmont)	Florentine State	Kingdom of Naples (Apulia)	Southern Low Countries	Dutch Republic
1500	20.8	23.3	21	3.2	34	20.4
1600	22.8	24.5	19	7.5	35	29.0
1700	18.2	22.9	18.5	6.2	34	37.4
1800	18.4	26.1	17.8	8.8	27	31.4

Sources: Own elaboration for the Republic of Venice starting with data from Zannini (2010) and Alfani and Percoco (2018); see Appendix (Section A.3) for details. Alfani (2015) for Piedmont(new estimate for 1500); Breschi and Malanima (2002) for Tuscany; Alfani and Sardone (2015) for Apulia; Alfani and Ryckbosch (2016, Appendix D) for the southern Low Countries; data kindly provided by Richard Paping for the Dutch Republic (new elaborations based on the same dataset used in Paping (2014). The estimates refer to the territory belonging to present-day the Netherlands).

22.8% in 1600 but dropped to 18.2% by 1700, mostly as the consequence of the 1629–30 plague (in 1650, the urbanization rate seems to have been as low as 15%: see Figure 4.3), and thereafter they stagnated until 1800. In the southern Low Countries, urbanization rates stagnated during the seventeenth century, and then declined in the eighteenth. The Dutch Republic is the only area for which an increase in urbanization rates is found during the seventeenth century – but it is followed by significant decline during the eighteenth. So if we are interested in urbanization rates as possible, region-specific indicators of economic growth (or economic development), we have another reason to reject the latter as a general explanation for preindustrial inequality growth. But urbanization rates are relevant also to assess the potential impact of 'Kuznetsian' dynamics in preindustrial Europe, a point already made, in a very effective way, by Van Zanden (1995, 655–56). Indeed, as he argued, if we replace Kuznets' (1955) original distinction between an 'industrial' and an 'agrarian' sector characterized by different wage levels with that between a 'urban' and a 'rural' sector, also characterized by a steep wage differential (and there is little doubt that in early modern Europe, average wages were higher in the city than in the country), then 'The gradual urbanization that typified this period probably contributed to a rise in income inequality through the mechanism described by Kuznets' (Van Zanden 1995, 656), i.e. as the simple consequence of the transfer of workforce from one sector to another (through migration from the country to the city) which is testified to by changes in urbanization rates. However, as is clear from Table 4.1, this could work for all the period considered here only in the case of the Dutch Republic – and indeed, *also for that case* Van Zanden expressed some doubts, preferring another explanation: changes in the functional distribution of income, which might have affected both sectors (although possibly with different intensity) leading to increasing within-sector inequality which added to the between-sectors inequality (about this distinction and different interpretations of the 'Kuznets Curve' see also Brenner et al. 1991). This has to do with a historical process which can be defined as one of 'proletarianization'.

By proletarianization, we refer to the process leading a share of the European population, growing throughout the early modern period, to lose the ownership of the means of production, thus becoming dependent on selling their labour for wages. In more or less recent times, this view has been strongly argued for by Tilly (1984), but it is also clearly rooted in the Marxist tradition of economic history. If we look at this process or at its main component – the crisis of small landownership – from the perspective of this literature, it can be easily qualified as a 'malign' phenomenon. The situation is more nuanced if we look at it from the point of view of the functional distribution of income in the tradition of Smith and Ricardo and indeed, proletarianization does not always lead to impoverishment, but quite clearly when we focus on these aspects we are moving away from an interpretation of preindustrial inequality growth as an altogether 'benign' phenomenon.

Many specific historical processes have been presented as a component of this overall tendency towards proletarianization, from the rural enclosures movement to the spread of the putting-out system. If we focus on the areas for which we have reconstructions of long-term inequality we find, for Italy, an ample literature detailing the crisis of small peasant property with the subsequent concentration of wealth in many areas, especially from the second half of the sixteenth century when population pressure on the available resources became acute (Cattini 1984; Alfani 2013a, 76–77; Alfani et al. 2017). Famines, like the terrible one which affected the whole of the Italian peninsula in 1590–93, accelerated the process (Alfani 2011), which also involved the crisis of common or 'communal' property, again to the advantage of economic elites (Alfani and Rao 2011; Di Tullio 2014a). Specifically, the crisis of peasant property has been singled out as a possible factor contributing to inequality growth in Piedmont (Alfani 2015), while for Tuscany this aspect is more difficult to assess owing to the earlier rise of urban ownership and the greater prevalence of sharecropping. However, although in Tuscany the concentration of land in the hands of rich urban elites began as early as the beginning of the fourteenth century, it continued in the following centuries (Alfani and Ammannati 2017). In the Republic of Venice, we have some evidence of proletarianization in the growing share of propertyless households (see Section 2.2). In the city of Bergamo, for example, propertyless households were 3.4% of the total in 1537, rising to 10% by 1610. The 1629–30 plague temporarily reduced their prevalence; thereafter the tendency became again orientated towards an increase. Across the entire *Terraferma*, a tentative estimate of the prevalence of propertyless households divides the trend into two phases of growth, separated by a drop caused by the 1629–30 plague: from 1.5% in 1500 to 4.7% in 1600, then from 2.3% in 1650 to 7.6% in 1750; see Appendix A.4 for details (note that although to calculate most of our inequality measures we exclude the propertyless, the prevalence of the 'relative' poor shows basically the same trend, suggesting that many households might have lost most, but not all, of their properties).

Similar processes have been detected also in the southern Low Countries and in the Dutch Republic (Alfani and Ryckbosch 2016; Ryckbosch 2016). In the first, we know that in the region of Flanders in the sixteenth century 60% of the agricultural land was owner-occupied, declining to 33% in the eighteenth century. In Holland in the Dutch Republic, 55% of the land had been owner-occupied in the sixteenth century but this share had already declined to just 27% in the seventeenth century. Additionally, a process of fragmentation of landholdings is to be found throughout the Low Countries, leading to a growing prevalence of small (<1 hectare) landholdings (Thoen 2001; Van Bavel et al. 2010; Brusse et al. 2010; Alfani and Ryckbosch 2016). In another area of Europe, Languedoc in South France, it was also found that periods of crisis during the early modern period repeatedly caused waves of wealth (land) concentration in the hands of a decreasing number of great landowners (Le Roy Ladurie 1966, 567–81).

Two additional aspects of proletarianization as a possible cause of inequality growth need to be underlined. First, as already mentioned, differently from other possible explanatory factors such as economic growth or urbanization increase, it was a general, pan-European phenomenon (Tilly 1984, 26–36; Van Zanden 1995, 656–58; Alfani and Ryckbosch 2016). Second, it was somehow connected to demographic developments – as phases of acute crisis of small ownership tend to coincide with major famines on a continental scale (Le Roy Ladurie 1966; Kamen 1976; Alfani 2013a, 76–77; Alfani and Ó Gráda 2017a), and these usually occurred in periods of intense demographic pressure on resources, as revealed by the most recent attempt to chart the famines throughout the continent (Alfani and Ó Gráda 2017b, 9–10, 16–18; Alfani and Ó Gráda 2018). This close connection between famines and phases of crisis of small ownership/quick concentration of capital (mostly but not exclusively, land) creates what many referred to as 'waves' of proletarianization – which is exactly why, although it was surely one of the main factors leading to inequality growth during the early modern period, proletarianization seems to fail to fully account for a process which is found to be overall monotonic in practically all areas during the entire period 1500–1800. This is a reason to look for possible causes of inequality growth that exerted a more constant influence throughout the early modern period. The rise of the fiscal state is by far the most probable culprit, as argued in the next section.

Before we move more generally to institutions and institutional change as possible culprits of long-term inequality growth, it is important to explore another interpretation, which is again connected to the tradition of the classical economists (from Smith to Marx)and more specifically, to the perspective of the functional distribution of income. Thomas Piketty, in his famous recent book *Capital in the Twenty-First Century* (2014) and elsewhere (Piketty and Zucman 2014) focused on wealth/income ratios as predictors of income inequality. He also argued that as long as the rate of return to capital (r) is higher than the growth rate of national income (g) and as long as wealth stays highly inheritable, inequality (of *both* income and wealth) will continue to increase. Although Piketty had very limited information for the pre-1800 period, in a very speculative section of his book he did argue for r being constantly >g across the world and throughout the period from year 0 to the eve of World War I (Piketty 2014, 353–58). In Piketty's theoretical framework, this equals to assuming a constantly growing preindustrial economic inequality.

There are a number of problems with this view of preindustrial inequality (admittedly, preindustrial times *were not* Piketty's main focus). First, the information we have about preindustrial growth rates of national income (g), albeit steadily improving in recent years, is still very hypothetical and of very varying quality. The situation is even worse for rates of return to capital (r). Second, and more importantly, the view of a constantly growing inequality does not fit the empirical finding that the Black Death caused a century-long phase of significant inequality decline. Indeed, as this catastrophe destroyed human capital and only marginally physical and financial capital, the wealth/income ratio very probably grew,[3] which does not support, at least for this specific period, the view that such a ratio would be positively correlated to income and wealth inequality. Another long phase of inequality decline has been reported at

---

[3] Although it is theoretically possible that wealth declined as much as income as a result of steep depreciation of assets, this seems to be an unlikely scenario.

the end of the Roman Empire (Scheidel 2017) – so that waves in long-run inequality trends are detectable, as also recently argued by Milanovic (2016a) and indeed, our new reconstruction for the Republic of Venice also supports such a view, given that we find a flat phase at the end of the Middle Ages (presumably the final lull in a process of inequality decline triggered by the Black Death: see Section 3.4) followed by continuous inequality growth during the early modern period.

It is not possible here to discuss further Piketty's views, which have been the object of intense debate (regarding in particular criticism about Piketty's implications for the study of inequality in the long run, see Lindert 2014). Instead, we need to introduce another family of possible explanations of inequality change: institutions. In Chapter 3 (Section 3.4), we have already discussed in detail the importance of inheritance systems – and particularly, we have argued that adaptation in inheritance systems explains why the seventeenth century plagues proved unable to cause inequality decline as the Black Death did instead (on this point see also Alfani 2010b; Alfani and Murphy 2017). Alfani and Ryckbosch (2016, 148) explored the hypothesis that differences in family institutions could determine inequality differences across space and time. However, in their comparison of parts of central-northern Italy and the Low Countries, they could not find any proof of this. Other potentially relevant institutions are closely connected to the state and the political system – they will be the topic of the next section.

4.2   The Redistributive Impact of the Early Modern Fiscal State

During the early modern period, the ability of the state to tax increased dramatically and indeed, improvements in the fiscal systems were a necessary condition in the development of stronger and 'deeper' state institutions. This process is generally referred to as the 'the rise of the fiscal state'. Sometimes, this new institutional arrangement is referred to as the 'fiscal-military state', which connects directly the increasing fiscal capacity of the state to the main use of the growing resources being collected (Bonney 1999; Glete 2002; Dincecco 2011; Yun-Casalilla and O'Brien 2012). Although the needs of the fiscal state were varied and included, for example, the expansion of bureaucracies or the support given to international trade (Yun-Casalilla 2012), there is no doubt that the main factor providing both the need, and the justification to the taxpayers for increasing the fiscal burden, was the growing cost of waging war in an effective way. This is connected to the so-called military revolution, which began with the Italian Wars of 1494–1559 (Alfani 2013a) and continued throughout the early modern period. The new and quickly changing methods of warfare led to the need for larger armies and better equipment, as well as for much improved military infrastructure and defence logistics in general (Parker 1988, 1995). This was a pan-European process: as all states had to play the same game to be able to compete effectively in the military arena – or even simply to survive as independent political entities – during the whole period 1500–1800 we find that both the overall, and more importantly, the per capita fiscal burden tend to increase everywhere. For the Republic of Venice, we have reconstructed in detail the development of its fiscal system in Chapter 1 (Section 1.2). Indeed, the increase in the per capita fiscal burden in this specific state was analogous to what is found elsewhere, as can be seen in Figure 4.4, where the Republic is compared to a selection of Italian and European states.

It is easy to see that everywhere in Europe, the per capita fiscal burden increased continuously during the early modern period. However, the Republic of Venice is far from being the Italian area where taxation increased more: that honour arguably goes to the Sabaudian State, where from 1620–29 to 1760–80 the per capita fiscal burden more than

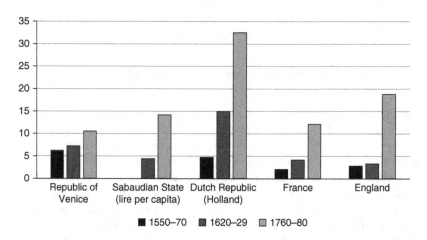

Figure 4.4 Estimates of per capita tax pressure across Europe, sixteenth to eighteenth centuries (measured in number of daily wages of labourers in the construction industry, exception made for the Sabaudian State for which per capita revenues in lire are provided).
Sources: Own elaboration from data published by Pezzolo 2006a, 66, exception made for the Sabaudian State for which we use estimates from Alfani and Ryckbosch (2016).

trebled, a striking result compared to the 'modest' +46% of the Republic of Venice (note that as the unit of measurement used for the Sabaudian State is different from all others, only percent change, and not absolute values, can be meaningfully compared). Of the countries considered here the one experiencing the most impressive proportional increase from the seventeenth to the eighteenth century is England, where the fiscal pressure grew almost five-fold, although it started from relatively low levels. In fact, the Republic of Venice stands out for having achieved a high fiscal capacity since early on: during 1550–70, its per capita fiscal pressure was the highest of all countries considered and surely one of the highest in Europe. Measured in daily wages of labourers in the construction industry,[4] it was equal to 6.2, versus 4.7 in the Dutch Republic, 2.8 in England and just 2.1 in France (Pezzolo 2006a, 66). By the eve of the 1630 plague, the Republic had managed to further increase it (+16%, to 7.2 daily wages), and it still compared favourably to other Italian and European states – but it had been vastly surpassed by Holland, which was already able to tax its inhabitants for the equivalent of fifteen daily wages (also see the estimates in Van Zanden and Prak 2009, 218). It is only during the eighteenth century, though, that the fiscal capacity of the Republic of Venice seems to have fallen behind that of the most advanced areas of Europe, as well as that of what had become the main military power of Italy, the Sabaudian State. This seems to go hand in hand with the general view that during the eighteenth century, the relative decline of the Republic of Venice became ever more intense and apparent – but to a degree at least, this is due to the fact that the Republic, which was now trying to avoid any major military confrontation and actively pursued neutrality (Scarabello 1995), simply did not need to increase its revenues beyond certain limits, as correctly pointed out by Fritschy (2017, 230).

Independently from their relative movements, all the states included in Figure 4.1, together with most other European states and some non-European ones (see Yun-Casalilla and O'Brien 2012 for examples) are characterized by vastly increasing overall and per capita revenues during the early modern period. This is very relevant to our analysis of the determinants of long-term inequality growth, as preindustrial fiscal systems had a marked 'regressive' nature. In other words, and contrary to what we are accustomed to thinking of today fiscal systems in Western countries, post-tax inequality was higher than pre-tax inequality, essentially because the poor were taxed proportionally more than the rich.

---

[4] Daily wages of labourers are a measure which is particularly helpful for comparisons across countries, as well as for comparisons across time as they are not altered by inflation. See Chapter 1, Section 1.4 for further discussion.

The reasons why fiscal systems were regressive are easy to understand. First of all (and generally speaking), many of the largest patrimonies were either partially, or entirely exempt from taxation. This was surely the case both for feudal property and for a large part of the patrimony of the Church. Nobles, who, as seen in Chapter 2, were an important component of the top rich in the Republic of Venice as elsewhere, paid fully their due on non-feudal properties inscribed in the local *estimi*, but were taxed at much lower rates on their feudal, or otherwise 'privileged', lands. This being said, 'the *Terraferma* was only marginally touched by feudal presence' (Gullino 1983, 185) and 'privileged lands accounted for a negligible portion of the whole assessed properties' (Pezzolo 2012, 272). We have a list of privileged properties for the whole province of Padua in 1642, allowing us to estimate the prevalence of non-institutional privileged property at just 1.1% of the value of all the real estate of the area (rising to 1.8% if we exclude the *clero* and the Venetians from the calculations: see Chapter 3, Section 3.5). More generally in central and northern Italy, in comparison with other European countries such as England or France, feudal property was much less prevalent (for example, in the Sabaudian State, feudal property was found to be 2.5% of the total in the territory of Ivrea in 1665 and 1.2% in Saluzzo in 1772: Alfani 2015, 1063), so large patrimonies were subject to relatively high taxation. Feudal property was much more abundant in southern Italy (Kingdom of Naples), although the extent of the immunities declined over time to meet the growing fiscal demands of the Spanish crown (Pezzolo 2012, 272). Another factor leading to lower taxation at the top, are the fiscal privileges of the citizens of capital cities. In Italy, these fiscal privileges often included the total or semi-total exemption from direct taxation (which is also why many capital cities such as Milan, Turin or Naples did not have *estimi*[5]) – and many of the richest inhabitants of any given state resided in its capital. In the Florentine State in 1427, for example, 'the richest 3,000 households of Florence were more wealthy [*sic*] than the remaining 57,000 Tuscan households, both inside and outside the city of Florence' (Herlihy 1977, 7). Nevertheless, 'Except for rare intervals, the Florentine government since the early fourteenth century had refrained from imposing direct taxes within the city; moneys collected from urban residents were considered interest-bearing, public obligations, eventually to be repaid. ... Fiscal policy not only protected the

[5] In fact, Turin did have them before becoming the capital of the Sabaudian State in 1563, but stopped thereafter (Alfani 2015, 1065) and also for Milan, there are some traces of medieval *estimi*, which, however, were discontinued in the early modern period (Barbieri 1937; Mainoni 1994).

great fortunes, but contributed to their growth' (9). In the Republic of Venice, residents of the capital did pay a tax on property, the *decima*, but the actual burden to which they were subjected remained somewhat lower than that paid by residents of the *Terraferma* through the system of the *estimo* (Gullino 1981, 208–10).

This recurrent situation of relative privilege of the capital compared to all other communities of the state was replicated at the local level, where the residents of the city were favoured over the rural dwellers (and again, the urban residents were, on average, richer than the rural; hence the system had regressive consequences). Specifically in the Republic of Venice, it has been underlined that the local fiscal bodies were particularly reticent to welcome the requests of the less-privileged components of the rural society (Maifreda 2002, 121; Vecchiato 1982, 360–61), determining the situation of unequal treatment which has been described in detail in Chapter 1. Here it will suffice to remember that this situation was regularly lamented also by the *rettori*, i.e. the local representatives of Venice. For example, Simon Contarini, Captain of Verona, wrote in 1654 that 'The weakest are those who are burdened by the heaviest [fiscal] weights ... consequently it is not surprising that they leave and that the [Veronese] countryside is left increasingly depopulated' (cit. in Vecchiato 1982, 360, our translation). To give a final example of this systematic inequality of fiscal treatment, until the 1530s across the provinces of the Republic the lands owned in the *contado* by citizens who managed them directly (*condotte a boaria*) had been entirely exempt from taxation. Then a coalition of territorial bodies lobbied with Venice to forbid such practice (Maifreda 2002, 120–21). Indeed, during the early modern period the central authorities of the Republic worked to slowly reduce the fiscal privileges of the urban taxpayers of the *Terraferma* (Pezzolo 2012, 270–71) – but they could never eliminate them entirely.

The second main reason why preindustrial fiscal systems were regressive, is that they relied much more on indirect taxation on consumption, than on direct taxation on wealth or income – and consumption taxes are intrinsically regressive, owing to the empirical regularity (also somehow connected to the 'Engel's Law'[6]) that the share of income that is consumed is inversely proportional to the income level. In other words, those having lower incomes will have to consume a greater part of it (100% if they are placed exactly at subsistence levels) compared to those belonging to the higher strata of the income distribution and as a consequence of this, they will be affected more than proportionally by consumption taxes.

---

[6] According to Engel's Law, as income grows the part of it spent on food declines in percentage even if it food expenditure increases in absolute terms.

Hence, any increase in indirect taxes on consumption will tend to have regressive, inequality-increasing consequences – in the past as well as today (Joumard, Pisu and Bloch 2012, 56–58). Indeed, across Europe, 'In the cities, the bulk of revenue usually came from excises on such basic consumption goods as beer, cereals, and meat, which proportionally took a larger chunk out of the budget of the poor than of the rich'(Alfani and Ryckbosch 2016, 150). In Italy, during the early modern period the general tendency was for the importance of indirect taxes on consumption to increase considerably, for example in the Sabaudian State and in the Florentine State, but also in the Republic of Venice, where it was partly a reaction to the decrease in revenues from international trade (Pezzolo 2012). In the southern Low Countries during the eighteenth century, consumption taxes accounted for about 55% of the overall fiscal revenues (Jenssen 2012), while in Britain during the years 1665–1810 overall indirect taxes always accounted for considerably more than 50% of the total, with taxes on domestic products and services rising from 25–30% of the total in the late seventeenth century to 50–55% in the second half of the eighteenth (O'Brien 1988, 9). The reasons why, across the continent, increases in indirect taxation on basic consumption goods were often preferred to those in direct taxation surely include the relative ease with which they could be enforced and collected (Bonney 1999; Yun-Casalilla and O'Brien 2012; Alfani and Ryckbosch 2016), as well the fact that excises helped to hide the real impact of taxation (Van Zanden and Prak 2009, 219).

It should be clear by now that preindustrial fiscal systems were regressive; hence any increase in the per capita fiscal burden tended to favour inequality growth.[7] But beyond this general statement, we need to have a better idea of their actual degree of regressiveness and of how they affected different segments of the population. An attempt to provide at least some orders of magnitude will be made in the next section. However, before doing so some concluding remarks are needed on the connection between changes in the fiscal capacity of the state and political institutions in general. For the history of the rise of the fiscal state is not only one of growing extractiveness achieved through increases in means of coercion of the state; rather, at least in some areas and more clearly in later periods, it went hand in hand with a deepening of political rights. Arguably, the European state where this is most clear is the Dutch Republic. Here, the

[7] Indeed, apart from the structure of taxation, the fiscal expansion of early modern states promoted inequality growth also due to the way in which taxation itself was organized (Yun-Casalilla 2012, 22–23).For example, it is not by chance that tax farmers are usually found among the richest, in the Republic of Venice as elsewhere (see discussion and examples in Chapter 2, Section 2.4).

increase in per capita fiscal burden went hand in hand with the progressive extension and deepening of rights of citizenship – and as has been convincingly argued (Van Zanden and Prak 2006, 2009, 217–24; Prak and Van Zanden 2009), this was instrumental to determine the kind of social contract which allowed the Dutch Republic to impose the highest fiscal burden in seventeenth- and eighteenth-century Europe. Additionally, it seems that the fiscal system of the Dutch Republic was the least regressive in Europe as indeed, in some provinces (such as Holland) the burden was heavier on cities than on rural communities, and from 1670 some forms of 'progressive' taxation were introduced. These included heavier consumption taxes on luxuries as well as some forms of (light) progressive taxation on wealth and, from 1715, on income. However, many of these fiscal innovations, experimented first by Holland and later spreading to other provinces of the Dutch Republic, proved unsuccessful in the medium to long run, mostly owing to the difficulties in collecting the needed information, so that income taxes remained basically emergency taxes, rather than ordinary financial instruments (Fritschy 2003; Van Zanden and Prak 2009). This being said, it has been estimated that in the period 1650–1750, the taxes paid by the 30% richest population of Holland increased three-fold and more, while the 70% poorest suffered just a 20% increase (De Vries and Van der Woude 1997, 112).

Overall, the fiscal system of the Dutch Republic remained regressive – but much less so than elsewhere, which might help to explain why, in relative terms, this state seems to have grown relatively less 'extractive' (if not necessarily less unequal) than all other European areas we can compare it with (Alfani and Ryckbosch 2016). What is more, even if we factor in some limited changes in the fiscal system aimed at reducing the disadvantaged situation suffered by the poorest strata of society, the dramatic increase in per capita taxation experienced by the Dutch Republic (Figure 4.4) more than compensated – as the overall power of a fiscal system to produce distributive effects depends on *both* its structure and the level of the fiscal pressure. As clarified in the next section, also in the Republic of Venice the increase in the 'regressive power' of the fiscal system depended solely upon the growth in per capita taxation.[8]

---

[8] Even though it seems probable that in the Dutch Republic, and maybe, in a much more limited way, also in the Republic of Venice the structure of the fiscal system evolved towards less regressiveness during the early modern period (albeit slowly and with great difficulties), it is also quite possible that in other European states this did not happen. There, the net result would be an even greater capacity for increases in the per capita fiscal burden to cause inequality growth. Although it is not possible to proceed here to additional comparisons, it is also worth remembering than in many areas of Europe a tendency for the structure of the fiscal system to evolve towards greater regressiveness seems to have

Indeed, there might be some additional points of resemblance between the Dutch Republic and the Republic of Venice – for example, a sentiment of belonging to a greater political entity, fuelled by opportunities for participating in various levels of government (as proper in a 'Republic', although we should be wary of replicating old political myths), might have been instrumental in enabling this state to achieve relatively very high levels of per capita taxation already from the sixteenth century. It is also probable that the Venetian fiscal system was more consensual, and less 'coercive' than that of other leading Italian states, particularly the Sabaudian State and the Florentine State (see Pezzolo 2012, 270–71) – but there is no doubt whatsoever that it was also intensely regressive.

4.3   Measuring Redistribution: Taxation

While it is easy to demonstrate that preindustrial fiscal systems were regressive, it is much harder to provide measures of their actual regressive power, upon which depends their ability to transform a pre-tax distribution into a more unequal post-tax one. As far as we know, no attempt to estimate the degree of regressiveness of a pre-industrial fiscal system has ever been attempted. What follows is not meant to provide perfect measures of fiscal regressiveness in the Republic of Venice – indeed, given the information and data currently available, any reconstruction of this kind can only be considered speculative. Our objective is simply to provide a first inroad into a promising new field for research, as well as to reach some basic conclusions about how the evolution in the European fiscal regimes described in the earlier section might have affected the overall regressiveness of the system, and not only the per capita fiscal burden which, as has been seen, was on the rise everywhere or almost.

An important assumption that we have to make is that the aggregate wealth distributions that we have reconstructed are also acceptable proxies of income distributions in the long run. As discussed in Chapter 3, this is not an entirely unrealistic hypothesis (although the actual income distribution of the Republic of Venice was surely less unequal). Additionally, assuming the same distribution for wealth and income

characterized the aftermath of the Black Death. This happened because the catastrophic disruption caused by the plague made it difficult to determine the amounts due by each community or fiscal body to the central state. As a consequence, a considerable part of the burden was transferred from direct to indirect taxation. This happened for example in the Florentine State (Cohn 1999), which might contribute to explaining why inequality in this area resumed growing very shortly after the Black Death, as found by Alfani and Ammannati (2017).

considerably simplifies the presentation and analysis of the results.[9] Our starting point, then, will be the aggregate distribution for the whole of the Republic (*Terraferma*; propertyless excluded) in 1550. As will be remembered from the earlier section, at this date the per capita fiscal burden corresponded to 6.2 daily wages of labourers in the construction industry. By 1760–80, this had increased to 10.5 daily wages of labourers (+69%), and we will assume this fiscal pressure also for 1750. But what we need in order to measure regressiveness is not the per capita fiscal burden, but the overall fiscal pressure of the central state. For the second half of the sixteenth century, this has been estimated at about 5% (Pezzolo 1990, 316). If we assume that the growth in fiscal pressure is directly proportional to that of per capita taxation (Figure 4.4), we can hypothetically place at about 8.5% the fiscal pressure in the Republic of Venice in 1750. These estimates seem coherent with those reported for Holland (taking into account the different trajectories of the two areas), where fiscal pressure has been estimated to be 1.9% of GDP in 1575, 5.2% in 1600, 5.4% in 1650, 9.7% in 1700 and 13.5% in 1750. For 1750 only, estimates for other provinces of the Dutch Republic are also available: 9.6% in Drenthe and 9.3% in Overjissel (Fritschy, 't Hart and Horlings 2012, 55). It is easy to see that the relative trend in the overall fiscal pressure in the Venetian and the Dutch Republics follows quite closely that reported in Figure 4.4. For Britain, O'Brien (1988, 3) estimates a lower fiscal pressure of about 3.4% in the mid-seventeenth century, rising to 10.5% in 1750: again in basic accordance with Figure 4.4.

We make our estimates starting with an extremely simplified version of the fiscal system of the Republic, notably one in which (1) all forms of taxation can easily be distinguished in direct or indirect (which is usually, but not always, the case: see Pezzolo 2006, 45); (2) all indirect taxation is on consumption; and (3) all direct taxation is on wealth.

The first aspect to determine is the relative share of the fiscal burden which can be referred to direct and to indirect taxation. As can be seen in Figure 4.5, in the Republic of Venice indirect taxation – which in the balance sheets of the state was referred to as *Dazi* ('duties') – always prevailed over direct taxation (the *Gravezze* or 'weights') to a considerable extent. Indeed, in the *Terraferma* the *Dazi* accounted for more than 80% of the total in 1550, thereafter slowly increasing until they peaked at almost 90% in 1670 (the percentages would be slightly lower if we factored in also other revenues, not classified by the Venetian central budget as either *Dazi* or *Gravezze*, and which we have disregarded for

---

[9] In particular, it allows us to measure the regressiveness of the fiscal system as the simple difference between the share of income/wealth earned/owned by each stratum of society and the share of the overall tax collected which was actually paid by that stratum (see Figure 4.6).

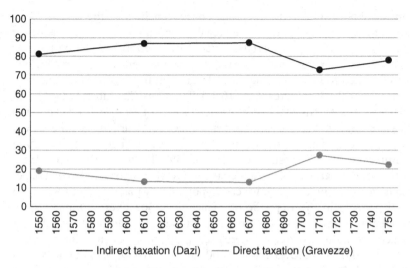

Figure 4.5 Direct and indirect taxation in the Republic of Venice (*Terraferma*), 1550–1750 (%).
Notes: We have excluded from the calculations a small residual amount of revenues which could not be classified as either direct (*Gravezze*) or indirect (*Dazi*) taxes. Additionally, the measures refer to the *Terraferma* only, for coherence with our aggregate distributions.
Sources: Own elaboration from data in Pezzolo 2016a, 47.

this exercise). Later it declined, to vary between 70% and 80% during the first half of the eighteenth century. But if we focus on the two extremes, which are those that we intend to compare, we see that the shares of *Dazi* and *Gravezze* were basically the same, so for simplicity here we will assume the same share of direct and indirect taxes in 1550 and 1750, fixed at 20% and 80% respectively. This means that for example in 1550 when the overall fiscal pressure is 5%, this can be split in 1% direct, and 4% indirect taxes.

The other aspect that we need to determine in order to assess the regressive impact of indirect taxation is its incidence on different strata of the population, which depends on the consumption habits of different socio-economic groups – or more properly, in our simplified model, on their propensity and/or ability to save or to elude taxes. We have very little information about the structure of consumption/saving at different levels of the social ladder, so we will have to make some tentative hypotheses, guided by the intuition that the higher the income, the lower the part of it which is consumed. The task is somewhat easier for the bottom of the distribution as indeed, the definition of relative poverty we used in

Chapter .2 (measured as those below 13% of the median wealth) can be operationalized by assuming that these poor had to consume their entire income to satisfy their basic needs. These account for an estimated 16.7% of the population in 1550. At the other extreme we have the rich (defined as those above 10 times the median), who were 5.1% of the population (Chapter 2, Table 2.4). For the sake of simplicity, for 1550 we set the share of the 'poor' consuming their entire income at 15%, and that of the rich at 5%. However, while we may have a good idea how many the rich numbered, we are still faced with the problem of defining how much of their income they saved, or subtracted to taxation in any other way (note that it is reasonable to assume that the ability to elude taxation grew with income, as relational/political power is closely related to income, too[10] – but as we could not disentangle the ability to save from the ability to elude taxation, we will just refer to the whole as 'saving'). We resort to simply setting a fairly broad range of variation, establishing that the rich saved, on average, between 20% and 40% of their income. We then define the share of income saved by those belonging to the rest of the distribution (above the poor, below the rich) through exponential interpolation.[11] What information we have about the capacity and propensity for saving of the top rich suggests that the above range is not unrealistic. For example, in Pavia in Lombardy in 1568–69, the humanist Bernardo Sacco – who can surely be placed at the top of the social ladder of his city – was able to save 22% of his revenue (Zanetti 2000, 210), albeit less in other periods. In Tuscany during 1690–1719, the extremely wealthy Riccardi family used just about 50% of their yearly income for current expenditures (Malanima 1977, 202). In the Republic of Venice during the years 1705–35, Piero Pisani Moretta (who at his death left an enormous patrimony worth one million ducats) was able to save and reinvest, on average, 86% of his revenues, mostly coming from the lands he owned in Montagnana and Este in the territory of Padua (Gullino 1984, 148) – but this was an exceptional man reputed for his 'angelic behavior' (*angelici costumi*), that is his frugality (although according to others, he had built his enormous patrimony through mean parsimony: *meschina parsimonia*; Gullino 1984, 5).[12] Of course, there are also many examples of wealthy families that spent more than their income, sold property, accrued debts

---

[10] Some confirmation of a greater ability of the elites to elude taxes is found in Ventura (1964), 405–16 and Gullino (1981).

[11] We also experimented with linear interpolation, but differences proved to be marginal. On principle, we prefer exponential interpolation because it emphasizes the differences in the relative ability to save of the upper and lower strata of society.

[12] To compare with today's societies, in a range of countries during 2003–10 it was found that the top 20% saved between 20–40% of their income, i.e. exactly the range that we

and ultimately declined – hence the choice of setting the average savings among the rich at no more than 20–40% of their income.

Regarding direct taxation, we take into account two aspects. First, we slightly reduce the fiscal burden on the rich to take into account privileged property exempt from taxation. We make the hypothesis that 5% of the patrimony of the rich was exempt from taxation, which is slightly higher than what would correspond to our estimate of non-institutional privileged property being 1.8% of the total in the province of Padua in 1642. We do this to account for probable differences across the *Terraferma*[13]. For Piedmont, it has been estimated that in the 1730s, 8% of the patrimony of the rich was exempt from taxation (Pezzolo 2012, 272) – an already low percentage, but it stands to reason that it was even lower in the Venetian mainland. This kind of fiscal privilege, however, affects only marginally our overall estimates. Much more importantly, we model a degree of differential treatment between urban and rural dwellers. As we have no information about the relative fiscal burden borne by these two kinds of taxpayers, we set a range of variation, establishing that the rural dwellers paid between 10% and 20% more per unit of wealth than the urban dwellers.[14] The prevalence of rural dwellers across society is measured directly from our aggregate distribution, and declines monotonically with income: it is 92% among the 10% poorest population, 88% in the second and third deciles, 83% in the deciles from fourth to seventh, 58% in the eighth, 50% in the percentiles 80–95, and finally, just 33% among the richest 5%.

The ranges of variation established for the share of income saved by the rich and for the fiscal disadvantage of the rural dwellers can be combined in four ways – but as we are interested in orders of magnitude, we focus only on the overall least regressive, and most regressive combinations, corresponding to the following hypotheses:

---

have attributed to the top 5% only in the early modern period (when per capita product was way lower). In particular, this share was slightly more than 40% in the United States and in Mexico, 20% in New Zealand, while countries like France and the Netherlands were in the middle (around 30%). At the other end of the distribution, the poorest 20% were characterized by negative savings everywhere, exception made for France where they were marginally above zero. In other words, the poorest 20% households were decumulating wealth, or becoming indebted, or receiving direct transfers from other households – whatever the case, they were placed, on average, in a precarious situation (Fesseau and Mattonetti 2013, 42–43).

[13] If we assumed privileged property to be about 2% across the *Terraferma*, then the share of non-taxable patrimony of the top 5% (under the assumption that they own all the non-taxable property) would be about 4%.

[14] We do not model another kind of fiscal privilege: that which favoured the capital city compared to all other communities. This is because for the Republic of Venice the actual differences in treatment are debatable and however very difficult to measure, and also because our distributions do not include the capital anyway.

Hypothesis 1, least regressive (HP1): the share of income saved by the rich is set at 20%. Rural dwellers pay 10% more taxes per unit of wealth than urban dwellers.

Hypothesis 2, most regressive (HP2): the share of income saved by the rich is set at 40%. Rural dwellers pay 20% more taxes per unit of wealth than urban dwellers.

Table 4.2 reports the outcome, in terms of fiscal pressure per capita and of the share of the overall tax burden, under the two different hypotheses. We organize the population, poorest to richest, in deciles but we split the top 10% into two brackets with 5% of the population each, to place in evidence what happens at the very top, where more than 50% of the overall wealth is concentrated. In the second and third columns, we measure the effective rate of indirect taxation on income, given the share of income saved at different levels of the socio-economic structure. As expected, this declines when we move up the social ladder: the bottom 10% (who are assumed to consume 100% of their income) are taxed at 4.41% of their overall income, while the top 5% at 3.53% under HP1, while under HP2 the poorest are taxed at 4.97% and the richest at 2.98%. If we look at direct taxation on wealth (fourth and fifth columns), it also declines as we move to the top: from 1.02% to 0.92% under HP1, and from 1.03% to 0.88% under HP2 (note the relatively large drop – from 0.96 to 0.88 under HP2 – when moving from the bracket 91–95 to the final one, 96–100, which is mostly due to the presence of some privileged property at the very top). Therefore if we take all the extreme values (combining HP1 and HP2), we can reasonably assume that in 1550 in the Republic of Venice, the effective tax rate was 5.43–6.00% for the bottom 10%, 4.86–4.96% in the mid-distribution (sixth decile) and 3.86–4.44% for the richest 5% of the population. The distance in fiscal pressure between bottom and top, then, might have been up to 2 percentage points, which given the assumed overall pressure of 5% for the whole of the Republic makes for a significantly regressive fiscal system.

The fact that the richest did not pay *proportionally* more taxes than the poor did not prevent them from paying more taxes overall – which obviously they did, on account of their much greater income and wealth. As we are assuming the income and wealth distributions to be the same (eight column), we can calculate the share of the overall fiscal revenue of the state paid by each percentile of the population simply by applying to this our estimates of the total fiscal pressure and recalibrating so that the resulting total is equal to 100 (ninth and tenth columns). If we do this, we obtain that the top 5% rich, who owned slightly more than 50% of the overall wealth, paid in-between 46.9% (HP2) and 48.68% (HP1) of all

Table 4.2 *Fiscal pressure per socio-economic stratum in the Republic of Venice (Terraferma) in 1550*

Population (poorest to richest)	Indirect Tax (HP1)[a]	Indirect Tax (HP2)[a]	Direct Tax (HP1)[a]	Direct Tax (HP2)[a]	Total pressure: direct + indirect (HP1)	Total pressure: direct + indirect (HP2)	% Wealth and Income[b]	% of Tax Burden (HP1)[c]	% of Tax Burden (HP2)[c]
10	4.41	4.97	1.02	1.03	5.43	6.00	0.21	0.25	0.30
10	4.38	4.89	1.01	1.02	5.40	5.92	0.68	0.80	0.97
10	4.27	4.61	1.01	1.02	5.28	5.63	1.08	1.24	1.47
10	4.16	4.34	1.01	1.02	5.17	5.35	1.66	1.87	2.15
10	4.05	4.08	1.01	1.02	5.06	5.10	2.58	2.84	3.18
10	3.95	3.85	1.01	1.02	4.96	4.86	3.87	4.17	4.54
10	3.84	3.62	1.01	1.02	4.85	4.64	5.50	5.81	6.16
10	3.74	3.41	0.99	0.97	4.73	4.38	8.47	8.72	8.96
10	3.65	3.21	0.98	0.96	4.63	4.17	12.85	12.94	12.93
5	3.58	3.07	0.98	0.96	4.55	4.03	12.79	12.68	12.44
5	3.53	2.98	0.92	0.88	4.44	3.86	50.32	48.68	46.90
Mean[d]	4	4	1	1	5	5			

[a] Effective tax rates.

[b] We assume the distribution of wealth to be the same as the distribution of income (see main text).

[c] Obtained by applying the estimates of the total percent fiscal pressure (under HP1 or HP2: columns 6 and 7) to the share of income/wealth of each percentile (column 8), then recalibrating so that the shares of the tax burden for all percentiles add up to 100.

[d] Means are weighted by % of population.

taxes. The contribution of the bottom 10% was marginal (0.25–0.3%) and indeed, overall the poorest 50% of the population paid just 7–8% of all taxes.

The rich pay more than the poor: this is what allowed the fiscal systems of preindustrial Europe to be perceived as 'just' – according to the ideal of 'distributive justice' that we have described in the Introduction, which required everybody to receive exactly what was due to him or her, but *not* equality of treatment for all (we will return to this in the concluding section). So the social pact on which preindustrial societies were built did not imply progressivity, or even just proportionality (everyone pays in exact proportion to his or her share of income/wealth). We, however, are interested in how far from proportional the system was, because from its regressiveness depends its ability to produce more and more inequality over time (as it allows for proportionally larger net incomes to be earned at the top, where they are saved at higher rates, thus translating into larger and larger wealth concentration as well as an ever greater concentration of income from capital, and so forth). A simple way to represent regressiveness is to analyse the difference between the share of wealth/income owned, and the share of the tax paid. This is done in Figure 4.6.

The figure clearly shows that, in our simplified model of the Republic's fiscal system, all strata of society paid more tax than would be due in a

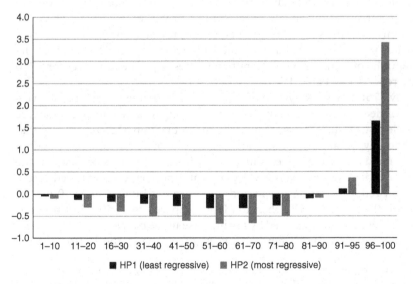

Figure 4.6 Regressiveness of the fiscal system of the Republic of Venice (*Terraferma*), 1550 (% wealth/income – % tax paid).

condition of proportional taxation (% wealth/income = % tax paid), bar from the top 10% which overall showed a positive imbalance of 1.75–3.77 percentage points (1.64–3.42 attributable to the top 5% only). The largest negative imbalances are found at the middle of the distribution, and especially for the sixth and seventh deciles, where the imbalance is about –0.3 under HP1 and –0.67 under HP2.[15] Indeed, the imbalances design a U curve – which is the result of the top managing to displace a significant part of what should be its due towards the bottom, which combines with a condition of effective rates of both direct and indirect taxation declining monotonically as wealth/income increases. In other words, even if those belonging to the upper middle of the distribution enjoy a relative privilege over the lower strata, this is balanced by their greater fiscal capacity – so they end up paying more, simply because they can afford to, whilst being unable to subtract from taxation as high a share of their income/wealth as the richest. This is an interesting and non-obvious result to which we will return, but before doing so we need to compare the situation in 1550 to that in 1750.

For 1750, we use the aggregate wealth distribution reconstructed for that year (also to estimate the share of rural population for each bracket), and we apply the higher fiscal pressure of 8.5%, as already discussed. We then make the additional adjustment of considering 'rich' the top 10% of the population, not just the top 5%. Consequently, the whole of the tenth decile now enjoys the maximum possible rates of income saved – but we still reserve to the top 5% ownership of privileged property, which we assume to be the same share of their patrimony as in 1550. Other changes in the parameters of our simplified model of the fiscal system of the Republic of Venice do not seem to be necessary. The estimates for 1750 are reported in Table 4.3.

By 1750, the fiscal system of the Republic remained highly regressive – and indeed, this could not have been different given that no attempts were made to introduce progressive elements of taxation and considering that some key parameters, and particularly the share of indirect taxation, remained about the same as in 1550. Admittedly, it is probable that the relative disadvantage suffered by the rural population compared to the urban reduced during the period – so it might be that in 1550 we are relatively closer to HP2 than to HP1 compared to 1750 – but this was more than counterbalanced by the increase in the per capita fiscal burden, which widened the distance between the top and the bottom of the

---

[15] Even though in absolute numbers the fiscal disadvantage was maximum for the sixth and seventh decile, in proportion (% tax /% wealth/income) it was still higher for the bottom 10% than for any other part of the distribution – which is the obvious result of the monotonically declining total rates shown in Table 4.2.

Table 4.3 *Fiscal pressure per socio-economic stratum in the Republic of Venice (Terraferma) in 1750*

Population (poorest to richest)	Indirect Tax (HP1)[a]	Indirect Tax (HP2)[a]	Direct Tax (HP1)[a]	Direct Tax (HP2)[a]	Total pressure: direct + indirect (HP1)	Total pressure: direct + indirect (HP2)	% Wealth and Income[b]	% of Tax Burden (HP1)[c]	% of Tax Burden (HP2)[c]
10	7.54	8.54	1.74	1.76	9.27	10.30	0.18	0.22	0.27
10	7.49	8.40	1.72	1.73	9.21	10.14	0.35	0.42	0.52
10	7.28	7.88	1.72	1.73	9.00	9.62	0.59	0.69	0.83
10	7.08	7.40	1.72	1.73	8.80	9.13	0.77	0.88	1.03
10	6.89	6.94	1.72	1.73	8.61	8.67	1.30	1.45	1.64
10	6.70	6.51	1.71	1.72	8.41	8.22	1.89	2.06	2.27
10	6.51	6.11	1.71	1.72	8.22	7.82	3.07	3.27	3.50
10	6.33	5.73	1.69	1.68	8.02	7.41	5.37	5.58	5.80
10	6.16	5.37	1.67	1.65	7.83	7.02	11.74	11.91	12.02
5	6.03	5.12	1.67	1.65	7.70	6.77	15.63	15.60	15.43
5	6.03	5.12	1.53	1.45	7.56	6.57	59.12	57.92	56.69
Mean[d]	6.8	6.8	1.7	1.7	8.5	8.5			

[a] Effective tax rates.

[b] We assume the distribution of wealth to be the same as the distribution of income (see main text).

[c] Obtained by applying the estimates of the total percent fiscal pressure (under HP1 or HP2: columns 6 and 7) to the share of income/wealth of each percentile (column 8), then recalibrating so that the shares of the tax burden for all percentiles add up to 100.

[d] Means are weighted by % of population.

distribution in terms of points of fiscal pressure. Looking at total pressure, in 1750 the effective rate on the poorest 10% was 9.27% and that of the top 5% was 7.56% under HP1, while under HP2 it was 10.3% and 6.57% respectively. This means that the distance in percentage points of taxation was in the range 1.71–3.73%, which compares rather unfavourably to the 0.98–2.13% of 1550 as indeed, the wedge between the two extremes seems to double. We can take this as a possible measure of the overall regressiveness of the fiscal systems in 1550 and 1750. We would reach the same conclusion by applying another popular measure of regressiveness: the sum of the absolute values of the differences between the effective rate and the proportional rate. Measured in this way, regressiveness would increase from the range 2.67–6 in 1550 to 4.77–10.71 in 1750. However, all these measures are heavily influenced by the increase in per capita taxation. A third possible indicator of overall regressiveness is the sum of the absolute values of the differences between % of income/wealth and % of tax paid at each level of the society (reported in Figure 4.6 for 1550). If we calculate it, we discover that in 1550 the total 'imbalance' varies in the range of 3.5–7.53 percentage points, declining to 2.5–5.25 in 1750. This decline occurred over time, as at an intermediate date, 1650, the range is 2.88–6.37.[16] In absolute values, the decline was monotonic for almost all social strata, with the exception of the ninth decile which shows an opposite tendency (hence experiencing a worsening of its relative situation), and partly of the eighth as seen in Figure 4.7, where for simplicity we report just the mean of HP1 and HP2 for all three dates.

While the aspect of the curve did not change, continuing to have its characteristic 'U-shape', the size of the in balances reduced in time. In other words, the poorest 80% of the population ended up paying a smaller share of the overall tax, while the richest 20% saw its burden increase. This result might seem surprising, due to the apparent contradiction of having an increase in the wedge between the effective tax rates paid by the extremes of the distribution, and a rebalancing towards a greater equality of treatment regarding the shares of the tax paid. This apparent contradiction, though, has a clear reason: the rebalancing in the tax paid is simply due to the increase in the concentration of wealth which occurred monotonically during the period. The top 5% in particular, who owned 50.32% of the total wealth in 1550, had seen their share increase to 52.62% by 1650, and even 59.12% by 1750. The large increase in their

[16] The estimate for 1650 has been obtained by using the relevant wealth distribution and setting the overall fiscal pressure at 5.8%, the share of indirect taxation at 87% (7 percentage points higher than in 1550 and 1750: see Figure 4.5 for the time trend followed by this variable), the prevalence of the poor at 10% and that of the rich at 5% (in accordance with Table 2.4 in Chapter 2).

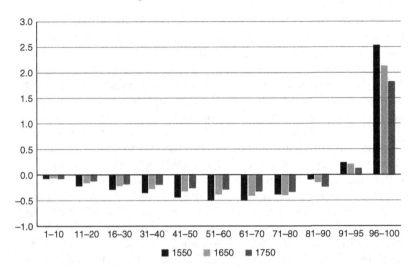

Figure 4.7 Regressiveness of the fiscal system of the Republic of Venice (*Terraferma*), 1550–1750 (% wealth/income – % tax paid; average of HP1 and HP2).

fiscal capacity – and the parallel reduction in that of the mid-distribution: the sixth decile for example experienced a share declining from 3.87% in 1550 to 1.89% – explains why they were now paying a much larger share of the overall tax. Indeed, imagine a dystopian society where the top 5% earns/owns 100% of the income/wealth. Then apply an extremely regressive fiscal system – as punishing to the poor as this could be in principle, in practice the overall regressiveness measured as the difference between share of income/wealth and share of tax paid would be zero, simply because the 95% poorest population will not have any income or wealth to be taxed.

The analyses conducted so far allow us to reach a number of relevant conclusions on the nature of the fiscal system of the Republic of Venice (and more generally, on European preindustrial fiscal systems, which had similar characteristics). Although our estimates are the result of a dramatic simplification of the way in which such system was actually structured, the key findings seem to be quite sound, and we do not expect that they could be upturned by more refined estimates. In synthesis:

1. The fiscal system of the Republic of Venice was highly regressive throughout the early modern period. Hence the ability of the reported continuous increases in per capita taxation to make the distribution of both income and wealth ever more unequal in time is fully confirmed.

2. In absolute terms, the most disadvantaged were those in the middle and upper middle of the distribution (fourth to eighth deciles), as they had relatively high fiscal capacity but a relatively low ability to save or more generally, to subtract part of their income from taxation. Regarding the poorest part of the population, paradoxically it was somewhat protected by its lack of means, and de facto it contributed only marginally to the overall revenues of the central state.

3. The time trend in the actual degree of regressiveness depends on the measure employed, as the difference in the effective rates paid by the richest and the poorest population increased, as well as the sum of the differences between effective and proportional rates, while the difference in the share of income/wealth and that of the tax paid declined. The latter outcome, however, is simply the result of increasing inequality. In other words, the higher the inequality, the lower the regressiveness, at least according to some parameters – but the system, if made to evolve ad infinitum, would converge towards fiscal proportionality and the maximum possible inequality (a Gini of wealth concentration of 1 or close to it), *not* towards progressivity.

4. Progressivity could only have been achieved through institutional innovations of a kind that was never attempted in the Republic of Venice in the period considered here, and only experimented (without much success) in very few other European areas, particularly Holland.

5. The marginal impact on inequality of an increase in the per capita fiscal burden depends on the initial distribution, itself the consequence of earlier iterations (savings translate into acquisition of new property) – as the overall regressiveness of the system depends in part on the distribution of taxable income/assets. Such impact will always be positive and can be expected to be greater, the lower the initial inequality. In other words, we have identified a mechanism which might have promoted, *ceteris paribus*, convergence towards high levels of inequality across Europe.

Until now, we have focused on central taxation. However, in the time period considered here, also local taxation increased very significantly. For example in Padua, the fiscal burden collected on each *lira* of *estimo* almost trebled from the 1550s to the 1710s while in Treviso, the same measure in the 1650s and 1660s was about two and a half that usual in the 1580s and 1590s. These taxes were collected to satisfy both the local, and the central financial needs, however, as the overall increase in the fiscal pressure of the central state was much more modest in these periods (see earlier), we have strong evidence of a very sizeable increase in the levy imposed by local institutions (Pezzolo 1990, 299; 2006a, 71–72). Both for reasons of synthesis and the lack of data, we will not develop further the analysis of local fiscal pressure. It will suffice to note that also local taxation had a markedly regressive character. Indeed, as direct local taxation was still based on the *estimo*, and as indirect taxation had the same characteristics of that imposed by the central state, the structure of the local fiscal systems was entirely comparable to the central one – hence they were similarly regressive. This being said, there were some significant differences between the local fiscal systems, which could for example have a different prevalence of direct and indirect taxation, as well as a different total fiscal pressure. We refer to Chapter 1 for details about the local fiscal systems. Here, we will conclude by stressing that not only did local fiscality contribute to the overall capacity of the system to lead to inequality increases, but it could also determine divergent distributional developments between each area. For example, provinces characterized by lower fiscal rates and greater reliance on direct taxation are expected to have suffered relatively less internal inequality growth compared with provinces having relatively high tax rates and more reliant on indirect taxation. These possible divergent trends would have some impact on the inequality levels throughout the whole of the *Terraferma* (i.e. those we measured from our aggregate distributions), however, in ways and with net effects that would be difficult to determine a priori, and which should be the object of additional and specific research.

4.4   Measuring Redistribution: Public Expenditure

In the fiscal systems of today in Western countries, not only is post-tax inequality lower than pre-tax due to the progressivity of taxation, but the very public expenditure contributes to a further reduction in inequality, through the offer of welfare. In 2016 the average for Organisation for Economic Co-operation and Development (OECD) countries was for social spending to be 21% of GDP (OECD 2016) – but if we compare it to state budgets instead of GDP, the share is obviously much higher. In 2015, for example, social protection, health services and education accounted for more than 60% of the budgets of almost all OECD countries, sometimes exceeding 70% (the most notable exception was South Korea with just below 50%). At the other extreme, expenses for 'defence' services usually accounted for no more than 2–3% of the state budget in these countries, the main outlier being the United States, where they reached almost 9% (OECD 2017).

The situation typical of preindustrial Europe was exactly the opposite. In the earlier sections we demonstrated that fiscal systems were highly regressive. Here we focus on the expenditures, arguing that there is no reason whatsoever to think that public provision of welfare and social services compensated for the tendency for inequality to increase as a result of regressive taxation – quite the contrary as indeed, it seems clear that in the long run public expenditure produced additional inequality. The first aspect to consider, is that social expenditure – which is the component of expenditure that can be safely assumed to be almost automatically inequality-reducing – was very low. In a recent, pioneering article, Van Bavel and Rijpma (2016) argued that across Europe from 1400 to 1850, total social spending (both private and public and both central and local) amounted to 1–2% of GDP (or lower in less developed areas), with a maximum of 2.9–3.3% reported for western Netherlands around 1760[17]. In central-northern Italy, social spending would have been around 1–1.1% of GDP in 1430, 1.8–2% in 1640, and 2–2.3% in 1790. These figures might be underestimating social spending in Italian countries, given that they seem to include only poor relief (and not, for example, education or central public health expenditures: see later), but probably not by much. Earlier estimates of 'relief expenditure' provided by Lindert (1998, 114) for England and Wales equal 1.22% in 1688, 0.99% in 1749, 1.59% in 1776, 1.75% in 1783–85, finally exceeding 2% only from ca. 1800. Also in this case, the figures include both private and public relief expenditure.

There are two ways of looking at these figures. On the one hand, if we take into account the fact that preindustrial European societies were still relatively poor compared to contemporary societies, a 1–2% of GDP absorbed by social spending is clearly not-negligible – perhaps even, in a sense, 'impressive', as stated by Van Bavel and Rijpma (2016, 183). On the other hand, if we are to assess the ability of this level of expenditure to upturn the redistributive consequences of regressive taxation, we have to conclude that it must, in fact, have been very limited. To demonstrate this point, we begin by looking at the expenditures of the central state. In Table 4.4 we report our estimates of the structure of public expenditures, distinguished between military expenditures (for equipment, maintenance of armies and fleets including wages paid to soldiers, sailors and officials, maintenance of fortifications, etc.), interest paid over the public debt, 'social expenditure' and finally 'other' expenditures which include state bureaucracy and administration.

As can be seen from the table, during the period 1582–1780 social expenditure was an almost-negligible component of the overall state expenditure, usually around 0.2% in the sixteenth and early seventeenth centuries, then usually a little more (0.4–0.5%) from the 1630s to 1740,

---

[17] About expenditure on poor relief in the Dutch Republic, see also De Vries and Van der Woude (1997) and Prak (1999).

Table 4.4 *Expenditures of the Republic of Venice by destination, 1582–1780 (% of total)*

Year	Military	Service of Debt	Social Expenditure	Other
1582	54.2	34.1	0.2	11.5
1587	40.9	12.8	0.5	45.8
1594	44.9	12.6	0.2	42.2
1602	55.9	8.2	0.2	35.7
1633	63.6	19.9	0.4	16.1
1637	59.2	19.0	0.5	21.3
1641	62.4	14.8	0.5	22.2
1679	40.3	42.0	0.1	17.6
1736	41.4	32.4	0.4	25.8
1740	23.4	34.4	0.5	41.7
1750	28.5	40.1	0.6	30.8
1760	30.8	35.0	0.7	33.4
1770	30.3	32.8	0.6	36.3
1780	30.4	26.9	1.3	41.3

Sources: Our estimates from information published in Bilanci I; Bilanci II; Bilanci III; Bilanci IV; Pezzolo 2006, 77; and only for 1582, Pezzolo 1990 (note that Pezzolo reported 3,000 ducats of expenditure for alms in 1582, to which we have added an estimated 1,200 ducats for the health office, i.e. the same value that we have estimated for 1594).

rising further, to 0.6–0.7%, during 1750–70. Interestingly, the highest share of social spending is found at the very end of the period, in 1780 (1.3%). These low figures are even more impressive as we have carefully included all the different possible components of social expenditure that were identified in the balance sheets of the Republic. In 1679 for example, out of 5,664 ducats of social expenditure, 35.6% went to alms paid to pious institutions (*elemosine a luoghi pii*), 25.5% to public teachers (*maestri di grammatica*, who provided basic education to whoever was interested in receiving it), 21.1% to the central health board (*Ufficio di Sanità*) and the remaining 17.7% to donations of various kinds. From the eighteenth century there is a greater consistency in the specific voices of social expenditure identified by the balance sheets of the Republic, which are summarized in Table 4.5.

During the eighteenth century, alms of various kinds represented by far the greatest component of the social spending of the central state, moving in the range 59.4–70.6% and even rising to 77.6–98.8% if we also include the contributions for the *Ospetal della Pietà*, an orphanage and later

Table 4.5 *Composition of the social expenditures of the Republic of Venice, 1736–1780 (ducats)*

	1736	1740	1750	1760	1770	1780
Alms	13,533	15,565	16,686	16,980	16,060	48,207
Alms for Dalmatia	55	165	141	141	186	153
Alms for the Levant	440	270	289	521	568	634
Alms for the *Terraferma*	1,995	2,272	2,152	4,326	3,800	3,532
Hospital (*Ospetal pietà*)	7,560	7,110	8,017	6,568	6,131	5,257
Salaries for the health office	252	966	580	1,283	2,834	4,109
Paper and books for the health office	31	100	40	95	137	110
Buildings for the health office	0	732	2,365	0	0	0
Expenses of the health office	0	0	1,006	2,526	2,980	5,428
Extraordinary expenses for the health office	0	0	0	3,312	2,000	7,011
TOT	23,866	27,180	31,276	35,752	34,696	74,441

Sources: Bilanci III; Bilanci IV.

conservatoire in Venice (Pullan 1971).[18] This fact provides some confirmation of the view that poor relief alone constitutes a good proxy for overall public social spending, as is implicit in the literature discussed earlier. The residual social expenditure was entirely absorbed by expenditures connected to the central institutions for public health. These increased in time, from just 1.2% of the total in 1736, to 20–22% during 1760–80, although almost half of such increase can be attributed to extraordinary expenses.[19] In these later sources we no longer find any trace of the public teachers, which were usually present in the balance sheets of the seventeenth century.

If we take these figures, which cover the entire Republic, as representative of the shares of social spending in the *Terraferma* alone, and if we remember (see the earlier section) that there, the fiscal pressure of the central state amounted to 5–8.5% of GDP during 1550–1750, we can hypothesize that the level of social spending as a % of GDP moved from about 0.01% in 1550 to 0.034–0.043% in 1750. In 1780 it might have just

[18] According to Pullan (1971, 413), in 1603 the *Ospetal della Pietà* sustained expenditures for 24,000 ducats, far exceeding its own revenues of 8,000 ducats. Hence the need for regular financial help.

[19] The increase might be partly due to the plagues that, coming from Ottoman lands, besieged Venetian territories in the Dalmatia in that period. For example, the port of Split was affected by plague during 1763–64 and 1784 (Andreozzi 2015).

exceeded 0.1% of GDP.[20] Although it would be erroneous to dismiss this public effort as 'negligible' *tout court*, surely its distributive impact was extremely limited, at least if seen from the point of view of its ability to moderate inequality. However, if we want to assess the power of public social spending as a whole to affect distribution, we must consider also the local governments. For them, the information we have is sparser. For example we can calculate that in rural communities of the province of Vicenza in 1607, expenses for public doctors amounted to 2% of the local budget, and those for public teachers to 0.7%. If we add to this the expenditure for other health services we reach an overall social expenditure of 3.9% of the budget (estimates based on data from Knapton 1981b, 400). In general, there are good reasons to think that across the *Terraferma*, local social spending might have been somewhat higher, at least as a percent of the budget, compared to state social spending – but in absolute terms it was still very limited and what is more, the resources used to fund it had been collected through local fiscal systems which were about as regressive as the central fiscal system.

Indeed, to assess the overall long-run distributive impact of public expenditure, we should focus on its main components: military spending and the service of public debt. In Figure 4.8, which covers a longer period (1575–1780) and more data points than would be possible if we had to distinguish social spending from the rest (as in Table 4.4), it can clearly be seen that until the mid-seventeenth century, the military absorbed on average more than 50% of the state budget. This share declined from the second half of the seventeenth century, with a parallel rise in the expenditure for servicing the public debt, which peaked at 42% of the state budget in 1679 and then started a path of slow decline. Throughout the eighteenth century, however, these two budget voices together accounted for 60–70% of all expenses. These observed trends are closely related to the general historical development of the Republic during the seventeenth and eighteenth centuries. In particular, the long War of Candia (1645–69) required huge increases in military spending and indeed, the overall expenses incurred for that war might have amounted to the enormous sum of 125 million ducats. To a significant degree, the war was financed by deficit spending, which led the yearly expenditures for interests on the public debt to increase dramatically. From 1670 attempts were made to reduce the public debt, but they were partly compromised by the need to finance another conflict against the Ottomans, the Morean War of 1684–99. Even though the Republic turned out victorious in this conflict, in a

---

[20] Estimates obtained by applying the % of social spending on the state budget to the % of GDP collected through central taxes.

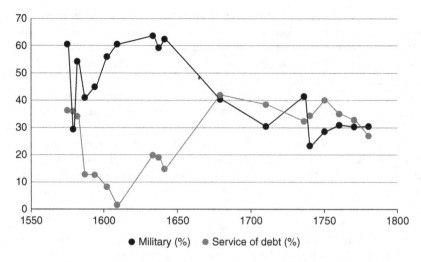

Figure 4.8 Share of the budget of the Republic of Venice spent on the military and on servicing the public debt, 1575–1780 (%).

sense the Morean War continued to incur sustained military spending also after its end, given that vast amounts of resources were invested in fortifying the newly acquired territories in Greece – which did not prevent the Ottomans from retaking the Morea (i.e. the Peloponnese peninsula) after the Second Morean War of 1714–18 (Pezzolo 2006a, 80–81). This was the last conflict that the Republic fought against the Ottomans, after which it started to actively pursue neutrality – a change in diplomatic attitude that allowed expenditures in the military to shrink to about 30% of the central budget.

It is difficult to think that military expenditure, given its nature, might have helped to reduce inequalities in the long run. On the contrary, as we argue below, it probably fostered further inequality. Before discussing this hypothesis, it should be clarified that, as has been rightly argued by Pezzolo (2006a, 83), a very significant part of the resources invested in the military did not go to the population of the Republic, so it could not have affected local household inequality directly. This was surely true for the expenditure related to the armies, given the tendency of the Republic of Venice to rely heavily upon mercenary *condottieri* and their troops recruited abroad, mostly from specialized areas of central Italy like the Marches. This was especially the case during the fifteenth and sixteenth centuries (Mallett 1974; Mallett and Hale 1984, 312–30; Alfani 2013a, 115–16). However, during the early modern period, 'the Venetian government favoured the stable placement of military units within its boundaries, units which, at least during peacetime, represented the largest share of the Venetian military potential' (Pezzolo 2006a, 83, our translation).

Even though the wages paid to these military units were mostly spent locally, including in the *Terraferma*, it is unclear to what degree the units themselves were recruited from the *Terraferma* or elsewhere. According to an estimate, at the end of the sixteenth century Venetian subjects might have accounted for just about 20% of the captains of the army, and about 15% of infantrymen, corporals and sergeants (Mallett and Hale 1984, 349). Consequently, the ability of the army expenditure to affect the income distribution in the *Terraferma* was mostly indirect, i.e. through the part of the wages earned by foreigners spent locally and through spending for the army maintenance. However, much of the cost of billeting was sustained, not by the central state, but by the local communities, promoting the rise in the local fiscal pressure reported previously – and thus contributing *locally* to increase inequality through regressive taxation, as well as to making the general fiscal structure of the state (central and local taxation taken together) even more regressive as the cost for billeting weighed heavily on rural communities while the cities were relatively spared, as was also common elsewhere (Knapton 1981a; 1981b; Pezzolo 2006, 67; Alfani 2013a; Buono, Di Tullio and Rizzo 2016). Finally, local expenditure was significant during peacetime, but it represented a much smaller share of the total military spending during wartime. The long War of Candia is the most striking case, as enormous amounts of money were syphoned towards territories that ultimately were lost to the enemy (Pezzolo 2006, 83). The overall situation might have been different in the case of the navy, given that arguably a larger part of the related expenditure stayed within the broader boundaries of the Republic (i.e. including the *Stato da Mar*); however, this might have only marginally affected the *Terraferma*.

Not only did a large part of the military expenditures not affect – either directly or indirectly – the population of the Republic, but the part which did probably helped to further increase inequality. A first aspect to consider is that a significant part of the expenditures for equipment and provisioning went through big military contractors, and other members of the social and economic elite. This point has been made for other European areas (Alfani 2015; Alfani and Ryckbosch 2016) and it is valid also for the Republic of Venice, as the central state relied regularly on merchants, both from the capital and from the *Terraferma*, to provide enormous amounts of equipment and raw materials to the army and, possibly even more importantly, to the fleet (Pezzolo 1990, 165).

A second aspect to consider is that the wage differentials within the army itself were so steep that they would presumably have tended to create inequality on their own. At the bottom of the hierarchy, soldiering seems to have been 'a subsistence occupation' (Mallett and Hale 1984, 500). Indeed, in 1616 an ordinary soldier earned 23 *soldi* a day, i.e. little more than half the pay of a labourer in the construction sector (41.63 *soldi*: Mallet and Hale 1984, 498) At the other extreme, a small number of *condottieri* or high commanders received vastly larger wages, probably 40–45 times those of an ordinary infantry soldier.[21] This strikingly high wage differential between bottom and top did not decline in the seventeenth century, if a comparison with the Spanish-controlled State of Milan in 1656 is indicative. There, the commander of the *Tercio de Lombardia* received a pay 47 times as large as that of a lowly soldier, while that of the *Tercio de Savoia*, 38.5 (Alfani and Di Tullio 2018). To make a comparison with today's societies, in Western Europe in 2001 the earnings ratio between production workers and chief executive officers (CEOs) varied in the range of 17 (Germany) to 32 (France) (Osberg and Smeeding 2006, 465). However, the *condottieri* of the Republic had to sustain large expenses to reaffirm their status and position, and it has been hypothesized that they must have spent their entire wage, or almost, in maintaining themselves and their personal retinue (Pezzolo 1990, 156–57) – although it goes without saying that the position that they occupied gave them many collateral opportunities for personal advancement and enrichment.

The final component of public spending that we have to consider is the service of the public debt. The amount of the public debt of the Republic of Venice fluctuated in time. After having grown during the wars of the first half of the sixteenth century, by the beginning of the seventeenth the Venetian public debt had been reduced to almost zero. However, in the subsequent decades it started to grow again, and boomed during the War of Candia (Pezzolo 2006, 88 ff.). The local elites provided most of the resources needed by the central state, thereby concentrating in their hands the shares of the public debt, as was commonly the case throughout Europe. For example, for Tuscany in 1427 it has been shown that the shares of the public debt were much more concentrated than any other component of wealth, in particular real estate (Herlihy 1978, 139), while in the Dutch Republic during the early modern period, increases in the entry sum needed to subscribe to public debt tended to reserve that kind of investment to the economic elites (Van Bavel 2016, 192). However, as

---

[21] Our estimate based on various pieces of information published in Mallett and Hale (1984). Additional details in Alfani and Di Tullio (2018).

per military spending, the expenditure for servicing the public debt did not flow entirely into the hands of the subjects of the Republic. In 1641, for example, it was found that about one seventh of the consolidated debt was owned by foreigners. This share grew during the seventeenth century, again as a consequence of the War of Candia as at the end of the war, the Genoese financiers alone owned over one third of at least some components of the public debt. During the century, though, the inhabitants of the *Terraferma* also increased their share of the public debt, spreading its ownership across the Republic's society to a certain extent – but without altering the fact that the lion's share was owned by patricians, merchants and other rich members of the bourgeoisie (Pezzolo 1990, 190–91; 2006, 96–97). The reason why both the foreigners and the local elites aspired to acquire shares of the public debt lies in the favourable conditions being offered. First of all, this form of investment was perceived as relatively safe, a perception which was strengthened by the involvement of the governing elites as lenders: 'rulers and oligarchies held large portions of debt and that reduced risk. Urban patricians were unlikely to default on loans that would endanger one of their most important sources of income' (Pezzolo 2012, 279). Second, the rates paid were non-negligible and could reach an annual nominal interest rate of 7–8%, and sometimes even higher, especially during wartime (Pezzolo 2006a, 2012). Given the extremely high concentration of public debt, interest payments clearly helped to further concentrate resources in the hands of precisely those social groups which had benefited from relatively lower effective tax rates, thus increasing the distance between the upper ranks of the income and wealth distribution, and the middling and lower ranks. As the share of the overall expenditure destined to servicing the Venetian debt showed an overall tendency to increase during the early modern period, it might be that the capacity of public spending to foster inequality also increased – if we make the additional hypothesis that interest payments had an even greater capacity for increasing inequality than military spending.

To sum up our discussion of the redistributive impact of central public spending, we have to underline that we found no reason whatsoever for arguing that it could have been mitigating the consequences of regressive taxation. This is because social spending was a very limited share of the total, and because both military spending and the service of the public debt had an inequality-promoting power of their own. The situation, then, is confirmed as perfectly specular to the current one, characterized by the prevalence of social spending among different kinds of public expenditure. Hence, we have confirmed the ability of the rise of the fiscal-military state to generate inequality. Indeed, we have identified what seems to have been a major cause of inequality growth during the early modern period, as discussed in the concluding section.

4.5   Conclusion: The Rise of the Fiscal State as a Main Driver of Inequality Growth across Early Modern Europe

The analysis of the redistributive consequences of taxation and public spending allowed us to connect the general reconstruction of the fiscal system of the Republic of Venice proposed in Chapter 1, with the study of long-term trends in economic inequality and social polarization in Chapters 2 and 3. Indeed, we have been looking for the roots of the tendency for both inequality and social polarization to increase which seems to have characterized the early modern period, both in the Venetian mainland and elsewhere in Europe. The aim of this concluding section is to make even more explicit some important connections, as well as the broader implications of our findings for the burgeoning research on economic inequality.

Throughout the period that we have covered, the fiscal system was highly regressive: the effective fiscal rate weighing on the poorest 10% of the population might have been as little as 20–25%, and as much as 55–60% higher than that paid by the top 5%. Regressiveness means that post-tax inequality is automatically higher than pre-tax inequality, hence simply by its structure, taxation is able to produce more income inequality. If we factor in some reasonable hypotheses about savings,[22] regressive taxation can also determine a continuous pressure for wealth inequality to grow.[23] During the early modern period, the fiscal system of the Republic did not undergo any radical changes – but the per capita fiscal burden did grow very significantly. This, which is surely one of the main features of the historical process known as the 'rise of the fiscal state', constitutes another factor leading inequality (of both income and wealth) also to grow over time: as the ability of a structurally regressive fiscal system to extract more and more inequality depends on the intensity of taxation. Such a phenomenon was in no way counterbalanced by public expenditure, given that social spending was only a marginal component of the budget of the central state, while military spending and the service of the public debt became

---

[22] A whole family of economic models connecting savings to wealth accumulation across generations has been generated by a seminal article by Meade (1964).Some of these models also underline the impact of impartible inheritance, which strongly increases the ability of savings to lead to greater wealth inequality across generations. For a synthesis, see Roine and Waldenström (2015, 552–54).

[23] Indeed, this would happen even if savings were proportional to income (as they are a share of post-tax income, and taxation was regressive). But they were not: as will be remembered from Section 4.3, the percent of income saved grows with income.

ever more important, especially from the War of Candia of 1645–69. Also from this point of view, such war proved to be a real turning point in the history of the Republic of Venice. As we have argued, both military spending and, even more clearly, the service of the public debt tended to direct the resources, already unevenly collected through regressive taxation, towards the hands of small elites of various kinds – thus favouring further inequality increase, instead of moderating it by provision of welfare and socio-economic protection.

But the structure and intensity of taxation might explain more than simply the monotonic growth in inequality found across the *Terraferma* in the early modern period. An important finding from our analysis of the prevalence of the rich and the poor is that both of them tended to become relatively more numerous (monotonically in the case of the rich, and with just a temporary interruption caused by the 1630 plague in that of the poor). This growing distance between the top and the bottom of the distribution was confirmed by our analysis of social and economic polarization. In 1500, the richest 50% owners had almost twelve times as much wealth as the poorest 50%, but by 1750, they owned over thirty times as much. The top 10% rich, which already at 1500 owned the lion's share (56.8%) of the overall wealth, in 1750 concentrated in their hands three-quarters of the whole (74.8%) – indeed, the top 1% alone owned 25.1% of the overall wealth of the *Terraferma*. By analysing the actual impact of taxation at different points in the overall distribution (i.e. by comparing the share of wealth/income owned or earned to the share of tax paid), we discovered that the most disadvantaged part of the population was the middle and upper-middle component of the wealth distribution (from the fourth to the eighth decile). In fact, while the rich were protected by relatively low effective rates so that the top 10% ended up paying a much inferior share of the overall tax than would have been their due under proportional taxation, the poor, too, were to some degree 'protected' by their low fiscal capacity. As a matter of fact, the fiscal advantages of the top were paid for by the middle of the distribution. And being in the middle constituted a factor of fiscal fragility of its own. In other words, we can hypothesize that either those placed there managed to climb to the top (thus reducing their effective fiscal rates), or they risked tumbling down to the bottom, emptying the middle strata. Of course, many other factors played a role and taxation could probably not, on its own, have been able to determine the impressive process of polarization suffered by the society of the Venetian mainland – but the distributional dynamics that we have reconstructed and the structure of the relative advantages or disadvantages dispensed by the fiscal system match so closely, that it seems assured that taxation was a key component in shaping distributional changes to a much finer degree than simply promoting overall inequality growth. Further studies will be needed to clarify the actual paths of upwards and downwards social and economic mobility in this area and period, but our research provides at the very least a powerful working hypothesis to understand these processes.

The fact that the rich enjoyed a relatively advantageous fiscal situation did not prevent them from paying, in absolute terms, more tax than anybody else. For example in 1550, the top 5% paid 47–49% of all taxes collected by the central state in the *Terraferma*, while the bottom 10% paid less than 0.3%. The fact that the rich paid more than the poor (albeit not *proportionally* more) was sufficient for the system to be perceived as fair according to the ideal of distributive justice of the time. This is an important point to make also in order to understand how inequality could increase for so long without causing acute social tensions. In fact, an unequal society is not necessarily perceived as an 'unjust' one. Preindustrial Europeans were well aware that their economies and societies were highly unequal, but this situation was usually seen as acceptable, 'natural' and coherent with God's plans (Levi 2003; Alfani 2009b). In other words, 'Although it was clearly recognized that in reality, the rich (*dives*) and the poor (*pauperes*) experienced deeply different social conditions, this situation was never understood as socially or economically unjust' (Alfani and Frigeni 2016, 53). Our analysis suggests that effective tax rates should also be included among these 'different social conditions'.

Another factor, beyond the cultural context, which allowed the system to be perceived as overall 'just', is that the rich gave back, in the form of private charity, part of their incomes. This was a specific requirement of Medieval European societies, clear for example in the tradition of thought related to St. Augustine's *De civitate Dei*, which continued throughout the early modern period: the rich were expected to provide alms for the poor, who in turn prayed for the rich (La Roncière 1974; Alfani and Frigeni 2016). In the Republic of Venice (and especially in Venice itself), it seems that the provision of alms and support to the poor was more based on private institutions and actions, and less on centrally organized institutions, than elsewhere: so, for example, the *scuole* and other confraternities managed a large array of hospices and hospitals for the poor and the sick (D'Andrea 2013, 430–31). These institutions, which we have briefly discussed in Chapter 2 as they had some influence in defining the social stratification of the Republic, significantly increased the poor's access to resources and surely contributed to social cohesion, not least by providing a kind of visible proof of the intrinsic 'justice' governing the system. Of course, seen from the perspective of the modern ideal of justice (which requires, at the very least, equality of rights and of opportunities), the picture is much bleaker. Even if private charity helped to reduce the imbalances generated by the fiscal system (to the sole detriment, once again, of the middling groups: as alms went from the top to the bottom), surely it stopped a long way from providing real equality of opportunities to the poorest strata of society. Additionally, this kind of private redistribution tended to make the poor dependent on the rich, a fact which made social structures more resilient, but not, as it seems, in the sense of helping to achieve in time a better and more open society for all – on the contrary, the expected outcome would be increasing social and economic polarization, which is exactly what we have observed.

The connection between social resilience and inequality should be considered carefully. Indeed, the behaviour of the rich, which might have contributed to an increase in inequality and polarization over time whilst also making the society more resilient, recalls what was found when discussing the ability of economic institutions such as the *fideicommissum* and the *fraterna* to make economic structures less susceptible to large-scale mortality crises like those caused by plague. In other words, we have a growing number of hints that resilience, for preindustrial societies, meant also the ability to tolerate more inequality, or to prevent dramatic (but inequality-reducing) shocks to property structures. The correlation between resilience and equality might, therefore, be negative (the more resilient societies are, or tend to become, more unequal) and not positive as hypothesized by some recent research. Although this is an aspect that should be explored further and from different angles, it leads us to also consider the view, connected to the political 'myths' that Venice purposefully spread but which are not entirely absent from more recent literature, that the Republic of Venice was as a relatively 'charitable' state, and also a somewhat more open one given its 'Republican' character (see critical discussion in D'Andrea 2013; Fusaro 2015). In actual fact, we found no proof whatsoever that the Republic of Venice was any less unequal a society, or any less socially and economically polarized, than other Italian states for which we had comparable information. In the period from 1500 to 1750, inequality across the *Terraferma* increased by +19% if measured with the Gini index (from 0.687 to 0.820), which is not far, for example, from the +24% found for the Sabaudian State, especially considering that this other part of northern Italy was still, by 1750 and with a Gini of 0.782, significantly less unequal that the Venetian mainland. So from the point of view of distribution, there is good reason to argue that the Republic should be seen as a 'normal' case within Italy, and not as an exception.

Not only was the Republic of Venice participating in a process which seems to have been common to all the main Italian pre-unification states, but that same process was also affecting the rest of Europe. In all the areas for which good-quality, data-rich reconstructions of long-term inequality trends are available, we find the same picture: over the five centuries from ca. 1300 to 1800, the only event able to interrupt what seems to have been a constant tendency for inequality to grow, is the Black Death plague of 1347–52. Especially during the early modern period, the general tendency was for inequality of both wealth and income to grow monotonically.[24] This led to a quickly growing debate about the causes of inequality growth, as no single factor seemed able to explain what was found both in economically (and/or demographically) booming or stagnating areas, with increasing or declining urbanization rates, and so on. Even the clearly inequality-promoting process of proletarianization, which is well known to have affected the whole of early modern Europe, did not exert its distributive impact in a continuous and homogeneous way through time. There were instead 'waves' of proletarianization, but we do not see any tendency for cycles in the period 1500–1800.

That is also the period of the rise of the fiscal state – or, if we want to account for the main use of the resources being collected, the 'fiscal-military' state (Bonney 1999; Yun-Casalilla and O'Brien 2012). Everywhere in Europe, the cost of waging war and of defending own boundaries increased, forcing all states aspiring to play an active role on the international scene, or simply to preserve their independence, to increase the per-capita fiscal burden. Even though fiscal systems were not exactly the same across Europe, all of them had a clearly regressive character, due to their high dependence upon indirect taxation (which weighs relatively more on the poor), the partial fiscal exemptions from which the elites benefited, and so on. As we have discussed, even the Dutch Republic, which was probably the European state graced by the more balanced and 'inclusive' fiscal system of the early modern period, still experienced a condition of regressive taxation. As the needs of war pressed on the states whatever their economic, social or demographic condition, and given the substantial institutional similitudes in the distributive character of their fiscal systems (and of their public expenditure, always dominated by military spending and interests on debt), the increase in the per capita fiscal burden is a feature of early modern Europe much more homogeneous and continuous in time than any other factor which has been proposed by earlier research as the possible cause of the widespread tendency for inequality to grow. Consequently,

---

[24] The only (partial) exception so far is Portugal (Reis 2017, 21).

we have identified a common factor that surely favoured the increase in economic disparities across the continent (and probably elsewhere, too: as the rise of the fiscal state also affected other world areas, especially in Asia). Indeed, the regressiveness of the Venetian fiscal system, which we believe could not differ radically from other European states in this respect, was so high and the increase in the per capita fiscal burden across the continent so large[25] that the rise of the fiscal state should probably be considered among the main causes (and maybe even the most important one) of the inequality growth experienced by Europe from the end of the Middle Ages and until the introduction of significantly progressive fiscal systems. The Lion of Venice (the central state) was actively favouring the concentration of the lion's share of the national wealth in the hands of the few.

The fact that we have identified a fundamental pan-European cause of early modern inequality growth does not mean that other factors did not also play a role. If we expand the timeframe to include the Middle Ages as well as the modern age, then we do find phases of inequality reduction, but they were triggered by huge catastrophes like the Black Death and the world wars (Piketty 2014; Milanovic 2016a; Alfani 2015; 2017; Alfani and Ammannati 2017; Scheidel 2017) – so the presence of apparent cycles is not the consequence of endogenous forces (surely not in the case of the Black Death, while the matter is more contentious regarding the world wars). On the contrary, the underlying trend was clearly orientated towards growth. Beyond taxation, factors like economic growth or proletarianization could also have favoured inequality growth in given periods and areas (Alfani and Ryckbosch 2016). What we argue is only that throughout the Middle Ages and the early modern period regressive taxation was surely always there to push societies towards an ever more unequal distribution of resources and of opportunities. But fiscal systems are devised and put in place by human beings and consequently, our study also clearly reaffirms that human agency has the power to shape distribution in the long run and indeed, the lull and even further decline in inequality after the end of World War II was arguably the effect of progressive taxation and of the development of welfare states from the 1950s to the early 1970s (Atkinson, Piketty and Saez 2011). Of course, it is a matter of debate if and why we *should* want a less unequal society – that is ultimately a political

---

[25] The rise in per capita taxation found across Europe was usually higher than that characterizing the Republic of Venice (see Section 4.4), hence our argument for Venice stands *a fortiori* for other European countries, too.

decision. History teaches us, not necessarily that inequality was too high in preindustrial Europe (even though there are some very good reasons to hold that opinion), but that *if* we want a less unequal society, then we have to act to achieve it as it will not come round by itself, and that we have the instruments to obtain this – because otherwise lions of all times and places have never been well known for letting go of their prey spontaneously.

Appendix: Building Regional Distributions of Wealth for the Republic of Venice and for Veneto

In this Appendix, we detail the procedure through which the regional times series of inequality measures used in the book have been produced. This also gives us the opportunity to explore some additional aspects of long-term economic change in the Republic of Venice. All the distributions we use here have been previously standardized by removing the propertyless (in the rare cases when they were present in the sources). This means that we are working with wealth distributions somewhat distorted towards a greater-than-real equality (see Chapter 3, Section 3.1 for further discussion). In the final section of this Appendix we also provide some tentative reconstructions of the complete distributions, propertyless included.

A.1 The Method Used: An Overview

There is a distinct advantage in obtaining inequality measures representative of entire regions or states. First, such measures are a useful synthesis of a number of relevant variables, and particularly of the local wealth or income distributions as well as of the differences in average wealth/income levels between different communities, territories, or environments (in particular, city vs. country).

Consequently, we need to find a way to aggregate the local/communal data in order to obtain measures representative of larger spatial units. We use a method introduced by Alfani (2015) in his case study of the Sabaudian State (Piedmont) and later applied to the Florentine State (Tuscany) as well as to the southern Low Countries by Alfani and Ryckbosch (2016), and to the Kingdom of Naples (Apulia) by Alfani and Sardone (2015). In fact, to build proper regional measures of inequality it does not suffice to calculate averages of local Gini indexes or of other inequality measures, as this would cause a loss of crucial information about between-community inequality. Instead, the methodology followed here constructs regional distributions starting from simplified, or 'fictitious' distributions modeled on information about deciles of income/wealth. For each community, a distribution of 100 elements, or 'fictitious households', is modeled: 10 fictitious households per decile, each having the same share of wealth (1/10 of the decile each). The tenth decile (the rich) is modeled in greater detail, using information about the top 5% and top 1% wealthy, as it is usually found empirically that what happens to the top rich disproportionately influences the overall trend in terms of Gini values.

Using these fictitious distributions it becomes easier to solve weighting problems and issues of comparability across sources, making the task of aggregating community-level data to produce regional reconstructions a relatively easy one (Alfani 2015, 1081–82). First, separate urban and rural inequality series are constructed, which are then weighed based on the urbanization rate in each time period to obtain the final, overall regional distribution. For example, Alfani and Ryckbosch (2016) in their reconstruction of the regional distribution of Tuscany assumed a 20% urbanization rate constant over time (coherently with the available information about urbanization trends in that region). This implied, for each year, building a regional distribution in which urban entries (i.e. the number of 'fictitious households') corresponded exactly to the above shares of the total. This procedure is similar in principle to that described by Milanovic (2005) for calculating 'weighted international inequality'. In the following section we will exemplify its use with reference to Veneto.

Sometimes, the lack of appropriate data requires additional assumptions to be made in order to build the regional distribution. Earlier applications of this method provide adequate and replicable solutions to many of these practical problems, and in order to increase comparability we will adopt the same solutions insofar as possible. For example, in the case of Piedmont, it was impossible to convert the values in the property tax registers of one community to another, except for the Canavese area in 1628–49 – so the assumption was made, that the urban–rural differential in average household wealth across Piedmont was the same as in the seventeenth-century Canavese (Alfani 2015, 1081–82). As shall be seen, we encountered a similar problem (though to a somewhat lesser scale) in our study of Veneto.

A.2   Building Rural and Urban Distributions

The first step in building our 'regional' reconstruction is to define more clearly the entity we want it to be representative of. In fact, differently from the reconstructions recently made available for other parts of Italy (Sabadian State/Piedmont; Florentine State/ Tuscany), the Venetian Republic – or more precisely, the *Terraferma* – does not even roughly correspond to any contemporary Italian administrative region, but to three: Veneto, which was comprised entirely within the Republic's

Table A.1 *Communities included in the reconstruction of the wealth distribution of the Republic of Venice* (Terraferma)

Province:	Bergamo	Padua	Verona	Vicenza	TOT
No. of cities	1	1	1	1	4
No. of rural communities	3	12	9	1	25

Notes: For Padua, *podesterie* and *vicarie* are listed. These rural administrative entities include more than one community.

boundaries,[1] the eastern part of nowadays Lombardy, and Friuli which includes two of the four provinces of the current region Friuli-Venezia Giulia. Here, our aim is to provide a reconstruction representative of the ancient state, not of the contemporary administrative region. As we do not have data for Friuli, we include in our reconstruction data for the provinces for which we have information (even if incomplete) for at least one city and one rural community: the provinces of Padua, Verona and Vicenza in nowadays Veneto, plus the province of Bergamo in nowadays Lombardy. To this overall reconstruction we add a sub-reconstruction related to nowadays Veneto only. Overall, we include in the reconstruction four cities and twenty-five rural communities (or *podesterie* and *vicarie* in the case of the province of Padua: see Chapter 1), as summarized in Table A1.

Building our aggregate series requires facing problems similar to those met by Alfani (2015) in his study of the Sabaudian State, namely the practical impossibility of converting the *estimo* values used in a given province with those of other provinces. This is because, generally speaking, each *estimo* recorded values expressed in the local *lire d'estimo*, i.e. a unit of measurement used solely for the purpose of distributing some fiscal burdens proportionally to each household's share of taxable wealth (see Chapter 1 for details about the inner workings of the local fiscal systems). Any attempt at converting the *lire d'estimo* in common currencies would be surely extremely difficult, maybe altogether impossible, and almost certainly destined to produce dubious results. When we have to compare local inequality measures this is not a problem, as Ginis, percentiles and the like are pure numbers (i.e. their value is independent from the unit of measurement in which the underlying data is expressed). However, when we have to aggregate local data into distributions representative of broader territories, we need to include some information

[1] Exception made for some alpine valleys which Italy acquired only after World War I.

about the relative per capita wealth of each community – as it is well known that urban dwellers tended to be richer than country dwellers, larger cities tended to have greater per capita wealth than smaller cities, and so on (see for example Herlihy 1978 and Alfani and Ammannati 2017 about Tuscany).

Luckily enough, our database comprises two large groups of communities whose fiscal data come from *estimi* covering broad territories: an entire province in the case of Padua, and the entire country (city excluded) in the case of Verona. This means that within the provinces of Padua and Verona, *estimo* values given to each household are directly comparable – exception made for the city of Verona, whose sources are different from those covering its *contado*. The problem, then, is making the distributions related to the province of Padua comparable to those of the Veronese country, to the city of Verona, and to other communities included in the reconstruction.

To solve this problem, and again adopting a solution similar in principle to that used by earlier studies, we recurred to fiscal sources of various kind in order to roughly estimate the differences in average wealth between provinces and, within each province, between the city and the country. Regarding the first aspect, we looked at the surviving balance sheets of the Republic of Venice, where we found information about the gross tax revenue from each province, which can be expected to be closely correlated to overall wealth. This information is available for three years – 1469, 1500, and 1641 – and we used it, together with the available information about provincial population size, to produce point estimates of average wealth differentials for years 1450, 1500 and 1650. We obtained estimates for 1550 and 1600 by means of simple linear interpolation, while for 1400 and 1700 we kept the estimates fixed at the 1450 and 1650 levels respectively (notice that there is no need to produce estimates of wealth differentials at later dates, as after 1700 we have information for communities in the province of Verona only). The weights we used in our reconstruction are summarized in Table A.2.

As can be seen from the table, Padua is the richest province throughout the period, and Bergamo the poorest. Verona and Vicenza occupy intermediary positions. From the sixteenth century, they start getting closer to Padua's average wealth levels, which parallels the growth of the silk industry (especially widespread in the province of Vicenza) relative to Padua's specialty: the wool industry (Ciriacono 1989, 49–52). From the mid-seventeenth century Vicenza swaps places with Verona in being the closest in average wealth to Padua, which seems to reflect the resilience of its textile and other proto-industrial productions compared to the difficulties faced by those of the provinces of both Verona and Padua, as confirmed by many studies (Molà 2000, 222–26; Demo 2001; Pezzolo 2011).

Table A.2 *Relative average household wealth in provinces of the* Terraferma

	Padua	Verona	Vicenza	Bergamo
1400	1	0.76	0.66	0.47
1450	1	0.76	0.66	0.47
1500	1	0.75	0.66	0.47
1550	1	0.78	0.73	0.46
1600	1	0.80	0.80	0.45
1650	1	0.82	0.87	0.44
1700	1	0.82	0.87	0.44

Notes: Value 1 = average wealth in the province of Padua.
Sources: Own elaboration from data published in Bilanci I, 148–49, 172–73, 566. Data about provincial population from Beloch (1994, 498).

At a first glance, the relative position of the province of Bergamo might seem too low – as for example in 1600, its average household wealth would be just 45% that of the province of Padua – but a closer look reveals it to be reasonable. Admittedly, Bergamo's relatively low position might reflect some residual fiscal advantage that the province continued to enjoy in the early modern period, although according to the literature, from the mid-sixteenth or early-seventeenth century this privileged regime had been almost entirely dismantled (see Pezzolo 2000, 217–20 as well as the discussion in Chapter 1). Instead, at least when we focus on cities only, this apparently large differential is more or less in line with what we know from studies about other areas. In fact, Bergamo was a considerably smaller city than the others in our database. Around 1600, for example, it had 18,362 inhabitants compared to the 36,054 of Padua (Beloch 1994, 633) and this contributes to explain, to a large degree at least, the difference in average wealth between the two provinces. Consider, for example, that in 1427 Tuscany, the average household wealth of small cities was only 50–60% that of large cities (Florence excluded. See Herlihy 1978, 136). Similar, and even starker, differences in average household wealth between smaller and larger cities have been reported by Alfani and Ryckbosch (2016, appendix D) in the southern Low Countries during 1600–1900.

When comparing the relative wealth of cities, then, the weights in Table A.2 seem realistic and adequate. Constructing a time series representative of all cities in the database is then a simple matter of (1) converting the actual distributions into fictitious distributions of 100 elements each and (2) using such fictitious distributions, opportunely modified to take into account the weight in Table A.2, to build the overall 'urban' distribution. The results are shown in Figure A.1, where the Ginis calculated from the fictitious distributions related to each city are also shown. As can easily be seen by comparing them with the measures calculated on the actual distribution in Chapter 3 (Figure 3.1), moving from the actual distributions to the related fictitious distributions only marginally alters the Gini values (more generally, the loss of information caused by the procedure is minimal, at least from the point of view of the calculation of basic inequality measures).

The urban series representative of the entire Republic of Venice (*Terraferma*) summarizes well the developments in local urban inequality. During the early modern period, it clearly shows a general trend orientated towards inequality growth (see discussion in Chapters 3 and 4). The actual levels of the Gini indexes reflect both within- and between-cities inequality. As the original distributions have been replaced by 100-terms fictitious distributions, each city contributes equally to the outcome, independently from its real size. This is a useful feature, as it allows to maximize the territorial representativeness of the sample.

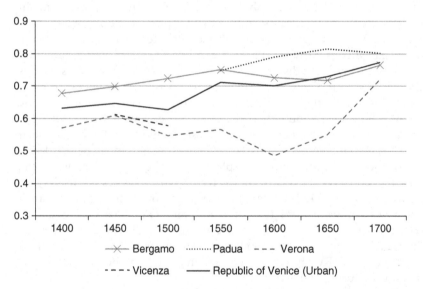

Figure A.1 Urban inequality in the Republic of Venice (*Terraferma*). *Notes*: Gini indexes of wealth inequality calculated on fictitious distributions (compare to Figure 3.1a for the actual distributions related to the four cities included).

The same overall procedure can be applied to the reconstruction of a distribution representative of the rural areas of the Republic. In this case, though, it is difficult to imagine that the average wealth of rural households may vary significantly from one province to the other. Coherently with earlier studies, then, we assumed that the average wealth in different *contadi* was about the same. Building an overall rural distribution was a simple matter of transforming the actual distributions in the *contadi* of Padua and Verona (where the values related to each community can be directly compared to those of others communities) into fictitious distributions and of building a distribution representative of the whole of the *contado* of Bergamo. For the *contado* of Vicenza we have just one series available, albeit of excellent quality (Arzignano). For the purpose of this reconstruction, we have to consider it representative of its entire *contado*, also because for the earlier (<1550) and later (>1700) dates Arzignano is one of the few rural communities for which any information is available (see Table 3.1). Notice that including or excluding Arzignano does not affect much the Gini values, nor does it alter the overall trend.[2]

Figure A.2 shows the overall rural distributions side by side that of each *contado*. As for the cities, the overall rural distribution summarizes well all the information available and also in this case, the tendency throughout the early modern period is clearly orientated towards inequality growth.

A.3   Building the Regional Distribution(s)

In the earlier section, we reconstructed two aggregate time series, related to the urban and the rural environment of the *Terraferma* respectively. To move from these to a series representative of the overall distribution, though, requires solving two additional weighting problems: (1) estimate the difference in the average wealth of cities versus rural communities; (2) weigh the partial urban and rural distributions to reflect the size of the population residing in the cities or in the country.

As already mentioned in Section A.2, to solve the first problem we have to resort to the province of Padua, which is the only one where we can compare directly the average *estimo* values of the city and the surrounding rural areas. We estimated that in the period 1550–1700, the ratio between the average wealth of rural and urban households oscillated within a tight band, from a minimum of 13% in the late sixteenth and early seventeenth centuries, to a maximum of 16% in the mid-seventeenth century. Padua,

---

[2] This is especially true after 1550, as in 1600 the rural Gini is 0.694 including Arzignano and 0.695 excluding it, in 1650 it is 0.727 and 0.722 respectively, 0.730 and 0.709 in 1700, and finally 0.771 and 0.770 in 1750.

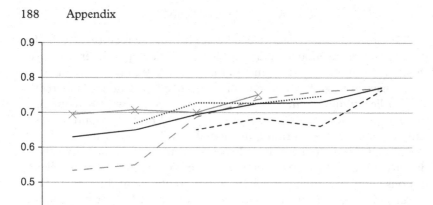

Figure A.2 Rural inequality in the Republic of Venice (*Terraferma*).
Notes: Gini indexes of wealth inequality calculated on fictitious
distributions (compare to Figure 3.1b for the actual distributions related
to rural areas included).

however, was the wealthiest city throughout the period we cover, so
that it is reasonable to assume that the average differences between
city and country were larger here compared to other provinces. As a
consequence, we adjusted the rural/urban wealth ratios to take in the
average position (compared to Padua) of all the communities in our
database, a task which could be easily accomplished by making use of
the weights presented in Table A.2. This resulted in slightly higher
ratios (from a minimum of 17% to a maximum of 21%) which better
represent the average situation across the *Terraferma*. For 1500 we
assumed the same value as in 1550, and for 1750 the same as 1700.
The ratios are shown in Figure A.3. Notice that these weights are in
line with those used in earlier studies. For example, in the case of the
Florentine State, Alfani and Ryckbosch (2016, appendix D) used a
rural/urban average wealth ratio varying from 29% in 1450 to 21% in
1750. A slightly lower ratio in the Republic of Venice reflects the
significantly larger size of its main cities compared to the Florentine
State.

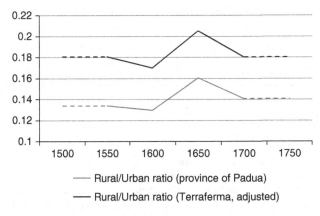

Figure A.3 Rural/urban average wealth ratio in the province of Padua, 1500–1750.

Regarding the relative weight to be given to the urban and rural components in the overall distribution, we used the urbanization rates provided by Zannini (2010, 160), which we integrated with recent findings (especially Alfani and Percoco 2018) to cover the period immediately following the 1630 plague (Table A.3; also represented graphically in Figure A.3). If we consider cities with more than 5,000 inhabitants, urbanization rates were about 21% in the late fifteenth century, rising to a maximum of 24% at around 1550 and later slowly declining. The 1630 plague opened huge holes in the urban population, which by 1650 was still just 15% of the total and later stabilized at slightly over 18%. For some dates, Zannini (2010) also provides information for cities with more than 10,000 inhabitants, whose share of the overall population was 21% in 1550, peaked at about 22.5% in 1600, declined abruptly due to the plague and stabilized at a level of 14–15% during the eighteenth century. The fact that the differences in urbanization rates for cities >5,000 and >10,000 are modest reflects the relatively large size of the urban centres of the Republic.

Given the relatively tight band within which the Republic's urbanization rates varied, and considering the very limited impact that these fluctuations would have in the aggregate distribution, we assumed a 20% urbanization rate throughout for the sake of simplicity, exception made for years 1550 and 1600 when we assumed 25% and 1650 when we assumed 15%. To clarify the implications of this, when the urbanization rate is 20% we have to maintain a 4:1 urban-to-rural ratio in the elements of the distributions. For example in 1600, when we have a 400-elements rural distribution (100 each for the four *contadi*) and a 300-elements urban distribution (100 each

Table A.3 *Overall population and urbanization rates in the Republic of Venice (Italian territories only), 1450–1800*

	Population	Urbanization rates (cities >5,000, %)	Urbanization rates (cities >10,000, %)
1500	1,400,000	20.8	
1550	1,650,000	24.1	21.2
1600	1,700,000	22.8	22.5
1650	1,500,000	15.1	
1700	2,000,000	18.2	
1750	2,175,000	18.4	15.1
1800	2,300,000	18.4	14.3

Sources and *notes:* Our elaboration from data published by Zannini (2010, 144,160) exception made for urbanization rates in 1650 (not provided by Zannini) for which we produced our own estimate from information provided by Alfani and Percoco (2018) about the consequences of the 1630 plague for the urban population of the Republic of Venice.

for the cities of Bergamo, Padua and Verona) we built a 1,500-elements distribution representative of the whole of the *Terraferma* by copying in three times the rural distribution and once the urban distribution. The results are shown in Figure A4, where we compare the overall reconstruction to its components, i.e. the urban and rural distributions introduced in the earlier section.

As can be see, the series representative of the Republic of Venice (or at least, of the *Terraferma*) clearly shows the tendency for inequality to grow during the early modern period. If we look at the aggregate, such growth is in fact monotonic, differently from the urban reconstruction which shows short periods of inequality decline (albeit the tendency is clearly orientated towards inequality growth in the cities, too) but similarly to the rural reconstruction. The series for the entire *Terraferma* follows more closely the trend of the rural series than of the urban, and this for the simple reason that the urban and rural components are weighted according to urbanization rates – and the vast majority of the population resided in the country. It is also interesting to notice that the Gini values for the aggregate are higher than both those of the cities and of the rural areas. This is not a statistical necessity (other cases show at least partly different behaviours: see, for example, the Sabaudian State in Alfani 2015, 1084), but is the consequence of the urban–rural differences in average household wealth which were higher than elsewhere, given the relatively large size of the cities of the *Terraferma*.

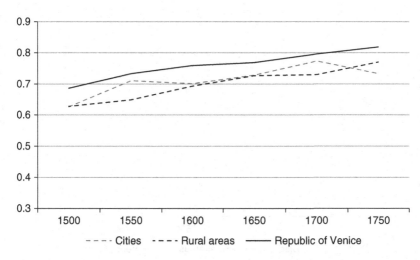

Figure A.4 Inequality in the Republic of Venice (*Terraferma*), 1500–1750 (Gini indexes of concentration).

As already discussed, in the case of the Republic of Venice there is no coincidence between the ancient state and a contemporary administrative region. It is clearly possible and useful, though, to also introduce a reconstruction related to the contemporary administrative region Veneto. Basically, this reconstruction makes use of the same data and hypotheses discussed earlier, with two changes: (1) the distributions of Bergamo and the communities of its *contado* have been excluded; (2) the rural/urban average wealth ratio has been slightly tweaked to take into account the removal of Bergamo. The result is a somewhat greater polarization between city and country, which is again the outcome of the particularly large size of the cities of Veneto.[3] The results are shown in Figure A.5 and it is easy to notice that they do not differ much from those related to the entire *Terraferma*. If anything, the tendency for inequality to grow during the early modern period is somewhat steeper.

Having reconstructed representative distributions for large territories, we are not constrained to analyze Ginis only, but we can explore such distributions in meaningful ways – for example by looking at the share of the top rich. In Figure A.6, trends in the share of the top 1, 5 and 10% rich are represented.

---

[3] For example, while in 1550 the rural–urban ratio calculated for the Republic was 18%, in the Veneto alone it was slightly smaller: 16%.

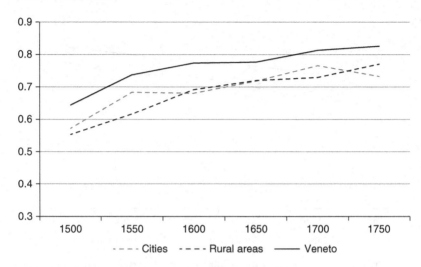

Figure A.5 Inequality in Veneto, 1500–1750
(Gini indexes of concentration).

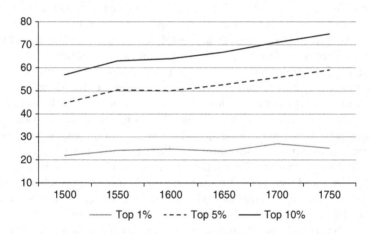

Figure A.6 Share of the top rich in the Republic of Venice (*Terraferma*),
1500–1750 (%).

Across the *Terraferma*, the share of wealth of the top rich grew over
time, confirming the empirical regularity noticed by many studies of both
past and contemporary societies, that what happens at the top tends to
shape the overall inequality trend as expressed by means of Gini indexes

or other indicators (Atkinson et al. 2011; Alvaredo et al. 2013; Piketty 2014; Alfani 2015; Alfani and Ryckbosch 2016). If we look, for example, at the top 10%, they owned 56.8% of the overall wealth in 1500 and their share grew steadily, reaching 74.8% in 1750. These figures are similar to those found in other Italian states, as in the same year in the Sabaudian State the share of the top 10% was 65.2% and in the Florentine State it was 78.3% (Alfani 2015; Alfani and Ammannati 2017). These findings are discussed in detail in Chapter 3.

A.4   Further Refinements: Accounting for the Propertyless and for the Capital City of Venice

The overall reconstruction which we introduced in the earlier section has been produced with the same methods which have recently been applied to other pre-unification Italian states, as well as to some other areas of Europe. However, it shares with such reconstructions a significant shortcoming: it does not take into account the propertyless, for the simple reason that they are almost always absent from our sources.

The case of the Republic of Venice is in fact exceptional in offering at least some indications about the prevalence of the propertyless during the early modern period in a couple of cities (Bergamo and Padua – although with much more continuity in the former than in the latter), as well as in at least one rural area, the *contado* of Padua, albeit for two years only: 1627 and 1694. This source material has been used in Chapter 2 to discuss the general issue of poverty in the Republic of Venice, and the actual information about the prevalence of the propertyless in different places and periods is summarized in Table 2.1. Such information can be used to provide an at least tentative reconstruction of inequality which also includes the propertyless. Notice that, given the limited amount of information we have about the propertyless, this has to be understood as a highly hypothetical and somewhat less reliable reconstruction compared to that which excludes them.

We clustered the information about the prevalence of the propertyless in Bergamo in the period 1537–1704 around our usual 50-years breakpoints. For 1700 we used the 1704 figure, then obtained an estimate for 1750 by projecting linearly the growth occurred in the period 1650–1700. As will be remembered from the discussion in Chapter 2, it seems that the 1630 plague strongly reduced, at least for a period, the prevalence of the propertyless throughout the Republic. Then, a further growth of the propertyless after 1700 is consistent both with the idea that their prevalence continued to recover after the fall in 1630, and with the general literature about the poor in northern Italy. For Padua we applied the same procedure as for Bergamo, with the additional complication that we also had to fill in a gap for year 1650. As for both 1600 and 1700 the observed prevalence of the propertyless was very similar in the two cities (10.04% in Bergamo and 10.16% in Padua in 1600, and respectively 5.4% and 6.74% in 1700), we hypothesized that in 1650, Padua differed from Bergamo in the same proportion as in 1700. We then assumed a prevalence of the propertyless equal to 4.99% in Bergamo and 6.23% in Padua in 1650. Finally, for 1550 Padua we assumed the same value as in 1500.

From the foregoing information, we estimated the prevalence of the propertyless in the cities of the *Terraferma* as the simple average of the cities of Bergamo and Padua. Regarding the country, we had information for the *contado* of Padua only. Here, in 1627 the propertyless households were 3.11%, i.e. about a third those in the city (10.16%). By 1694 the relative position of city and *contado* had inverted, as now rural propertyless households were about one-fifth more than in the city (8.11% vs. 6.74%). Given that these are the only years for which we have measures of the prevalence of the propertyless directly comparable between city and country, we had to assume that the ratio between the rural and urban propertyless was the same as that found in the province of Padua in 1627. Only for 1700 and 1750 we used the ratio calculated for year 1694 instead.

Based on the above assumptions, we obtained estimates of the prevalence of the propertyless in the entire Venetian mainland by calculating the average of the urban and rural prevalence weighted by the urbanization rates presented in Table A.3. All these estimates are summarized in Figure A.7.

As can easily be noticed, our reconstruction of the prevalence of the propertyless is entirely consistent with the finding (discussed in Chapter 2) that the numbers of the poor peaked in the decades immediately preceding the 1630 plague, collapsed after the plague and then recovered during the rest of the early modern period. As always, given that the majority of the population resided in the country, the series of the overall propertyless closely follows that of the rural propertyless. Generally speaking, the propertyless tended to become more numerous throughout the early modern period – with the terrible plague of the mid-seventeenth century being the only shock able to temporarily rebalance the situation. This being said, the scarcity of information about the rural areas might have led to some distortions. In particular, the prevalence of propertyless households in the *contado* in 1627 seems relatively low; therefore it might not represent correctly the overall situation of the Republic. Underestimation of the poor until the early seventeenth century also

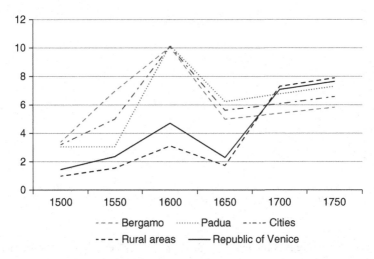

Figure A.7 The prevalence of the propertyless in the Republic of Venice (*Terraferma*), 1500–1750 (estimates).

implies some risk of overestimation of their growth throughout that century. However, a marked growth in the prevalence of the poor is exactly what should be expected based on the literature on the condition of the peasants, the crisis of small ownership and on 'proletarianization' during the late sixteenth and the seventeenth centuries, which has been discussed in Chapter 4 (Section 4.1).

Starting with the information shown in Figure A.7, obtaining a reconstruction of the wealth distribution is a simple matter of adding to the distributions introduced in the earlier section a number of fictitious households with zero wealth which matches exactly the presumptive prevalence of the poor. The results are shown in Figure A.8.

As can easily be noticed by comparing Figure A.8 with Figure A.4, the inclusion of the (estimated) propertyless does not alter the long-term trends in inequality, which continue to be orientated towards inequality increase throughout the early modern period. This is an important finding, as it gives support to what has been argued by other studies (Alfani 2015; Alfani and Ryckbosch 2016; Alfani and Ammannati 2017) and also confirms the ability of inequality measures built from distributions which do not include the propertyless to rightly represent general dynamics. Of course, if one looks at the *level* of inequality and not at the *trend*, excluding the propertyless means distorting the measures (for example, the Ginis) towards a greater-than-real equality. Our reconstructions make it possible

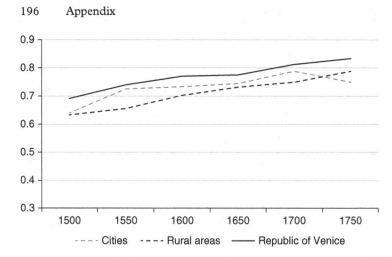

Figure A.8 Inequality in the Republic of Venice (*Terraferma*) including the propertyless, 1500–1750 (Gini indexes of concentration).

to provide some estimates of such distortion. If we focus on the Republic of Venice as a whole, the Gini excluding the propertyless is systematically 0.012–0.015 points lower than that which includes them. Only for year 1600 the distortion is greater (0.031 Gini points), as a consequence of the fact that the prevalence of the propertyless peaked in the pre-1630 plague decades. Further discussion of the topic is provided in Chapter 2.

Including the capital city, Venice, in the reconstruction is an altogether trickier task, basically because we do not have a usable distribution of wealth for the city at any date. Some information about patrimonies and their values has been provided by Chauvard (2005, 2009), but unfortunately this is not enough to proxy even a partial distribution. This being said, we should remember that the main reason why including Venice would alter the distribution that we have reconstructed for the *Terraferma*, is not its presumably very high 'internal' inequality, but the difference between the wealth of its inhabitants and that of the subject territories in the Italian mainland. As we do have the information needed to roughly measure such difference over time, it seems worthwhile to try to provide at least some orders of magnitude about wealth inequality in the whole of the Italian territories of the Republic, then including the capital city.

In brief, to do this:

1. We assume for the city of Venice the same internal distribution of wealth characterizing Padua, the largest and most unequal city

included in our database[4]. Note that, given the very high inequality levels found in Padua (the reported Gini is 0.81 in 1650: see Chapter 3, Table 3.1), we do not expect the actual internal inequality of Venice to have been much higher. To make a comparison, in another capital city, Florence, the Gini index of real estate inequality was 0.705 in 1427 (Herlihy 1978, 139) – although admittedly this value is related to a much earlier epoch, and we know that inequality tended to grow in the Florentine State throughout the early modern period (Alfani and Ammanati 2017, as well as our discussion in Chapter 3, Section 3.6).

2. We calculate the average wealth differential between inhabitants of Venice and inhabitants of the *Terraferma*. To do this, we use data made available by Pezzolo (2006a, 47) about the overall fiscal revenue (direct and indirect taxes together: see Chapter 4, Section 4.3) from Venice and the *Terraferma* in the period 1490–1780. We then use the population data discussed in Section A.3 as well as information about the population of Venice from Alfani and Percoco (2018) to produce measures of per capita fiscal revenue. On the assumption that the average fiscal pressure is about the same in the capital and in the *Terraferma*, we can estimate that an average household of Venice was much wealthier than an average household of the *Terraferma*: usually 5.5 to 6.5 times as wealthy (the minimum estimated value is 3.44 in 1550, and the maximum is 7.12 in 1800). If we restrict the comparison to Venice and the richest city of the *Terraferma*, Padua, we can estimate – by using the same information as in Section A.2 – that the average household of Venice was 1.55 times as wealthy as the average household in Padua in 1500, 2.15 in 1600 and 1.83 in 1800. Compared to a poorer and smaller city, Bergamo, a Venetian household would be 3.32 times wealthier in 1500, 4.79 in 1600 and 4.18 in 1700. Again, this seems to be in line with what has been found by Herlihy (1978, 136–39) for Tuscany, where in 1427 the average Florentine household was about three times richer than those of the medium-sized cities under its rule and up to six times richer than those of the smaller cities.

3. As for the purposes of our reconstruction we have expressed relative wealth of different areas in relation to Padua (see Table A.2), we can now do the same for Venice and simply add it to our aggregate reconstructions. When doing this, however, the number of 'urban' elements in each aggregate distribution needs to be recalibrated in order to maintain the right proportion of urban and rural elements (matching urbanization rates).

[4] We use for 1500 the same distribution as for 1550, and for 1750 the same distribution as for 1650.

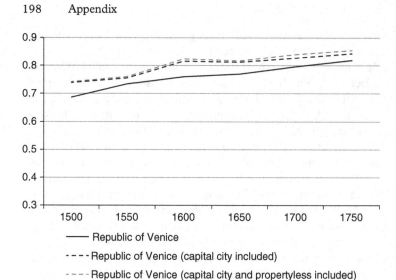

Figure A.9 Inequality in the Republic of Venice (*Terraferma* plus Venice), 1500–1750 (Gini indexes of concentration).

The results of this process are presented in Figure A.9, with and without propertyless (the reconstruction of aggregate distributions including both Venice and the propertyless is a simple matter of reapplying the procedure introduced at the beginning of this section).

As can easily be seen, including Venice does lead to higher inequality, as was expected (the Gini, propertyless excluded, increases from 0.687 to 0.739 in 1500, from 0.760 to 0.816 in 1600 and from 0.797 to 0.828 in 1700). Indeed, the increase is considerably more significant than that resulting from the inclusion of the propertyless. However, the trend does not change. This basically confirms our intuition that the absence of Venice from most of our reconstructions does not alter significantly the overall picture.

For completeness and for easier consultation, in Table A.4 we present detailed information (including all deciles as well as the share of the richest 5%) about the distribution that we have reconstructed for different aggregates.

Table A.4 *Wealth concentration in the Republic of Venice (various aggregates), 1500–1750*

Year	1500	1550	1600	1650	1700	1750
Gini index						
Terraferma	0.687	0.734	0.76	0.77	0.797	0.82
Veneto only	0.645	0.738	0.773	0.777	0.813	0.826
Terraferma plus Venice	0.739	0.755	0.816	0.813	0.828	0.844
Terraferma, propertyless included	0.692	0.74	0.771	0.776	0.812	0.834
Terraferma plus Venice, propertyless included	0.743	0.76	0.825	0.817	0.84	0.856
Share of the top 10%						
Terraferma	56.8	63.1	64.0	67.0	71.1	74.8
Veneto only	54.1	64.6	65.9	67.7	73.4	75.4
Terraferma plus Venice	64.8	66.3	73.2	73.6	75.9	78.6
Terraferma, propertyless included	57.1	63.5	64.9	67.4	72.5	76.1
Terraferma plus Venice, propertyless included	65.1	66.8	74.1	74.0	77.1	79.8

Note: The measures related to the *Terraferma* and Veneto, propertyless excluded, have to be considered the most reliable. Those including the propertyless are more hypothetical, while those including the city of Venice have to be considered tentative and are are only meant to provide an order of magnitude.

Archival Sources

Biblioteca Civica A. Mai, Bergamo (BCBg)
Archivio Storico del Comune di Bergamo-Sezione antico regime-Serie Estimi, folders 1.2.16-II (1430), 1.2.16–14 (1448), 1.2.16-XXI (1537), 1.2.16-XIII A and B (1555)
Archivio di Stato, Bergamo (ASBg)
Estimo Veneto, folders 1 and 2 (1610), 6 and 7 (1640), 11–14 (1704)
Archivio di Stato, Padova (ASPd)
Estimi Miscellanea, folders 2 (1549), 24 (1627 and 1642)
Estimo 1518, folders 382 (Venetians with the *contado* 1549), 379 (Venetians with the city 1549), 412 (exempts 1549)
Estimo 1575, folder 170 (Venetians with the *contado* 1627)
Estimo 1615, folders 166–170 (*clero* 1627)
Estimo 1668, folders 415–420 (*contado* 1694), 376–389 (city 1694), 557–558 (*clero* 1694), 555 (Venetians with the city), cart. 556 (Venetians with the *contado*)
Archivio di Stato, Verona (ASVr)
Antico Archivio del Comune, registers 249 (1409), 255 (1456), 260 (1502), 264 (1545), 270 (1605), 273 (1635)
Antichi Estimi Provvisori, registers 103 (1696) and 169–170 (1800); folders 390 (Parona), 489 (Nogara), 469 (Visegna), 605 (Prun), 609 (Sant'Ambrogio), 616 (Ceredello), 626 (Rivalta) 646 (Garda), 662 (Peschiera)
Archivio di Stato, Vicenza (ASVi)
Estimi, folders 1061 (1443), 1065 (1500), 1074 (1547–1549), 1085 (1602), 1094 (1650), 1103 (1696), 1105 (1718–1756) (all related to Arzignano)
Archivio Storico del Comune, Clusone (ASCClu)
Estimi, folders 108 (1579), 111 (1618), 112 (1624), 120 (166), 136 (1700)
Archivio Storico del Comune, Romano di Lombardia (ASCRom)
Estimi, unnumbered registers (1522, 1605 and 1663)

Printed Sources

Bilanci I, *Bilanci generali della repubblica di Venezia*, Vol. 1, edited by F. Besta, Venezia, 1912

Bilanci II, *Bilanci generali della repubblica di Venezia*, Vol. 2, Venezia, 1903

Bilanci III, *Bilanci generali della repubblica di Venezia*, Vol. 3, Venezia, 1903

Bilanci IV, *Bilanci generali della repubblica di Venezia*, Vol. 4, edited by A. Ventura, Venezia, 1972

Bibliography

Acemoglu, D., Johnson, S. and Robinson, J. 2005. 'The rise of Europe: Atlantic trade, institutional change, and economic growth'. *The American Economic Review* 95(3), 546–79.

Ago, R. 1998. *Economia barocca: Mercato e istituzioni nella Roma del Seicento*. Roma: Donzelli.

Albini, G. 1999. 'La popolazione di Bergamo e del suo territorio nei secoli XIV e XV'. In G. Chittolini (ed.), *Storia economica e sociale di Bergamo. I primi mille anni. Il comune e la signoria*. Bergamo: Fondazione per la storia economica e sociale di Bergamo, 213–55.

Albini, G. 2002. *Carità e governo della povertà (secoli XII–XV)*. Milano: Unicopli.

Alfani, G. 2009a. 'Prima della curva di Kuznets: dinamiche della ricchezza tra Medioevo ed Età Moderna'. In G. Alfani and M. Barbot (eds.), *Ricchezza, valore, proprietà in età preindustriale 1400–1850*. Venezia: Marsilio, 143–67.

Alfani, G. 2009b. 'Proprietà, ricchezza e disuguaglianza economica'. In G. Alfani and M. Barbot (eds.), *Ricchezza, valore, proprietà in età preindustriale 1400–1850*. Venezia: Marsilio, 11–22.

Alfani, G. 2009c. 'Crisi demografiche, politiche di popolazione e mortalità differenziale (ca. 1400–1630)'. *Popolazione e Storia*, 1, 57–75.

Alfani, G. 2010a. 'Wealth inequalities and population dynamics in northern Italy during the early modern period'. *Journal of Interdisciplinary History*, 40(4), 513–49.

Alfani, G. 2010b. 'The effects of plague on the distribution of property: Ivrea, Northern Italy 1630'. *Population Studies*, 64(1), 61–75.

Alfani, G. 2010c. 'Pestilenze e 'crisi di sistema' in Italia tra XVI e XVII secolo. Perturbazioni di breve periodo o cause di declino economico?'. In S. Cavaciocchi (ed.), *Le interazioni fra economia e ambiente biologico nell'Europa preindustriale*. Firenze: Florence University Press, 219–44.

Alfani, G. 2010d. 'Pestilenze e 'crisi di sistema' in Italia tra XVI e XVII secolo. Perturbazioni di breve periodo o cause di declino economico?'. In S. Cavaciocchi (ed.), *Le interazioni fra economia e ambiente biologico nell'Europa preindustriale*. Firenze: Florence University Press, 219–44.

Alfani, G. 2011. 'The famine of the 1590s in Northern Italy. An analysis of the greatest "system shock" of the sixteenth century'. *Histoire & Mesure*, 26(1), 17–49.

Alfani, G. 2012. 'Immigrants and formalisation of social ties in Early Modern Italy (Ivrea, sixteenth–seventeenth centuries)'. In G. Alfani and V. Gourdon (eds.), *Spiritual Kinship in Europe, 1500–1900*. London: Palgrave, 47–73.

Alfani, G. 2013a. *Calamities and the Economy in Renaissance Italy*. Basingstoke: Palgrave Macmillan.

Alfani, G. 2013b. 'Plague in seventeenth century Europe and the decline of Italy: An epidemiological hypothesis'. *European Review of Economic History*, 17, 408–30.

Alfani, G. 2013c. 'Fiscality and territory: Ivrea and Piedmont between the fifteenth and seventeenth centuries'. M. Vester (ed.), *Sabaudian Studies: Political Culture, Dynasty, & Territory 1400–1700*. Kirksville, MO: Truman State University Press, 213–39.

Alfani, G. 2013d. 'Cittadinanza, immigrazione e integrazione sociale nella prima età moderna: il caso di Ivrea'. In *Mélanges de l'École française de Rome. Moyen Âge*, 125(2), 2–15.

Alfani, G. 2014. 'Back to the peasants: New insights into the economic, social, and demographic history of northern Italian rural populations during the early modern period'. *History Compass*, 12(1), 62–71.

Alfani, G. 2015. 'Economic inequality in northwestern Italy: A long-term view (fourteenth to eighteenth centuries)'. *The Journal of Economic History*, 75(4), 1058–96.

Alfani, G. 2016a. 'La popolazione dell'Italia settentrionale nel XV e XVI secolo: scenari regionali e macro-regionali'. In G. Alfani, A. Carbone, B. Del Bo and R. Rao (eds.), *La popolazione italiana del Quattrocento e del Cinquecento*. Udine: Forum, 19–40.

Alfani, G. 2016b. 'Review of Daniel R. Curtis, "Coping with crisis: The resilience and vulnerability of pre-industrial settlements"'. *Continuity and Change*, 31(1), 1–3.

Alfani, G. 2017. 'The rich in historical perspective: Evidence for preindustrial Europe (ca. 1300–1800)'. *Cliometrica*, 11(3), 321–48.

Alfani, G. and Ammannati, F. 2017. 'Long-term trends in economic inequality: The case of the Florentine State, ca. 1300–1800'. *Economic History Review*, 70 (4), 1072–102.

Alfani, G. and Barbot, M. (eds.) 2009. *Ricchezza, valore, proprietà in età preindustriale 1400–1850*. Venezia: Marsilio.

Alfani, G. and Caracausi, A. 2009. 'Struttura della proprietà e concentrazione della ricchezza in ambiente urbano: Ivrea e Padova, secoli XV–XVII'. In G. Alfani and M. Barbot (eds.), *Ricchezza, valore, proprietà in età preindustriale 1400–1850*. Venezia: Marsilio, 185–209.

Alfani G. and De Franco, D. 2015. *Economic and social inequality in a preindustrial society: building a social table for northern Italy (Sabaudian State, 1613)*. Paper presented at the *European historical economics society conference*, Pisa, 4–5 September 2015.

Alfani, G. and Di Tullio, M. 2018. 'Reconstructing the wage structures of early modern armies'. Working Paper, forthcoming.

Alfani, G. and Frigeni R. 2016. 'Inequality (un)perceived: The emergence of a discourse on economic inequality from the Middle Ages to the Age of Revolution'. *Journal of European Economic History*, 45(1), 21–66.

Alfani, G. and Melegaro, A. 2010. *Pandemie d'Italia. Dalla peste nera all'influenza suina: l'impatto sulla società*. Milano: Egea.

Alfani, G., Mocarelli, L. and Strangio, D. 2017. 'Italy'. In G. Alfani and C. Ó. Gráda (eds.), *Famine in European History*. Cambridge: Cambridge University Press, 25–47.

Alfani, G. and Murphy, T. 2017. 'Plague and lethal epidemics in the pre-industrial world'. *Journal of Economic History*, 77(1), 314–43.

Alfani, G. and Ó Gráda, C. (eds.). 2017a. *Famine in European History*. Cambridge: Cambridge University Press.

Alfani, G. and Ó Gráda, C. 2017b. 'Famines in Europe: An overview'. In G. Alfani and C. Ó Gráda (eds.), *Famine in European History*. Cambridge: Cambridge University Press, 1–24.

Alfani, G. and Ó Gráda, C. 2018. 'The timing and causes of famines in Europe'. *Nature Sustainability*, 1, 283–88.

Alfani, G. and Percoco, M. 2018. 'Plague and long-term development: The lasting effects of the 1629–30 epidemic on the Italian cities'. *Economic History Review*, forthcoming.

Alfani, G. and Rao R. (eds.). 2011. *La gestione delle risorse collettive. Italia settentrionale, secoli XII-XVIII*. Milano: Franco Angeli.

Alfani, G. and Ryckbosch, W. 2015. 'Was there a "Little Convergence" in inequality? Low Countries and Italy compared, ca. 1500–1900'. IGIER Working Paper, 557. Milano: Innocenzo Gasparini Institute for Economic Research.

Alfani, G. and Ryckbosch, W. 2016. 'Growing apart in early modern Europe? A comparison of inequality trends in Italy and the Low Countries, 1500–1800'. *Explorations in Economic History*, 62, 143–53.

Alfani, G. and Sardone, S. 2015. 'Long-term trends in economic inequality in southern Italy. The Kingdom of Naples and Sicily, 16th–18th centuries: First results'. Paper presented at the Economic History Association Annual Meeting, Nashville.

Alimento, A. 2008. *Finanza e amministrazione: un'inchiesta francese sui catasti nell'Italia del Settecento (1736–1764)*, Vol. I: *Il viaggio di François-Joseph Harvoin: con uno scritto inedito di Pompeo Neri*. Firenze: Olschki.

Allen, R. C. 2001. 'The great divergence in European wages and prices from the Middle Ages to the First World War'. *Explorations in Economic History*, 38, 411–77.

Alvaredo, F., Atkinson, A. B., Piketty, T. and Saez, E. 2013. 'The top 1 percent in international and historical perspective'. *Journal of Economic Perspectives*, 27(3), 3–20.

Ammannati, F. 2009. 'Florentine woolen manufacture in the sixteenth century: crisis and new entrepreneurial strategies'. *Business and Economic History On-Line*, 7, 1–9.

Andreozzi, D. 2015. 'The "Barbican of Europe". The plague of split and the strategy of defence in the Adriatic area between the Venetian Territories and the Ottoman Empire (eighteenth century)'. *Popolazione e Storia*, 2, 115–37.

Arbel, B. 2013. 'Venice's maritime empire in the early modern period'. In E. R. Dursteler (ed.), *A Companion to Venetian History. 1400–1797*. Leiden: Brill, 125–253.

Atkinson, A. B., Piketty, T. and Saez, E. 2011. 'Top incomes in the long run of history'. *Journal of Economic Literature*, 49(1), 3–71.

Azpitarte, F. 2012. 'Measuring poverty using both income and wealth: An empirical comparison of multidimensional approaches using data for the U.S. and Spain'. *Review of Income and Wealth*, 58(1), 24–50.

Barbero, A. 2008. *Storia del Piemonte. Dalla preistoria alla globalizzazione*. Torino: Einaudi.

Barbieri, G. 1937. 'I redditi dei milanesi all'inizio della dominazione spagnola'. *Rivista internazionale di scienze sociali*, 45, 759–81.

Barbot, M. 2007. 'Appartenere. Inclusione ed esclusione nelle città italiane di Antico regime'. *Zapruder*, 14, 9–22.

Barbot, M. 2009. 'Gli estimi, una fonte di "valore"'. In G. Alfani and M. Barbot (eds.), *Ricchezza, valore, proprietà in età preindustriale 1400–1850*. Venezia: Marsilio, 23–7.

Béguin, K. (ed.) 2015. *Ressources publiques et construction étatique en Europe. XIIIe-XVIIIe siècle*. Paris: IGPDE.

Belfanti, C. M. 1994. *Mestieri e forestieri. Immigrazione ed economia urbana a Mantova fra Sei e Settecento*. Milano: Franco Angeli.

Belfanti, C. M. 1995. 'Dalla stagnazione alla crescita: la popolazione di Bergamo dal Cinquecento a Napoleone'. In A. De Maddalena, M. Cattini and M. A. Romani (eds.), *Storia economica e sociale di Bergamo. Il tempo della Serenissima. L'immagine della Bergamasca*. Bergamo: Fondazione per la storia economica e sociale di Bergamo, 173–214.

Bellavitis, A. 2001. *Identité, mariage, mobilité sociale: citoyennes et citoyens à Venise au XVIe siècle*. Roma: École française de Rome.

Bellavitis, A. 2013. 'Family and society'. In E. R. Dursteler (ed.), *A Companion to Venetian History. 1400–1797*. Leiden: Brill, 319–51.

Beloch, K. J. 1994. *Storia della popolazione italiana*. Firenze: Le Lettere (original edition Berlin-Leipzig: Walter de Gruyter & Co., 1937–61).

Beltrami, D. 1954. *Storia della popolazione di Venezia dalla fine del secolo XVI alla caduta della Repubblica*. Padova: Cedam.

Beltrami, D. 1961. *La penetrazione economica dei veneziani in Terraferma. Forze di lavoro e proprietà fondiaria nelle campagne venete dei secoli XVII e XVIII*. Venezia: Istituto per la collaborazione culturale.

Bengtsson, E., Missiaia, A., Olsson, M. and Svensson, P. 2018. 'Wealth inequality in Sweden, 1750–1900'. *Economic History Review*, 71(3), 772–94.

Beonio-Brocchieri, V. 2000. *"Piazza universale di tutte le professioni del mondo". Famiglie e mestieri nel Ducato di Milano in età spagnola*. Milano: Unicopli.

Berengo, M. 1975. 'Patriziato e nobilita: il caso veronese'. *Rivista Storica Italiana*, 3, 493–517.

Berengo, M. 1999. *L'Europa delle città. Il volto della società urbana europea tra Medioevo e Età moderna*. Torino: Einaudi.

Bianchi, F. and Demo, E. 2013. 'Tra mercati e mendicanti: amministrare la carità nella terraferma veneta del Rinascimento'. In F. Ammannati (ed.), *Assistenza e solidarietà in Europa. Secc. XIII–XVIII*. Firenze: Florence University Press, 307–16.

Bolt, J. and Van Zanden, J. L. 2014. 'The Maddison Project: Collaborative research on historical national accounts'. *Economic History Review*, 67(3), 627–51.

Bonney, R. (ed.) 1999. *The Rise of the Fiscal State in Europe (1200–1815)*. Oxford: Oxford University Press.

Borelli, G. 1974. *Un patriziato della Terraferma veneta tra XVII e XVIII secolo. Ricerche sulla nobiltà veronese*. Milano: Giuffrè.

Borelli, G. 1980. 'Il problema degli estimi'. *Economia e Storia*, 1, 127–30.

Borelli, G. 1982. 'Introduzione'. In G. Borelli, P. Lanaro and F. Vecchiato (eds.), *Il sistema fiscale veneto. Problemi e aspetti XV–XVIII secolo*. Verona: Libreria Universitaria Editrice, 7–12.

Borelli, G. 1983. 'I corpi territoriali nella Repubblica veneta'. *Economia e storia*, 1, 103–08.

Borelli, G. 1986a. 'Il meccanismo dell'estimo civico in epoca in epoca veneta'. In *Città e campagna in età preindustriale XVI–XVIII secolo*. Verona: Libreria università editrice, 325–34.

Borelli, G. 1986b. 'Per una tipologia della proprietà fondiaria della villa tra XVII e XVIII secolo. In *Città e campagna in età preindustriale XVI–XVIII secolo*. Verona: Libreria università editrice, 141–72.

Borelli, G. 1986c. 'La ricchezza degli enti ecclesiastici e monastici di Verona tra secolo XVI e XVIII. In *Città e campagna in età preindustriale XVI–XVIII secolo*. Verona: Libreria università editrice, 369–407.

Borelli, G., Lanaro, P. and Vecchiato, F. (eds.) 1982. *Il sistema fiscale veneto. Problemi e aspetti XV–XVIII secolo*. Verona: Libreria Universitaria Editrice.

Bossy, J. 1970. 'The Counter-Reformation and the people of Catholic Europe'. *Past and Present*, 47, 51–70.

Bossy, J. 1973. 'Blood and baptism: Kinship, community and Christianity in Western Europe from the fourteenth to the seventeenth century'. *Studies in Church History*, 10, 129–43.

Braudel, F. 1984. *Civilization and Capitalism, 15th–18th Century*, Vol. 3. *The Perspective of the World*. New York: Harper and Row (first French ed. 1979).

Brenner, Y.S., Kaelble, H. and Thomas, M. (eds.). 1991. *Income Distribution in Historical Perspective*. Cambridge: Cambridge University Press.

Breschi, M. and Malanima, P. (eds.) 2002. *Prezzi, redditi, popolazioni in Italia: 600 anni (dal secolo XIV al XX)*. Udine: Forum.

Brolis, M. T. 1995. 'Confraternite bergamasche bassomedievali. Nuove fonti e prospettive di ricerca'. *Rivista di Storia della Chiesa in Italia*, 49, 337–54.

Brusse, P., Schuurman, A., Van Molle, L. and Vanhaute, E. 2010. 'The low countries, 1750–2000'. In B. Van Bavel and R. Hoyle (eds.), *Rural Economy and Society in North-western Europe, 500–2000. Social Relations: Property and Power*. Turnhout: Brepols, 199–225.

Bulgarelli Lukacs, A. 1993. *L'imposta diretta nel Regno di Napoli in età moderna*. Milano: Franco Angeli.

Bulgarelli Lukacs, A. 2012. *La finanza locale sotto tutela*, 2 vols. Venezia: Marsilio.

Buono, A. 2009. *Esercito, istituzioni, territorio: alloggiamenti militari e case herme nello Stato di Milano (secc. XVI–XVII)*. Florence: Firenze University Press.

Buono, A., Di Tullio, M. and Rizzo, M. 2016. 'Per una storia economica e istituzionale degli alloggiamenti militari in Lombardia tra XV e XVII secolo'. *Storia economica*, 1, 187–218.

Campbell, B. S. 2010. 'Nature as historical protagonist: Environment and society in pre-industrial england'. *Economic History Review*, 63(2), 281–314.

Canbakal, J. 2013. 'Wealth and Inequality in Ottoman Bursa, 1500–1840'. Paper presented at the Economic History Society Annual Conference, York.

Capra, C. 1980. 'Alcuni aspetti del riordinamento tributario in Lombardia nell'età Teresiana'. In *La fiscalité et ses implications sociales en Italie et en France aux XVIIᵉ et XVIIIᵉ siècles*. Roma: École Française de Rome, 3–16.

Caracausi, A. 2008. *Dentro la bottega. Culture del lavoro in una città d'età moderna*. Venezia: Marsilio.

Carmichael, A. G. 1986. *Plague and the Poor in Renaissance Florence*. Cambridge: Cambridge University Press.

Cattini, M. 1984. *I contadini di San Felice. Metamorfosi di un mondo rurale nell'Emilia dell'età moderna*. Torino: Einaudi.

Cattini, M. and Romani, M. A. 'Per lo studio delle élites municipali di due capitali di Stato: Parma e Modena nei secoli dell'Età Moderna'. In M. Cattini, M. A. Romani and J. M. de Bernardo Ares (eds.), *Per una Storia sociale del Politico. Ceti dirigenti urbani italiani e spagnoli nei secoli XVI–XVIII*, special number of *Cheiron*, 41, 101–33.

Cavaciocchi, S. (ed.) 2008. *La fiscalità nell'economia europea (secc. XIII–XVIII)*, Firenze: Firenze University Press.

Cavallo, S. 1995. *Charity and Power in Early Modern Italy. Benefactors and Their Motives in Turin, 1541–1789*. Cambridge: Cambridge University Press.

Cavazzana Romanelli, F. and Orlando, E. (eds.) 2006. *Gli estimi della podesteria di Treviso*. Roma: Ministero per i beni e le attività culturali.

Cerutti, S. 2003. *Giustizia sommaria. Pratiche e ideali di giustizia in una società di Ancién Régime (Torino XVIII secolo)*. Milano: Feltrinelli.

Cerutti, S. 2012. *Étrangers: étude d'une condition d'incertitude dans une société d'Ancien regime*. Montrouge: Bayard.

Chauvard, J.-F. 2005. *La Circulation des biens à Venise. Stratégies Patrimoniales et Marché Immobilier (1600–1750)*. Roma: École Française de Rome.

Chauvard, J.-F. 2009. 'Dietro l'immobilità della struttura proprietaria. Mutamento sociale e ricomposizione dei patrimoni a Venezia (1661–1712)'. In G. Alfani and M. Barbot (eds.), *Ricchezza, valore, proprietà in età preindustriale 1400–1850*. Venezia: Marsilio, 211–25.

Chauvard, J. F. 2015. 'Adaptabilité versus inaliénabilité. Les dérogations des fidéicommis dans la Venise du XVIIIe siècle'. *Annales HSS*, 4, 849–78.

Chilese, V. 2002. *Una città nel seicento veneto. Verona attraverso le fonti fiscali del 1653*. Verona: Accademia di agricoltura, scienze e lettere.

Chilosi, D. 2014. 'Risky institutions: Political regimes and the cost of public borrowing in early modern Italy'. *Journal of Economic History*, 74(3), 887–915.

Chittolini, G. 1979a. *La formazione dello stato regionale e le istituzioni del contado (sec. XIV e XV)*. Torino: Einaudi.

Chittolini, G. 1979b. *La crisi degli ordinamenti comunali e le origini dello stato del Rinascimento*. Bologna: Il Mulino.

Chittolini, G. 1983. 'Le terre separate nel ducato di Milano in età sforzesca'. In *Milano nell'età di Ludovico il Moro*, Milano: Comune di Milano, Archivio storico civico e Biblioteca Trivulziana, Vol. I, 115–28.

Chittolini, G. 1990. 'Quasi-città. Borghi e terre in area lombarda nel tardo medioevo'. *Società e storia*, 47, 3–26.

Chittolini, G., Molho A. and Schiera P. (eds.) 1994. *Origini dello Stato. Processi di formazione statale in Italia fra medioevo ed età moderna*. Bologna: Il Mulino.

Chojnacki, S. 2004. *Women and Men in Renaissance Venice: Twelve Essays on Patrician Society*. Baltimore, MD: Johns Hopkins University Press.

Cipolla, C. M. 1981. *Fighting the Plague in Seventeenth-Century Italy*. Madison: University of Wisconsin Press.

Ciriacono, S. 1989. 'L'economia regionale veneta in epoca moderna. Note a margine del caso bergamsco'. In *Venezia e la Terraferma. Economia e Società*. Bergamo: Assessorato alla cultura, 49–52.

Ciriacono, S. 1994. *Acque e Agricoltura. Venezia, l'Olanda e la bonifica europea in età moderna*. Milano: Franco Angeli.

Cohn, S. K. 1999. *Creating the Florentine State: Peasants and Rebellion, 1348–1434*. Cambridge: Cambridge University Press.

Cohn, S. K. 2006. *Lust for Liberty. The Politics of Social Revolt in Medieval Europe, 1200–1425*. Cambridge, MA: Harvard University Press.

Cohn, S. K. 2007. 'After the Black Death: Labour legislation and attitudes towards labour in late-medieval Western Europe'. *Economic History Review*, 60(3), 486–512.

Cohn, S. K. 2009. *Cultures of Plague. Medical Thought at the End of the Renaissance*. Oxford: Oxford University Press.

Cohn, S. K. 2010. 'The changing character of plague in Europe, 1348–1800'. In S. Cavaciocchi (ed.), *Le interazioni fra economia e ambiente biologico nell'Europa preindustriale*. Firenze: Florence University Press, 33–56.

Collins, J. B. 1988. *Fiscal Limits of Absolutism. Direct Taxation in Early Seventeenth-Century France*. Berkeley: University of California Press.

Colombo, E. 2005. *Il contado di Vigevano e la forza di una comunità. Gambolò e la provincia nel Seicento*. Vigevano: Arkè.

Colombo, E. 2008. *Giochi di luoghi. Il territorio lombardo nel seicento*. Milano: Franco Angeli.

Comba, R. 1982. 'Méthodes, bilan provisoire et perspectives des recherches en cours sur les villes piémontaises aux xiv e et xve siècles'. *Annales de démographie historique*, 21–30.

Coppola, G. 1973. 'L'agricoltura di alcune pievi della pianura irrigua Milanese nei dati catastali della metà del secolo XVI'. In M. Romani (ed.), *Contributi dell'Istituto di Storia economica e sociale*, Vol. I, *Aspetti di vita agricola lombarda (sec. XVI–XIX)*. Milano: Vita e Pensiero, 185–286.

Corritore, R. P. 1993. 'Il processo di "ruralizzazione" in Italia nei secoli XVII-XVIII. Verso una regionalizzazione'. *Rivista di storia economica*, 10, 353–86.

Corritore, R. P. 1997. 'Una fondamentale discontinuità padana: la linea dell'Oglio'. In Brambilla, E. and G. Muto, (eds.), *La Lombardia spagnola. Nuovi indirizzi di ricerca*. Milano: Unicopli, 139–53.

Coşgel, M. and Boğaç, A. E. 2012. 'Inequality of wealth in the Ottoman Empire: War, weather, and long-term trends in eighteenth century Kastamonu'. *Journal of Economic History*, 72(2), 308–31.

Covini, N. 1987. '"Alle spese di Zoan Villano". Gli alloggiamenti militari nel dominio visconteo-sforzesco'. *Nuova Rivista Storica*, LXXXI, 531–85.

Covini, N. 1998. *L'esercito del duca. Organizzazione militare e istituzioni al tempo degli Sforza, 1450–1480*. Roma: Istituto Storico Italiano per il Medioevo.

Cowan, A. 2007. *Marriage, Manners and Mobility in Early Modern Venice*. Aldershot: Ashgate.

Cozzi, G. 1995. 'Venezia nei secoli XVI e XVII'. In *Storia d'Italia*, XII, *La Repubblica di Venezia nell'età moderna*, II. Torino: Utet, 5–200.

Curtis, D. R. 2014. *Coping with Crisis. The Resilience and Vulnerability of Pre-Industrial Settlements*. Farnham: Ashgate.

D'Amico, S. 2004. 'The question of economic decline in seventeenth century Italy: Myth or Reality?'. *History Compass*, 2, 1–7.

D'Andrea, D. 2013. 'Charity and confraternities'. In E. R. Dursteler (ed.), *A Companion to Venetian History. 1400–1797*. Leiden: Brill, 421–47.

Davies, J. B. and Shorrocks, A. F. 2000. 'The distribution of wealth'. In A. B. Atkinson and F. Bourguignon (eds.), *Handbook of Income Distribution*. London: Elsevier, 605–75.

Davis, J. C. 1962. *The Decline of the Venetian Nobility as a Ruling Class*. Baltimore, MD: Johns Hopkins University Press.

Deaton, A. 2013. *The Great Escape: Health, Wealth and the Origins of Inequality*. Princeton, NJ: Princeton University Press.

de La Roncière, C. 1974. 'Pauvres et pauvreté à Florence au XIVe siècle'. In M. Mollat (ed.), *Etudes sur l'histoire de la pauvreté (Moyen age–XVI siècle)*. Paris: Publications de la Sorbonne, Vol. II, 661–745.

De Luca, G., Pezzolo, L. and Sabatini, R. 2003. 'La storiografia più recente sulla finanza italiana dell'età moderna'. *Rivista di Storia finanziaria*, 10, 11–128.

Della Misericordia, M. 2006. *Divenire comunità. Comuni rurali, poteri locali, identità sociali e territoriali in Valtellina e nella montagna lombarda nel tardo medioevo*.Milano: Unicopli.

Del Torre, G. 1986. *Venezia e la terraferma dopo la guerra di Cambrai. Fiscalità e amministrazione (1515–1530)*. Milano: Franco Angeli.

De Maddalena, A. 1961. *Le finanze del ducato di Mantova all'epoca di Guglielmo Gonzaga*. Milano-Varese: Istituto Editoriale Cisalpino.

De Maddalena, A. and Kellenbenz, H. (eds.) 1984. *Finanze e ragion di Stato in Italia e in Germania nella prima Età moderna*. Bologna: Il Mulino.

Demo, E. 2001. *L'Anima della Città: l'Industria Tessile a Verona e Vicenza: 1400–1550*. Milano: Unicopli.

Demo, E. 2013. 'Industry and production in the Venetian Terraferma (15th–18th centuries)'. In E. R. Dursteler (ed.), *A Companion to Venetian History. 1400–1797*. Leiden: Brill, 291–318.

De Vries, J. 1976. *The Economy of Europe in an Age of Crisis, 1600–1750*. Cambridge: Cambridge University Press.

De Vries, J. and Van Der Woude, A. 1997. *The First Modern Economy: Success, Failure, and Perseverance of the Dutch Economy, 1500–1815*. Cambridge: Cambridge University Press.

Dincecco, M. 2011. *Political Transformation and Public Finances (Europe, 1650–1913)*. Cambridge: Cambridge University Press.

Di Tullio, M. 2009. 'Rese agricole, scorte alimentari, strutture famigliari. Le campagne dello stato di Milano a metà Cinquecento'. In G. Alfani and M. Barbot (eds.), *Ricchezza, valore, proprietà in età preindustriale 1400–1850*. Venezia: Marsilio, 293–318.

Di Tullio, M. 2011. 'L'estimo di Carlo V (1543–1599) e il perticato del 1558. Per un riesame delle riforme fiscali nello stato di Milano del secondo Cinquecento'. *Società e Storia*, 131, 1–35.

Di Tullio, M. 2014a. *The Wealth of Communities: War, Resources and Cooperation in Renaissance Lombardy*. Farnham: Ashgate.

Di Tullio, M. 2014b. 'Dynamiques du travail et ménages paysans dans la Lombardie du XVIème siècle'. In F. Boudjaaba (ed.), *Le travail et la famille dans le monde rural (16–21ᵉ siècles)*. Rennes: Presses Universitaires de Rennes, 35–52.

Di Tullio, M. 2018. 'Cooperating in time of crisis: War, commons, and inequality in Renaissance Lombardy'. *Economic History Review*, 71(1), 82–105.

Di Tullio, M. and Fois, L. 2014. *Stati di guerra. I bilanci della Lombardia francese del primo Cinquecento*. Roma: École Française de Rome.

Di Tullio, M., Maffi, D. and Rizzo, M. 2015. 'Il fardello della guerra. Governo della finanza pubblica e crisi finanziarie nello Stato di Milano fra centri e periferie (secc. XV–XVII)', in *Le crisi finanziare: gestione, implicazioni sociali e conseguenze nell'età preindustriale*. Firenze: Firenze University Press, 239–60.

Di Vittorio, A. 1993. *La finanza pubblica in età di crisi*. Bari: Cacucci.

Dompnier, B. and Vismara, P. 2008. 'De nouvelles approches pour l'histoire des confréries'. In B. Dompnier and P. Vismara (eds.), *Confréries et dévotions dans la Catholicité moderne (mi-XVe–debut XIXe siècle)*. Roma: Ecole Française de Rome, 405–23.

Donati, C. 1988. *L'idea di nobiltà in Italia. Secoli XIV–XVIII*. Laterza, Bari.

Donazzolo, P. and Saibante, M. 1926. 'Lo sviluppo demografico di Verona e della sua Provincia dalla fine del sec. XV ai giorni nostri'. *Metron. Rivista internazionale di statistica*, IV(3–4), 56–180.

Downing, B. M. 1992. *The Military Revolution and Political Change: Origins of Democracy and Autocracy in Early Modern Europe*. Princeton, NJ: Princeton University Press.

Dubet, A. and Legay, M.-L. 2011. *Avant-propos*. In A. Dubet and M.-L. Legay (eds.), *La Comptabilité publique en Europe. 1500–1850*. Rennes: Presses Universitaries de Rennes, 9–16.

Dursteler, E. R. (ed.) 2013. *A Companion to Venetian History. 1400–1797*. Leiden: Brill.

Dyer, C. 1995. 'Taxation and communities in late medieval England'. In R. H. Britnell and J. Hatcher (eds.), *Progress and Problems in Medieval England*. Cambridge: Cambridge University Press, 168–80.

Elliott, J. H. 1992. 'A Europe of composite monarchies'. *Past and Present*, 137(1), 48–71.

Epstein, S. R. 2000. *Freedom and Growth: The Rise of States and Markets in Europe, 1300–1750*. New York: Routledge.

Faccini, L. 1988. *La Lombardia fra '600 e '700. Riconversione economica e mutamenti sociali*. Milano: Franco Angeli.

Favaretto, I. 1998. *L'istituzione informale. Il territorio padovano dal quattrocento al cinquecento*. Milano: Unicopli.

Felloni, G. 1999. 'Temi e problemi nella storia della finanza degli stati italiani'. *Rivista di Storia finanziaria*, 2, 101–12.

Fernández, E. and Santiago-Caballero, C. 2013. 'Income inequality in Madrid, 1500-1850'. Paper presented at the Economic History Society Annual Conference, York.

Ferrarese, A. 2009. 'Fonti estimali nella Terraferma veneta tra Quattrocento e Cinquecento. Approcci comparativi e nuove prospettive di ricerca'. In G. Alfani and M. Barbot (eds.), *Ricchezza, valore, proprietà in età preindustriale 1400–1850*. Venezia: Marsilio, 43–62.

Fesseau, M. and Mattonetti, M. L. 2013. 'Distributional measures across household groups in a national accounts framework'. OECD Statistics Working Paper, 53.

Fontaine, L. 2008. *L'économie morale. Pauvreté, crédit et confiance dans l'Europe préindustrielle*. Paris: Gallimard.

Fontaine, L. 2013. 'Assistance et solidarité en Europe, XIIIe-XVIIIe siècle'. In F. Ammannati (ed.), *Assistenza e solidarietà in Europa. Secc. XIII–XVIII*. Firenze: Florence University Press, 3–13.

Fontana, G. L. and Gayot, G. (eds.) 2004. *Wool: Products and Markets (13th–20th century)*. Padova: Cleup.

Fornasin, A. 2001. 'La popolazione del Friuli in età moderna. Conferme e nuove evidenze'. *Memorie Storiche Forogivliesi*, 81, 208–34.

Fornasin, A. and Zannini, A. 1999. 'Crisi e ricostruzione demografica nel seicento Veneto'. In *La popolazione italiana nel Seicento*. Bologna: Clueb, 103–40.

Fouquet, R. and Broadberry, S. N. 2015. 'Seven centuries of European economic growth and decline'. *Journal of Economic Perspective*, 29(4), 227–44.

Fritschy, W. 2003. 'A "financial revolution" reconsidered: Public finance in Holland during the Dutch Revolt, 1568–1648'. *Economic History Review*, 56 (1), 57–89.

Fritschy W. 2017. *Public Finance of the Dutch Republic in Comparative Perspective: The Viability of an Early Modern Federal State (1570s–1795)*. Leiden: Brill.

Fritschy, W., 't Hart, M. and Horlings, E. 2012. 'Long-term trends in the fiscal history of the Netherlands, 1515–1913'. In B. Yun-Casalilla and P. K. O'Brien (eds.), *The Rise of Fiscal States: A Global History. 1500–1914*. Cambridge: Cambridge University Press, 39–66.

Fusaro, M. 2007. 'Gli uomini d'affari stranieri in Italia'. In *Il Rinascimento Italiano e l'Europa*, 12 vols., Vol. iv: *L'Italia e l'economia europea nel Rinascimento*, ed. by F. Franceschi, R. A. Goldthwaite and R. C. Mueller. Treviso: Colla, 369–95.

Fusaro, M. 2012. 'Cooperating mercantile networks in the early modern Mediterranean'. *Economic History Review*, 65(2), 701–18.

Fusaro, M. 2015. *Political Economies of Empire in the Early Modern Mediterranean*. Cambridge: Cambridge University Press.

Galasso, G. 1994. *Alla periferia dell'impero: il Regno di Napoli nel periodo spagnolo (secoli XVI–XVII)*. Torino: Einaudi.

Gamberini, A. and Lazzarini, I. (eds.) 2012. *The Italian Renaissance State*. Cambridge: Cambride University Press.

Garbellotti, M. 2013. *Per Carità: Poveri e politiche assistenziali nell'Italia moderna*. Roma: Carocci.

García-Montero, H. 2015. 'Long-term Trends in Wealth Inequality in Catalonia, 1400–1800: Initial Results'. Dondena Working Paper, 79.

Gazzini, M. 2004. 'Bibliografia medievistica di storia confraternale'. *Reti Medievali. Rivista*, 5(1), www.rmoa.unina.it/1858/1/292-992-1-PB-1.pdf

Gazzini, M. 2006. 'Le confraternite italiane: periodi, problemi, storiografie'. In *Confraternite e società cittadina nel medioevo italiano*. Bologna: Clueb, 22–57.

Gazzini, M. (ed.) 2009. *Studi confraternali: orientamenti, problemi, testimonianze*. Firenze: Florence University Press.

Geremek, B. 1994. *Poverty: A History*. Oxford: Blackwell.

Ginatempo, M. 2001. 'Spunti comparativi sulle trasformazioni della fiscalità nell'Italia post-comunale'. In P. Mainoni (ed.), *Politiche finanziarie e fiscali nell'Italia settentrionale (secoli XIII–XV)*. Milano: Unicopli, 125–220.

Gioia, C. 2004. *Lavoradori et brazzenti, senza trafichi né mercantie: Padroni, massari e braccianti nel Bergamasco del Cinquecento*. Milano: Unicopli.

Glete, J. 2002. *War and the State in Early Modern Europe. Spain, the Dutch Republic and Sweden as Fiscal-Military States, 1500–1660*. New York: Routledge.

Grendi, E. 1975. 'Pauperismo e Albergo dei poveri nella Genova del Seicento'. *Rivista Storica Italiana*, 4, 621–65.

Grubb, J. S. 1982. 'Patriarcate and Estimo in Vicentine Quattrocento'. In G. Borelli, P. Lanaro, and F. Vecchiato (eds.), *Il sistema fiscale veneto. Problemi e aspetti XV–XVIII secolo*. Verona: Libreria Universitaria Editrice. 149–73.

Grubb, J. S. 1986. 'When myths lose power: Four decades of Venetian historiography'. *Journal of Modern History*, 58/1, 43–94.

Grubb, J. S. 1996. *Provincial Families on the Renaissance: Private and Public Life in the Veneto*. Baltimore, MD: Johns Hopkins University Press.

Gullino, G. 1981. 'Nobili di Terraferma e Patrizi Veneziani di fronte al sistema fiscale della campagna nell'ultimo secolo della Repubblica'. In A. Tagliaferri (ed.), *Venezia e la Terraferma attraverso le relazioni dei rettori*. Milano: Giuffré, 203–25.

Gullino, G. 1982. 'Considerazioni sull'evoluzione del sistema fiscale veneto tra il XVI e il XVII secolo'. In G. Borelli, P. Lanaro, and F. Vecchiato (eds.), *Il sistema fiscale veneto. Problemi e aspetti XV–XVIII secolo*. Verona: Libreria Universitaria Editrice. 59–91.

Gullino G. 1983. 'Un problema aperto: Venezia e il tardo feudalesimo'. *Studi veneziani*, VII, 183–96.

Gullino G. 1984. *I Pisani Dal Banco e Moretta: Storia di due famiglie veneziane in età moderna e delle loro vicende patrimoniali fra 1705 e 1836*. Roma: Istituto Italiano per l'età moderna e contemporanea.

Gullino, G. 1985. 'I patrizi veneziani e la mercatura negli ultimi tre secoli della Repubblica'. In G. Borelli (ed.), *Mercanti e vita economica nella Repubblica veneta (secoli XIII–XVIII)*. Verona: Banca Popolare di Verona, 403–51.

Gullino, G. 1994. 'Quando il mercante costruì la villa: proprietà fondiaria dei veneziani in Terraferma'. In G. Cozzi and P. Prodi (eds.), *Storia di Venezia, VI, Dal Rinascimento al Barocco*. Roma: Isitituo della Enciclopedia Italiana, 875–924.

Gutton, J.-P. 1974. *La société et les pauvres en Europe*. Paris: Presses Universitaires de France.

Hamon, Ph. 1994. *L'argent du roi. Les finances sous François Ier*. Paris: Comité pour l'histoire économique et financière de la France.

Hanus, J. 2013. 'Real inequality in the early modern Low Countries: The city of 's-Hertogenbosch, 1500–1660'. *Economic History Review*, 66(3), 733–56.

Herlihy, D. 1967. *Medieval and Renaissance Pistoia*. New Haven, CT: Yale University Press.

Herlihy, D. 1968. 'Santa Maria Impruneta: A rural commune in the late Middle Ages'. In N. Rubinstein (ed.), *Florentine studies: Politics and Society in Renaissance Florence*. Evanston: Northwestern University Press, 242–76.

Herlihy, D. 1973. 'The population of Verona in the first century of Venetian rule'. In J. R. Hale (ed.), *Renaissance Venice*. London: Faber & Faber, 91–120.

Herlihy, D. 1977. 'Family and property in renaissance Florence'. In H. A. Miskimin, D. Herlihy and A. L. Udovitch (eds.), *The Medieval City*. New Haven, CT: Yale University Press, 3–24.

Herlihy, D. 1978. 'The distribution of wealth in a Renaissance Community: Florence 1427'. In P. Abrams and E. A. Wrigley (eds.), *Towns in Societies: Essays in Economic History and Historical Sociology*. Cambridge: Cambridge University Press, 131–57.

Herlihy, D. and Klapisch-Zuber, C. 1985. *Tuscans and Their Families: A Study of the Florentine Catasto of 1427*. New Haven, CT: Yale University Press.

Hoffman, P. T., Jacks, D., Levin, P. A. and Lindert, P. H. 2002. 'Real inequality in Europe since 1500'. *Journal of Economic History*, 62(2), 322–55.

Hunecke, V. 1997. *Il patriziato veneziano alla fine della Repubblica*. Roma: Jouvence.

Janssens, P. 2012. 'Taxation in the Habsburg Low Countries and Belgium, 1579–1914'. In B. Yun-Casalilla and P. K. O'Brien (eds.), *The Rise of Fiscal States: A Global History. 1500–1914*. Cambridge: Cambridge University Press, 67–92.

Joumard, I., Pisu, M. and Bloch, B. 2012. 'Tackling income inequality: The role of taxes and transfers'. *OECD Journal: Economic Studies*, 1, 37–70.

Jütte, R. 1994. *Poverty and Deviance in Early Modern Europe*. Cambridge: Cambridge University Press.

Kamen, H. 1976. *The Iron Century: Social Change in Europe, 1550–1660*. London: Cardinal.

Knapton, M. 1981a. 'I rapporti fiscali tra Venezia e la Terraferma: il caso padovano nel secondo '400'. *Archivio Veneto*, CXII, 15–58.

Knapton, M. 1981b. 'L'organizzazione fiscale di base nello stato veneziano: estimi e obighi fiscali a Lisiera fra '500 e '600'. In C. Povolo (ed.), *Lisiera. Immagini, documenti e prolemi per la storia e cultura di una comunità veneta*. Lisiera: Parrocchia di Lisiera, 377–418.

Knapton, M. 1982. 'Il fisco nello stato veneziano di Terraferma tra '300 e '500: la politica delle entrate'. In G. Borelli, P. Lanaro and F. Vecchiato (eds.), *Il sistema fiscale veneto. Problemi e aspetti XV–XVIII secolo.* Verona: Libreria Universitaria Editrice, 17–57.

Knapton, M. 1984. 'Il Territorio vicentino nello Stato veneto del '500 e primo '600: nuovi equilibri politici e fiscali'. In G. Cracco and M. Knapton (eds.), *Dentro lo "Stato italico". Venezia e la Terraferma fra Quattrocento e Seicento.* Trento: Biblioteca Cappuccini, 33–115.

Knapton, M. 1986. 'Guerra e finanza (1308–1508)'. In G. Galasso (ed.), *Storia d'Italia, XII, La repubblica di Venezia nell'età moderna dalla guerra di Chioggia al 1517.* Torino: Utet, 273–353.

Knapton, M. 1995. 'Tra dominante e dominio (1517–1630)'. In *Storia d'Italia,* tomo XII, *La Repubblica di Venezia nell'età moderna.* Torino: Utet, Vol. II, 201–550.

Knapton, M. 1998. '"Nobiltà e popolo" e un trentennio di storiografia veneta'. *Nuova Rivista Storica,* LXXXII, 1, 167–92.

Knapton, M. 2010. 'Le campagne trevigiane: i frutti di una ricerca'. *Società e storia,* 130, 771–800.

Knapton, M. 2012. 'Venice and the Terraferma'. In A. Gamberini and I. Lazzarini (eds.), *The Italian Renaissance State.* Cambridge: Cambride University Press, 132–55.

Kuznets, S. 1955. 'Economic growth and income inequality'. *American Economic Review,* 45(1), 1–28.

Lanaro, P. 1982a. 'Radiografia della soglia di povertà in una città della Terraferma veneta: Verona alla metà del XVI secolo'. *Studi Veneziani,* 6, 45–85.

Lanaro, P. 1982b. 'L'esenzione fiscale a Verona nel '400 e '500: un momento di sconto tra ceto dirigente e ceti subalterni'. In G. Borelli, P. Lanaro and F. Vecchiato (eds.), *Il sistema fiscale veneto. Problemi e aspetti XV–XVIII secolo.* Verona: Libreria Universitaria Editrice, 189–215.

Lanaro, P. 1984. 'Patrizi e poveri. Assistenza, controllo sociale e carità nella Verona rinascimentale'. In A. Tagliaferri (ed.), *I ceti dirigenti in Italia in età moderna e contemporanea.* Udine: Del Bianco, 131–49.

Lanaro, P. 1991a. 'Scelte economichferre e politica corporativa tra Cinque e Seicento in Terraferma veneta'. *Studi Storici Luigi Simeoni,* n. 41, 183–96.

Lanaro, P. 1991b. 'Un patriziato in formazione: l'esempio veronese del '400'. In *Il primo dominio veneziano a Verona (1405–1509).* Verona: Accademia di Agricoltura di Verona, 35–51.

Lanaro, P. 1992. *Un'oligarchia urbana del Cinquecento veneto. Istituzioni, economia, società.* Torino: Giappichelli.

Lanaro, P. 1999. *I mercati della Repubblica veneta: Economie cittadine e stato territoriale (secoli XV–XVIII).* Venezia: Marsilio.

Lanaro, P. 2000. 'Familia est substantia: la trasmissione dei beni nella famiglia patrizia'. In P. Lanaro, P. Marini and G. M. Varanini (eds.), *Edilizia privata nella Verona rinascimentale.* Milano: Electa, 98–117.

Lanaro, P. 2003a. 'Economic space and urban policies: Fairs and markets in the Italy of the early modern age'. *Journal of Urban History,* 30, 37–49.

Lanaro, P. 2003b. 'Periferie senza centro. Reti fieristiche nello spazio geografico della Terraferma in età moderna'. In P. Lanaro (ed.), *La pratica dello scambio.*

Sistemi di fiere, mercati e città in Europa e in Italia, 1400–1700. Venezia: Marsilio, 21–51.

Lanaro, P. 2003c. 'La crisi della proprietà nobiliare veneziana e veneta nel XVIII secolo'. In S. Cavaciocchi (ed.), *Il mercato della Terra. Secc. XIII–XVIII.* Florence: Le Monnier, 431–44.

Lanaro, P. (ed.) 2006. *At the Centre of the Old World. Trade and Manufacturing in Venice and the Venetian Mainland, 1400–1800.* Toronto: CRRS.

Lanaro, P. 2012. 'Fedecommessi, doti, famiglia: la trasmissione della ricchezza nella repubblica di Venezia (XV–XVIII secolo). Un approccio economico'. *Mélanges de l'École française de Rome – Italie et Méditerranée modernes et contemporaines,* 124/2, 519–31.

Lane, F. C. 1973a. *Venice: A Maritime Republic.* Baltimore, MD: Johns Hopkins University Press.

Lane, F. C. 1973b. 'Public debt and private wealth: Particularly in sixteenth century Venice'. In *Mélange en l'honneur de Fernarnd Braudel.* Tolouse: Privat, Vol. I, 317–25.

Le Goff, J. 2010. *Le Moyen Age et l'argent: Essai d'anthropologie historique.* Paris: Perrin.

Le Roy Ladurie, E. 1966. *Les Paysans de Languedoc.* Paris: SEVPEN.

Leverotti, F. 2005. *Famiglia e Istituzioni nel Medioevo Italiano dal Tardo Antico al Rinascimento.* Rome: Carocci.

Leverotti, F. 2007. 'Uomini e donne di fronte all'eredità: il caso italiano'. In *Aragòn en la Edad Media.* Zaragoza: Universidad de Zaragoza, 39–52.

Levi, G. 2003. 'Aequitas vs fairness. Reciprocità ed equità fra età moderna ed età contemporanea'. *Rivista di storia economica,* 2, 195–204.

Lindert, P. H. 1991. 'Toward a comparative history of income and wealth inequality'. In Y. S. Brenner, H. Kaelble and M. Thomas (eds.), *Income Distribution in Historical Perspective.* Cambridge: Cambridge University Press, 212–31.

Lindert, P. H. 1998. 'Poor relief before the welfare state: Britain versus the continent, 1780–1880'. *European Review of Economic History,* 2, 101–40.

Lindert, P. H. 2000. 'Three centuries of inequality in Britain and America'. In A. B. Atkinson and F. Bourguignon (eds.), *Handbook of Income Distribution.* London: Elsevier, 167–216.

Lindert, P. H. 2004. *Growing Public: Social Spending and Economic Growth since the Eighteenth Century.* Cambridge: Cambridge University Press.

Lindert, P. H. 2014. *Making the Most of Capital in the 21st Century.* NBER Working paper no. 20232.

Lindert, P. H. and Williamson, J. G. 2016. *Unequal Gains: American Growth and Inequality since 1700.* Princeton, NJ: Princeton University Press.

Little, L. K. 1988. *Libertà, carità, fraternità: Confraternite laiche a Bergamo nell'età del comune.* Bergamo: Lubrina.

Little, L. K. (ed.) 2007. *Plague and the End of Antiquity: The Pandemic of 541–750.* Cambridge: Cambridge University Press.

Lorenzini, C. 2011. 'Monte versus bosco: Gestione delle risorse collettive e mobilità in area alpina: il caso della Carnia fra Sei e Settecento'. In G. Alfani and R. Rao (eds.), *La gestione delle risorse collettive. Italia settentrionale, secoli XII–XVIII*.Milano: Franco Angeli, 95–109.

Lucas, R. E. 2004. 'The Industrial Revolution: Past and future'. *The Region. 2003 Annual Report of the Federal Reserve Bank of Minneapolis*, 1 May 2004.

Luzzatto, G. 1967. *Per una storia economica d'Italia*. Roma-Bari: Laterza.

Lynch, K. A. 2003. *Individuals, Families and Communities in Europe, 1200–1800. The Urban Foundations of Western Society*. Cambridge: Cambridge University Press.

Maffi, D. 1999. 'Alloggiamenti militari e comunità locali: Pavia e il suo contado nel '600'. *Annali di storia pavese*, 27, 325–38.

Maffi, D. 2007. *Il Baluardo della corona: Guerra, esercito, finanze e società nella Lombardia seicentesca (1630–1660)*. Firenze: Le Monnier.

Maifreda, G. 2002. *Rappresentanze rurali e proprietà contadina: Il caso veronese tra Sei e Settecento*. Milano: Franco Angeli.

Maifreda, G. 2009. 'Estimi, fiscalità e istituzioni in Terraferma veneta tra Cinque e Seicento. Considerazioni a partire dal caso veronese'. In G. Alfani and M. Barbot (eds.), *Ricchezza, valore, proprietà in età preindustriale 1400–1850*. Venezia: Marsilio, 77–100.

Mainoni, P. 1994. *Economia e politica nella Lombardia medievale: Da Bergamo a Milano tra XIII e XV secolo*. Cavallemaggiore: Gribaudo.

Mainoni, P. 2001. 'La gabella del sale nell'Italia del nord (sec. XIII-XIV)'. In P. Mainoni (ed.), *Politiche finanziarie e fiscali nell'Italia settentrionale (secoli XIII–XV)*. Milano: Unicopli, 39–86.

Malanima, P. 1977. *I Ricciardi di Firenze: Una famiglia e un patrimonio nella Toscana dei Medici*. Firenze: Olschki.

Malanima, P. 1982. *La decadenza di un'economia cittadina: L'industria di Firenze nei secoli XVI–XVIII*. Bologna: Il Mulino.

Malanima, P. 1983. 'La formazione di una regione economica: la Toscana nei secoli XIII-XV'. *Società e Storia*, 20, 229–69.

Malanima, P. 1998. 'Italian cities: a quantitative approach'. *Rivista di Storia economica*, 14, 91–126.

Malanima, P. 2006. 'An age of decline: Product and income in eighteenth century Italy'. *Rivista di Storia Economica*, 22, 91–133.

Malanima, P. 2009. *Pre-Modern European Economy*. Leiden: Brill.

Malanima, P. 2011. 'The long decline of a leading economy: GDP in central and northern Italy, 1300–1913'. *European Review of Economic History*, 15, 169–219.

Malanima, P. 2013. 'When did England overtake Italy? Medieval and early modern divergence in prices and wages'. *European Review of Economic History*, 17, 45–70.

Malinowski, M. and Van Zanden, J. L. 2017. 'Income and its distribution in preindustrial Poland'. *Cliometrica*, 11(3), 375–404.

Mallett, M. E. 1974. *Mercenaries and Their Masters: Warfare in Renaissance Italy*. London: Bodley Head.

Mallett, M. E. and Hale, J. R. 1984. *The Military Organization of a Renaissance State. Venice c. 1400 to 1617*. Cambridge: Cambridge University Press.

Mannori, L. 1990. 'Per una preistoria della funzione amministrativa. Cultura giuridica e attività dei pubblici apparati nell'età del tardo diritto comune'. *Quaderni Fiorentini per la Storia del Pensiero Giuridico Moderno*, XIX, 345–415.

Mannori, L. (ed.) 1997. *Comunità e poteri centrali negli antichi Stati italiani*, Napoli: Cuen.

Meade, J. E. 1964. *Efficiency, Equality, and the Ownership of Property*. London: Allen and Unwin.

Medeiros, M. 2006. 'The rich and the poor: The construction of an affluence line from the poverty line'. *Social Indicators Research*, 78, 1–18.

Medeiros, M. and Ferreira de Souza, P. H. G. 2014. 'The Rich, the Affluent and the Top Incomes: A Literature Review'. IRLE Working Paper, 105–14.

Milanovic, B. 2005. *Worlds Apart. Measuring International and Global Inequality*. Princeton, NJ: Princeton University Press.

Milanovic, B. 2013. 'The Inequality Possibility Frontier. Extensions and New Applications'. The World Bank. Policy Research Working Paper, 6449.

Milanovic, B. 2016a. *Global Inequality: A New Approach for the Age of Globalization*, Cambridge, MA: Harvard University Press.

Milanovic, B. 2016b. 'Towards an Explanation of Inequality in Pre-Modern Societies: The Role of Colonies and High Population Density'. MPRA Paper, 74877.

Milanovic, B., Lindert, P. H. and Williamson, J. G. 2011. 'Pre-industrial inequality'. *The Economic Journal*, 121, 255–72.

Mirri, M. 1986. 'Formazione di una regione economica. Ipotesi sulla Toscana, sul Veneto, sulla Lombardia'. *Studi Veneziani*, XI, 47–59.

Mocarelli, L. 2006. 'Manufacturing activity in Venetian Lombardy: Specialized products and the formation of a regional market (17th–18th centuries)'. In P. Lanaro (ed.), *At the Centre of the Old World. Trade and Manufacturing in Venice and the Venetian Mainland, 1400–1800*. Toronto: CRRS, 317–41.

Molà, L. 2000. *The Silk Industry of Renaissance Venice*. Baltimore: Johns Hopkins University Press.

Molho, A. 1994. *Marriage Alliance in Late Medieval Florence*. Cambridge, MA: Harvard University Press.

Mollat, M. 1978. *Les pauvres au Moyen Âge. Étude sociale*. Paris: Hachette.

Mueller, R. C. 1997. *The Venetian Money Market: Banks, Panics and Public Debt, 1200–1500*. Baltimore, MD: Johns Hopkins University Press.

Muir, E. 1981. *Civic Ritual in Renaissance Venice*. Princeton, NJ: Princeton University Press.

Muldrew, C. 1998. *The Economy of Obligation: The Culture of Credit and Social Relations in Early Modern England*. London: Houndmills.

Munro, J. H. 2003. 'Wage-stickiness, monetary changes, and real incomes in late-medieval England and the Low Countries, 1350–1500: Did money matter?' *Research in Economic History*, 21, 185–297.

Nicolini, E. A. and Ramos Palencia, F. 2016a. 'Decomposing income inequality in a backward pre-industrial economy: Old Castile (Spain) in the middle of the 18th century'. *Economic History Review*, 69(3), 747–72.

Nicolini, E. A. and Ramos Palencia, F. 2016b. 'Comparing Income and Wealth Inequality in Pre-Industrial Economies: Lessons from 18th-Century Spain'. EHES Working Papers, 95.

North, D. 1981. *Structure and Change in Economic History*. New York: W. W. Norton.

O'Brien, P. K. 1988. 'The political economy of British taxation, 1660–1815'. *Economic History Review*, 41(1), 1–32.

OECD. 2011. 'Income inequality'. In *OECD Factbook 2011–2012: Economic, Environmental and Social Statistics*. Paris: OECD Publishing, 80–81.

OECD. 2013. *OECD Guidelines for Micro Statistics on Household Wealth*. Paris: OECD Publishing.

OECD. 2016. Social Expenditure Update 2016, www.oecd.org/els/soc/OECD2016-Social-Expenditure-Update.pdf.

OECD. 2017. *Government at a Glance 2017*. Paris: OECD Publishing.

Ongaro, G. 2017. *Peasants and Soldiers: The Management of the Venetian Military Structure in the Mainland Dominion between the 16th and 17th Centuries*. London: Routledge.

Osberg, L. and Smeeding T. 2006. '"Fair" inequality? Attitudes toward pay differentials: The United States in comparative perspective'. *American Sociological Review*, 71, 450–73.

Oscar, P. and Belotti, O. 2000. *Atlante Storico del territorio bergamasco: Geografia delle circoscrizioni comunali e sovra comunali dalla fine del XIV secolo a oggi*. Bergamo: Provincia di Bergamo.

Pamuk, Ş. 2007. 'The Black Death and the origins of the 'Great Divergence' across Europe, 1300–1600. *European Review of Economic History*, 11(3), 289–317.

Panciera, W. 1996. *L'arte matrice. I lanifici della Repubblica di Venezia nei secoli XVII e XVIII*. Treviso: Fondazione Benetton studi e ricerche.

Panciera, W. 2006. 'The industries of Venice in the seventeenth and eighteenth centuries'. In Lanaro, P. (ed.), *At the Centre of the Old World. Trade and Manufacturing in Venice and the Venetian Mainland, 1400–1800*. Toronto: CRRS, 185–214.

Paping, R. 2014. *General Dutch Population Development 1400–1850: Cities and countryside*. Paper presented at 1st ESHD conference, Alghero, Italy.

Parker, G. 1988. *The Military Revolution: Military Innovation and the Rise of the West, 1500–1800*. Cambridge: Cambridge University Press.

Parker, G. 1995. 'Guerra e rivoluzione militare (1450–1789)'. In M. Aymard (ed.), *Storia d'Europa, IV, L'Età moderna. Secoli XVI–XVIII*. Torino: Einaudi, 435–71.

Parrott, D. 2012. *The Business of War: Military Enterprise and Military Revolution in Early Modern Europe*. Cambridge: Cambridge University Press.

Pastore, A. 2000. 'Il problema dei poveri agli inizi dell'età moderna. Linee generali'. In V. Zamagni (ed.), *Povertà e innovazioni istituzionali in Italia. Dal Medioevo ad oggi*. Bologna: Il Mulino, 185–205.

Pederzani, I. 1992. *Venezia e lo "Stado de Terraferma". Il governo delle comunità nel territorio bergamasco (sec. XV–XVIII)*. Milano: Vita e Pensiero.

Peichl, A., Schaefer, T. and Scheicher, T. 2010. 'Measuring richness and poverty: A micro data application to Europe and Germany'. *Review of Income and Wealth*, 56(3), 597–619.

Pezzolo, L. 1982. 'Dal contado alla comunità: finanze e prelievo fiscale nel Vicentino (XVI–XVIII)'. C. Povolo (ed.), *Dueville. Storia e identificazione di una comunità del passato*. Vicenza: Neri Pozza, 381–428.

Pezzolo, L. 1990. *L'oro dello Stato. Società, finanza e fisco nella Repubblica veneta del secondo Cinquecento*. Venezia: Il cardo.

Pezzolo, L. 1994. 'Sistema di potere e politica finanziaria nella Repubblica di Venezia (secoli XV–XVII)'. In G. Chittolini, A. Molho and P. Schiera (eds.), *Origini dello Stato. Processi di formazione statale in Italia fra medioevo ed età moderna*. Bologna: Il Mulino, 303–27.

Pezzolo, L. 1998. *Finanza e fiscalità nel territorio di Bergamo (1450–1630)*. In M. Cattini and M. A. Romani (eds.), *Storia economica e sociale di Bergamo. Il tempo della Serenissima. Il lungo Cinquecento*. Bergamo: Fondazione per la storia economica e sociale di Bergamo, 49–70.

Pezzolo, L. 2000. 'Fiscalità e congiuntura in città e nel territorio (1630–1715)'. In A. De Maddalena, M.A. Romani and M. Cattini (eds.), *Storia economica e sociale di Bergamo. Il Tempo della Serenissima. Un Seicento in controtendenza*. Bergamo: Fondazione per la Storia economica e social di Bergamo, 217–34.

Pezzolo, L. 2006a. *Una finanza d'ancien regime: La repubblica veneta tra XV e XVIII secolo*. Napoli: Edizioni Scientifiche Italiane.

Pezzolo, L. 2006b. 'La rivoluzione militare: una prospettiva italiana 1400–1700'. In A. Dattero and S. Levati (eds.), *Militari in età moderna: La centralità di un tema di confine*. Milano: Cisalpino, 15–62.

Pezzolo, L. 2007. 'Stato, guerra e finanza nella Repubblica di Venezia fra medioevo e prima età moderna'. In R. Cancila (ed.), *Mediterraneo in armi (sec. XV–XVIII)*. Palermo: Associazione Mediterranea, I, 67–112.

Pezzolo, L. 2011. 'La storia agraria veneta. Risultati, ipotesi, prospettive'. *Archivio Veneto*, 142, 79–210.

Pezzolo, L. 2012. 'Republics and principalities in Italy'. In B. Yun-Casalilla and P. K. O'Brien (eds.), *The Rise of Fiscal States: A Global History. 1500–1914*. Cambridge: Cambridge University Press, 267–84.

Pezzolo, L. and Stumpo, E. 2008. 'L'imposizione diretta in Italia dal Medioevo a fine dell'ancien régime'. In S. Cavaciocchi (ed.), *La fiscalità nell'economia europea (secc. XIII–XVIII)*, Firenze: Firenze University Press, Vol. I, 75–98.

Piketty, T. 2014. *Capital in the Twenty-First Century*. Cambridge, MA: Belknap Press of Harvard University Press.

Piketty, T. 2015. 'Putting distribution back at the center of economics: Reflections on capital in the twenty-first century'. *Journal of Economic Perspectives*, 29(1), 67–88.

Piketty, T., Postel-Vinay, G. and Rosenthal, J.-L. 2006. 'Wealth concentration in a developing economy: Paris and France, 1807–1994'. *American Economic Review*, 96(1), 236–56.

Piketty, T., Postel-Vinay, G. and Rosenthal, J. L. 2014. 'Inherited vs self-made wealth: Theory and evidence from a rentier society (Paris 1872–1937)'. *Explorations in Economic History*, 51, 21–40.

Piketty, T. and Zucman, G. 2014. 'Capital is back: Wealth–income ratios in rich countries, 1700–2010'. *The Quarterly Journal of Economics*, 109(3), 1255–1310.

Pini, A. I. 1981. 'Dal comune città-stato al comune ente amministrativo'. In O. Capitani, R. Manselli, G. Cherubini, A. I., Pini and G. Chittolini (eds.), *Comuni e signorie: istituzioni, società e lotte per l'egemonia*. Torino: Utet, 451–590.

Piola Caselli, F. 1997. *Il buon governo. Storia della finanza pubblica nell'Europa preindustriale*. Torino: Giappichelli.

Piola Caselli, F. (ed.) 2008. *Government Debts and Financial Markets in Europe*. Londra: Pickering & Chatto.

Podestà, G. L. 1995. *Dal delitto politico alla politica del delitto. Finanza pubblica e congiure contro i Farnese nel Ducato di Parma e Piacenza dal 1545 al 1622*. Milano: Egea.

Podestà, G. L. 2007. *La finanza pubblica nel Ducato di Parma e Piacenza in età farnesiana*. In G. De Luca and A. Moioli (eds.), *Debito pubblico e mercati finanziari in Italia. Secoli XIII–XX*. Milano: Franco Angeli, 167–75.

Pomeranz, K. 2002. *The Great Divergence: China, Europe, and the Making of the Modern World Economy*. Princeton, NJ: Princeton University Press.

Porisini, G. 1963. *La proprietà terriera nel Comune di Ravenna dalla metà del secolo XVI ai giorni nostri*. Milano: Giuffré.

Povolo, C. 1981. *Evoluzione demografica della valle nei secoli XVI–XVIII*. In P. Preto (ed.), *La valle del Chiampo. Vita civile ed economica in età moderna e contemporanea*. Vicenza: Neri Pozza, I, 137–206.

Prados de la Escosura, L. 2008. 'Inequality, poverty and the Kuznets curve in Spain, 1850–2000'. *European Review of Economic History*, 12, 287–324.

Prak, M. 2005. *The Dutch Republic in the Seventeenth Century*. Cambridge: Cambridge University Press.

Prak, M. and Van Zanden, J. L. 2009. 'Tax morale and citizenship in the Dutch Republic'. In O. Gelderblom (ed.), *The Political Economy of the Dutch Republic*. Franham: Ashgate, 143–66.

Preto, P. 1978. *Peste e società a Venezia (1576)*. Vicenza: Neri Pozza Editore.

Preto, P. 1980. 'Le grandi pesti del 1575–77 e 1630-31'. In *Venezia e la peste*. Venezia: Marsilio, 123–26.

Preto, P. 1981. 'La valle del Chiampo nell'età della Repubblica di Venezia (1404–1797)'. In Id. (ed.), *La valle del Chiampo. Vita civile ed economica in età moderna e contemporanea*. Vicenza: Neri Pozza, I, 31–133.

Pullan, B. 1971. *Rich and Poor in Renaissance Venice*. Oxford: Blackwell.

Pullan, B. 1978. 'Poveri, mendicanti e vagabondi (secoli XIV–XVII)'. In *Annali della Storia d'Italia*, I. C. Vivanti and R. Romano (eds.), *Dal feudalesimo al capitalismo*. Torino: Einaudi, 981–1047.

Pullan, B. 1992. 'Plague and perceptions of the poor in early modern Italy'. In T. Ranger and P. Slack (eds.), *Epidemics and Ideas: Essays on the Historical Perception of Pestilence*. Cambridge: Cambridge University Press, 101–23.

Rapp, R. 1976. *Industry and Economic Decline in Seventeenth-Century Venice*. Cambridge, MA: Harvard University Press.

Ravallion, M. 2009. 'Poverty lines'. In J. Haughton and S. R. Khandker (eds.), *Handbook on Poverty and Inequality*. Washington, DC: World Bank, 556–61.

Ravallion, M. and Bidani, B. 1994. 'How robust is a poverty profile?' *The World Bank Economic Review*, 8(1), 75–102.

Ravallion, M., Datt, G. and Walle, D. 1991. 'Quantifying absolute poverty in the developing world'. *Review of Income and Wealth*, 37(4), 345–61.

Rawls, J. 1971. *A Theory of Justice*. Cambridge, MA: Harvard University Press.

Reis, J. 2017. 'Deviant behaviour? Inequality in Portugal 1565–1770'. *Cliometrica*, 11(3), 297–319.

Ricci, G. 1996. *Povertà, vergogna, superbia. I declassati fra Medioevo e Età moderna*. Bologna: Il Mulino.

Rizzo, M. 1987. 'Militari e civili nello Stato di Milano durante la seconda metà del Cinquecento. In tema di alloggiamenti militari'. *Clio*, XXIII, 563–69.

Rizzo, M. 2001. *Alloggiamenti militari e riforme fiscali nella Lombardia spagnola fra Cinque e Seicento*. Milano: Unicopli.

Rizzo, M. 2007. '"Rivoluzione dei consumi", "state-building" e "rivoluzione militare". La domanda e l'offerta di servizi strategici nella Lombardia spagnola, 1535–1659'. In I. Lopane and E. Ritrovato (eds.), *Tra vecchi e nuovi equilibri. Domanda e offerta di servizi in età moderna e contemporanea*. Bari: Cacucci, 447–74.

Rizzo, M. 2008. '"La maggiore et più sentita gravezza, che si provi in questo stato". Oneri militari, politica fiscale e corpi contribuenti nella Lombardia spagnola (1550–1620)'. In S. Cavaciocchi (ed.), *La fiscalità nell'economia europea (secc. XIII–XVIII)*, Firenze: Firenze University Press, II, 881–95.

Roberts, M. 1956. *The Military Revolution, 1560–1660*. Belfast: Boyd.

Rogers, C. J. (ed.) 1995. *The Military Revolution Debate: Readings on the Military Transformation of Early Modern Europe*. Boulder, CO: Westview Press.

Roine, J. and Waldenström, D. 2015. 'Long run trends in the distribution of income and wealth'. In A. Atkinson and F. Bourguignon (eds.), *Handbook of Income Distribution*, Vol. 2A. Amsterdam: North-Holland, 469–592.

Romani, M. A. 1978. 'Finanza pubblica e potere politico: il caso dei Farnese (1545–1593)'. In M. A. Romani (ed.), *Le corti farnesiane di Parma e Piacenza (1543–1662)*. Roma: Bulzoni, Vol. I, 3–85.

Romani, M. A. 1994. 'Regions in Italian history (XVth–XVIIth centuries)'. *Journal of European Economic History*, 23(1), 177–91.

Rossi, N., Toniolo, G. and Vecchi, G. 2001. 'Is the Kuznets curve still alive? Evidence from Italian household budgets, 1881–1961'. *Journal of Economic History*, 61(4), 904–25.

Rossini, A. 1994. *Le campagne bresciane nel Cinquecento. Territorio, Fisco, società*. Milano: Franco Angeli.

Rossini, E. 1982. 'Ceti urbani: terra e proprietà fondiaria nel basso Medioevo'. In G. Borelli (ed.), *Uomini e civiltà agraria in territorio veronese*. Verona: Banca Popolare di Verona, I, 77–118.

Rossini, E. 1993. 'La normativa sugli estimi veronesi (parte prima)'. *Studi storici Luigi Simeoni*, 125–46.

Rossini, E. 1994. 'La normativa sugli estimi veronesi (parte seconda)'. *Studi storici Luigi Simeoni*, 63–90.

Rotelli, C. 1966. *La distribuzione della proprietà terriera e delle colture a Imola nel XVII e XVIII secolo*. Milano: Giuffré.

Ryckbosch, W. 2016. 'Economic inequality and growth before the industrial revolution: The case of the Low Countries (fourteenth to nineteenth centuries)'. *European Review of Economic History*, 20, 1–22.

Saba, F. 1995. 'La popolazione del territorio bergamasco nei secoli XVI–XVIII'. In A. De Maddalena, M. Cattini and M. A. Romani (eds.), *Storia economica e sociale di Bergamo. Il tempo della Serenissima. L'immagine della Bergamasca*. Bergamo: Fondazione per la storia economica e sociale di Bergamo, 215–73.

Saito, O. 2015. 'Growth and inequality in the great and little divergence debate: A Japanese perspective'. *Economic History Review*, 68(2), 399–419.

Santiago-Caballero, C. 2011. 'Income inequality in central Spain, 1690–1800'. *Explorations in Economic History*, 48(1), 83–96.

Saviolo, P. 1667. *Compendio delle origini et relazione delli estimi della città di Padova*, Padova: Frambotto.

Sbriziolo, L. 1967–1968. 'Per la storia delle confraternite veneziane: dalle deliberazioni miste (1310–1476) del consiglio dei Dieci. "Scolae comunes", artigiane e nazionali'. *Atti dell'Istituto veneto di scienze, lettere ed arti*, 126, 405–42.

Scarabello, G. 1995. 'Il Settecento'. In *Storia d'Italia, XII, La Repubblica di Venezia nell'età moderna, II*. Torino: Utet, 553–67.

Scheidel, W. 2017. *The Great Leveller: Violence and the Global History of Inequality from the Stone Age to the Present*. Oxford: Oxford University Press.

Scherman, M. 2009. 'La distribuzione della ricchezza in una città: Treviso e i suoi estimi (1434–1499)'. In G. Alfani and M. Barbot (eds.), *Ricchezza, valore, proprietà in età preindustriale 1400–1850*. Venezia: Marsilio, 169–84.

Scherman, M. 2013. *Famille et travail à Trévise à la fine du Moyen Âge*. Roma: École Française de Rome.

Schumpeter, J. A. 1991. 'The crisis of the tax state'. In R. Swedberg (ed.), *J. Schumpeter: The Economics and Sociology of Capitalism*. Princeton, NJ: Princeton University Press, 99–140.

Sella, D. 1968. 'Crisis and transformation in Venetian trade'. In B. Pullan (ed.), *Crisis and Change in the Venetian Economy in the Sixteenth and Seventeenth Centuries*. London: Methuen, 88–105.

Sella, D. 1979. *Crisis and Continuity: The Economy of Spanish Lombardy in Seventeenth Century*. Cambridge, MA: Harvard University Press.

Sella, D. 1997. *Italy in the Seventeenth Century*. London: Longman.

Sella, D. 2010. 'Sotto il dominio della Spagna'. In D. Sella and C. Capra (eds.), *Il Ducato di Milano 1535–1796*. Torino: Utet, 3–149.

Silini, G. 1996. 'L'estimo generale di Bergamasca del 1547'. *Bergomum*, 1, 125–44.

Slack, P. 1985. *The Impact of Plague in Tudor and Stuart England*. London: Routledge & Kegan Paul.

Soltow, L. and Van Zanden, J. L. 1998. *Income and Wealth Inequality in the Netherlands, 16th–20th Centuries*. Amsterdam: Het Spinhuis.

Stevens Crawshaw, J. L. 2012. *Plague Hospitals: Public Health for the City in Early Modern Venice*. Farnham: Ashgate.

Tabacchi, S. 2007. *Il Buon Governo: le finanze locali nello Stato della Chiesa (secoli XVI-XVIII)*. Roma: Viella.

Tagliaferri, A. 1966. *L'economia veronese secondo gli estimi dal 1409 al 1635.* Milano: Giuffrè.

Tagliaferri, A. 1978. *Per una storia sociale della Repubblica Veneta: La rivolta di Arzignano del 1655.* Trieste: Istituto di storia economica, Università degli Studi di Trieste.

Tagliaferri, A. (ed.) 1984. *I ceti dirigenti in Italia in età moderna e contemporanea.* Udine: Del Bianco.

Tanzini, L. 2012. 'Tuscan states: Florence and Siena'. In A. Gamberini and I. Lazzarini (eds.), *The Italian Renaissance State.* Cambridge: Cambride University Press, 90–111.

Tedoldi, L. 2003. 'Cittadinanza, vocazioni e integrazione sociale nella Brescia veneta (XVII-XVIII secolo)'. *Quaderni Storici,* 2, 381–98.

Tedoldi, L. 2004. *Cittadini minori. Cittadinanza, integrazione sociale e diritti reali nella Brescia veneta, secc. XVI–XVIII.* Milano: Franco Angeli.

Terpstra, N. 2000. 'The politics of confraternal charity: Centre, periphery, and the modes of confraternal involvement in early modern civic welfare'. In V. Zamagni (ed.), *Povertà e innovazioni istituzionali in Italia. Dal Medioevo ad oggi.* Bologna: Il Mulino, 153–73.

Thoen, E. 2001. 'A commercial survival economy in evolution. The Flemish countryside and the transition to capitalism (Middle Ages–19th century)'. In P. Hoppenbrouwers and J. L. Van Zanden (eds.), *Peasants into Farmers: The Transformation of Rural Economy and Society in the Low Countries (Middle Ages–19th Century) in the Light of the Brenner Debate.* Turnhout: Brepols, 102–57.

Tilly, C. 1984. 'Demographic origins of the European proletariat'. In D. Levine (ed.), *Proletarianization and Family History.* Orlando: Academic Press, 1–85.

Todeschini, G. 2002. *I mercanti e il tempio: La società cristiana e il circolo virtuoso della ricchezza fra Medioevo ed età Moderna.* Bologna: Il Mulino.

Todeschini, G. 2004. *Ricchezza francescana.* Bologna: Il Mulino.

Trivellato, F. 2006. 'Murano glass, continuity and transformation'. In P. Lanaro (ed.), *At the Centre of the Old World. Trade and Manufacturing in Venice and the Venetian Mainland, 1400–1800.* Toronto: CRRS, 143–84.

Ulvioni, P. 1989a. 'I quattro cavalieri dell'Apocalisse nella Repubblica veneta'. In *Venezia e la Terraferma. Economia e Società,* 3. Bergamo: Assessorato alla cultura, 77–91.

Ulvioni, P. 1989b. *Il gran castigo di Dio. Carestia ed epidemie a Venezia e nella Terraferma 1628–1632.* Milano: Franco Angeli.

Van Bavel, B. 2016. *The Invisible Hand? How Market Economies Have Emerged and Declined since AD 500.* Oxford: Oxford University Press.

Van Bavel, B., van Cruyningen, P. and Thoen, E. 2010. 'The Low Countries, 1000–1750'. In B. Van Bavel and R. Hoyle (eds.), *Rural Economy and Society in North-western Europe, 500–2000. Social Relations: Property and Power.* Trunhout: Brepols, 169–98.

Van Bavel, B. and Rijpma, A. 2016. 'How important were formalized charity and social spending before the rise of the welfare state? A long-run analysis of selected western European cases, 1400–1850'. *Economic History Review,* 69 (1), 159–87.

Van Zanden, J. L. 1993. *The Rise and Decline of Holland's Economy*. Manchester: Manchester University Press.

Van Zanden, J. L. 1995. 'Tracing the beginning of the Kuznets curve: Western Europe during the early modern period'. *Economic History Review*, 48(4), 643–64.

Van Zanden, J. L. 2009. *The Long Road to the Industrial Revolution: The European Economy in a Global Perspective, 1000–1800*. Leiden: Brill.

Van Zanden, J. L. and Prak, M. 2006. 'Towards an economic interpretation of citizenship: the Dutch Republic between medieval communes and modern nation-states'. *European Review of Economic History*, 10(2), 111–45.

Van Zanden, J. L. and Prak, M. 2009. 'State formation and citizenship'. In J. Van Zanden, L., *The Long Road to the Industrial Revolution: The European Economy in a Global Perspective, 1000–1800*. Leiden: Brill. 205–32.

Varanini, G. M. 1979. 'La Curia di Nogarole nella pianura veronese fra Tre e Quattrocento. Paesaggio, amministrazione, economia e società'. *Studi di storia medioevale e di diplomatica*, IV, 45–263.

Varanini, G. M. 1980. *Il distretto veronese nel Quattrocento: Vicariati del comune di Verona e vicariati privati*. Verona: Fiorini.

Varanini, G. M. (ed.) 1987. *La Valpolicella nella prima età moderna (1500 c.–1630)*. Verona: Centro di documentazione per la storia della Valpolicella.

Varanini, G. M. 1992. *Comuni cittadini e stato regionale. Ricerche sulla Terraferma veneta del Quattrocento*. Verona: Libreria editrice universitaria.

Varanini, G. M. 1996. 'Proprietà fondiaria e agricoltura'. In V. A. Tenenti and U. Tucci (eds.), *Storia di Venezia, Il Rinascimento. Società ed economia*. Roma: Istituto della enciclopedia italiana, 807–79.

Varanini, G. M. 2011. 'La Terraferma veneta del Quattrocento e le tendenze recenti della storiografia'. In *1509–2009. L'ombra di Agnadello. Venezia e la Terraferma*, Venezia: Ateneo Veneto, 13–63.

Vecchiato, F. 1982. 'Il mondo contadino nel Seicento'. In G. Borelli (ed.), *Uomini e civiltà agraria in territorio veronese*, I, secc. *IX–XVII*. Verona: Banca Popolare di Verona, 347–94.

Ventura, A. 1964. *Nobiltà e popolo nella società veneta del '400 e '500*. Bari: Laterza.

Ventura, A. 1968. 'Considerazioni sull'agricoltura veneta e sulla accumulazione originaria di capitale nei secolo XVI e XVII'. *Studi Storici*, 1, 674–722.

Vigato, M. 1989. 'Gli estimi padovani tra XVI e XVII secolo'. *Società e Storia*, 43, 45–82.

Vigo, G. 1979. *Fisco e società nella Lombardia del Cinquecento*. Bologna: Il Mulino.

Wade, R. H. 2014. 'The strange neglect of income inequality in economics and public policy'. In E. Giovanni, A. Cornia and F. Steward (eds.), *Toward Human Development: New Approaches to Macroeconomics and Inequality*. Oxford: Oxford University Press, 99–121.

Wall, R., Robin, J. and Laslett, P. (eds.) 1984. *Forme di famiglia nella società europea*. Bologna: Il Mulino.

Williamson, J. G. 1985. *Did British Capitalism Breed Inequality?* Boston: Allen & Unwin.

Williamson, J. G. and Lindert, P. H. 1980. *American Inequality: A Macro Economic History*. New York: Academic Press.

Woolf, S. J. 1988. *Porca miseria. Poveri e assistenza nell'età moderna*. Roma-Bari: Laterza.

Yun-Casalilla, B. 2012. 'Introduction: The rise of the fiscal state in Eurasia'. In B. Yun-Casalilla and P. K. O'Brien (eds.), *The Rise of Fiscal States: A Global History. 1500–1914*. Cambridge: Cambridge University Press, 1–35.

Yun-Casalilla, B. and O'Brien, P. K. (eds.) 2012. *The Rise of Fiscal States: A Global History. 1500–1914*. Cambridge: Cambridge University Press.

Zalin, G. 1987. *Dalla bottega alla fabbrica: La fenomenologia industriale nelle province venete tra '500 e '900*. Verona: Libreria universitaria editrice.

Zamperetti, S. 1981. 'Aspetti e problemi delle comunità del territorio vicentino durante il XVI secolo nell'ambito dei rapporti città-contado nello stato regionale veneto'. In C. Povolo (ed.), *Lisiera. Immagini, documenti e prolemi per la storia e cultura di una comunità veneta*. Lisiera: Parrocchia di Lisiera, 501–32.

Zamperetti, S. 1987. 'I "sinedri dolorosi". La formazione e lo sviluppo dei corpi territoriali nello Stato regionale veneto tra '500 e '600'. *Rivista Storica Italiana*, XCIC, 269–320.

Zanetti, D. 2000. *Fra le antiche torri. Scritti di storia pavese*. Pavia: Università di Pavia.

Zangheri, R. 1980. *Catasti e storia della proprietà terriera*. Torino: Einaudi.

Zaninelli, S. 1963. *Il nuovo censo dello Stato di Milano dall'editto del 1718 al 1733*. Milano: Vita e Pensiero.

Zannini, A. 1993. *Burocrazia e burocrati a Venezia in età moderna: i cittadini originari (secc. XVI-XVIII)*. Venezia: Istituto Veneto di Scienze.

Zannini, A. 1999. 'L'economia veneta nel Seicento. Oltre il paradigma della "crisi generale"'. In *La popolazione italiana nel Seicento*. Bologna: Clueb, 473–502.

Zannini, A. 2010. 'Sempre più agricola, sempre più regionale. L'economia della Repubblica di Venezia da Agnadello al Lombardo-Veneto (1509–1817)'. In *Ateneo Veneto*, CXCVII, Terza serie, 9/1, 137–71.

Zannini, A. 2012. 'Un ecomito? Venezia (XV–XVIII sec.)'. In G. Alfani, M. Di Tullio and L. Mocarelli (eds.), *Storia economica e ambiente italiano (ca. 1400–1850)*. Milano: Franco Angeli, 100–13.

Zappa, A. 1986. 'Il paesaggio pavese. Campagne, Lomellina e Oltrepò, attraverso le fonti catastali della metà del '500'. *Nuova Rivista Storica*, LXX(1-2), 33–106.

Zardin, D. 1987. 'Le confraternite in Italia settentrionale fra XV e XVIII secolo'. *Società e Storia*, 35, 81–137.

Železnik, U. 2015. 'Peste sul e oltre il confine asburgico-veneto: un'epidemia per ricostruire la popolazione (Capodistria, 1630–31)'. *Popolazione e Storia*, 2, 73–94.

Index

232   Index

Printed in the United States
by Baker & Taylor Publisher Services